D0325655

BLOOD AND STEEL 3

Other Books by Donald E. Graves

Scarlet and Blue: The History of The Royal Regiment of Canada, 1861–2014 (The Regiment, 2015)

Blood and Steel 2: The Wehrmacht Archive: Retreat to the Reich, September to December 1944 (Frontline, 2015)

Blood and Steel: The Wehrmacht Archive: Normandy 1944 (Frontline, 2013)

And All Their Glory Past: Fort Erie, Plattsburgh and the Last Battles in the North (Robin Brass Studio, 2013)

First Campaign of an A.D.C.: The War of 1812 Memoir of Lt. William Jenkins Worth, U.S. Army (Old Fort Niagara Press, 2012)

Dragon Rampant: The Royal Welch Fusiliers at War, 1793–1815 (Frontline Books & Robin Brass Studio, 2010)

Fix Bayonets! A Royal Welch Fusilier at War, 1796–1815 (Robin Brass Studio & Spellmount Publishing, 2007)

Century of Service: The History of the South Alberta Light Horse (The South Alberta Light Horse Regiment Foundation & Robin Brass Studio, 2005)

More Fighting for Canada: Five Battles, 1760–1944 (Robin Brass Studio, 2004)

Another Place, Another Time: A U-boat Officer's Wartime Album (with Werner Hirschmann; Robin Brass Studio, 2004, 2011)

In Peril on the Sea: The Royal Canadian Navy and the Battle of the Atlantic (Canadian Naval Memorial Trust & Robin Brass Studio, 2003)

Quebec, 1759: The Siege and the Battle (by C. P. Stacey; edited and with new material by Donald E. Graves; Robin Brass Studio, 2002)

Guns Across the River: The Battle of the Windmill, 1838 (Friends of Windmill Point & Robin Brass Studio, 2001, 2013)

Fighting for Canada: Seven Battles, 1758–1945 (Robin Brass Studio, 2000)

Field of Glory: The Battle of Crysler's Farm, 1813 (Robin Brass Studio, 1999)

The Incredible War of 1812: A Military History (by J. Mackay Hitsman; updated by Donald E. Graves; Robin Brass Studio, 1999)

South Albertas: A Canadian Regiment at War (South Alberta Regiment Veterans Association & Robin Brass Studio, 1998, 2004)

Where Right and Glory Lead! The Battle of Lundy's Lane, 1814 (Robin Brass Studio, 1997, 2013)

Soldiers of 1814: American Enlisted Men's Memoirs of the Niagara Campaign (Old Fort Niagara Press, 1996)

Redcoats and Grey Jackets: The Battle of Chippawa, 1814 (Dundurn Press, 1994)

Merry Hearts Make Light Days: The War of 1812 Journal of Lieutenant John Le Couteur, 104th Foot (Carleton University Press, 1993; Robin Brass Studio, 2012)

Normandy 1944: The Canadian Summer (with W. J. McAndrew and M. J. Whitby; Art Global, 1993)

BLOOD AND STEEL 3

The Wehrmacht Archive: The Ardennes Offensive, December 1944 to January 1945

Donald E. Graves

Frontline Books, London

Blood and Steel 3: The Wehrmacht Archive:
The Ardennes Offensive, December 1944 to January 1945

This edition published in 2015 by Frontline Books,
an imprint of Pen & Sword Books Ltd,
47 Church Street, Barnsley, S. Yorkshire, S70 2AS
www.frontline-books.com

ISBN: 978-1-84832-236-3

CIP data records for this title are available from the British Library.

For more information on our books, please visit
www.frontline-books.com, email info@frontline-books.com
or write to us at the above address.

Printed and bound by CPI Group (UK) Ltd, Croydon, CR0 4YY
Typeset in 10.8/13.5 point Minion Pro Regular

Contents

List of Plates

Introduction

Although some American intelligence officers suspected that the enemy was preparing a major operation, the German Ardennes offensive came as a complete surprise to the Allies. Shortly before dawn on 16 December 1944, some 1,600 artillery pieces, ranging in calibre from 75mm to 210mm, opened a heavy 90-minute bombardment on the forward positions of the First U.S. Army in the Ardennes and then the infantry moved forward. For the next six weeks, desperate fighting took place in some of the most inhospitable terrain in western Europe in sub-zero temperatures amid snow squalls and blizzards. When the battle ended in the last week of January 1945 with a total defeat for the Wehrmacht, about 160,000 men in both armies had been killed, wounded or captured. The third volume of the *Blood and Steel, The Wehrmacht Archive* series is concerned with this hard-fought military operation, popularly known as the 'Battle of the Bulge'.

Like the preceding volumes in this series, *Blood and Steel 3* is not a history of the campaign it documents – indeed the story of the Ardennes offensive has been ably told elsewhere.[1] Rather, it is a collection or anthology of translated German wartime documents taken from the daily Intelligence Summaries of First Canadian Army. It should be noted, however, that as most of the fighting on the Allied side was done by American troops, the greater part of the documents below come from United States sources.

1. The Ardennes offensive has attracted many authors. The official American history is Hugh M. Cole, *The Ardennes: Battle of the Bulge* (Washington, 1965). An excellent study, which has held up very well since it was first published in 1984, is Charles B. Macdonald, *A Time for Trumpets: The Untold Story of the Battle of the Bulge* (New York, 1985). Macdonald had the advantage of being an infantry company commander during the Ardennes fighting and also an historian with the U.S. Army. An extensive new examination of the Ardennes offensive can be found in Christer Bergstrom, *The Ardennes 1944–1945: Hitler's Winter Offensive* (Haverstown, 2014) while a useful pictorial record is Jean-Paul Pallud, *Battle of the Bulge. After the Battle* (London, 1984).

The origins of the Ardennes campaign go back to the summer of 1944. Adolf Hitler began planning a major counter-offensive in the west almost at the same time as his armies were experiencing disastrous defeats on all fronts. The German leader seems to have conceived the idea in late July 1944 and, by September, his concept had advanced far enough for him to order plans drawn up for an operation codenamed *Wacht am Rhein*,[2] which would be a massive assault directed against the American First Army in the Ardennes area. Toward that end, he brought back *Feldmarschall* Gerd von Rundstedt, a highly respected senior officer whom he had fired three months before, to serve as the nominal commander-in-chief on the Western Front. The operation was scheduled to take place about the middle of December and its purpose, as explained by Hitler to a group of selected officers, was to be:

(1) the encirclement of 48 Allied divisions or a general Allied withdrawal;
(2) to gain time, viz. at least four weeks, for the consolidation of German war industry, particularly the synthetic oil industry;
(3) by accentuating political difficulties on the Continent and by propaganda, to detach one of the Allies from the war.[3]

Hitler, one historian has written, hoped with this operation to create conditions in which one Allied nation would 'blame the other for the debacle that engulfed its troops, to sow mutual mistrust, to deal such a blow' that the citizens of America, Britain and Canada 'would demand that their leaders bring the boys home'.[4] A successful offensive that more or less destroyed First U.S. Army and captured the port of Antwerp would accomplish these objectives.

Hitler's senior commanders were not impressed with *Wacht am Rhein*. Von Rundstedt, the nominal commander-in-chief on the Western Front, was particularly disparaging. As he later remarked:

> I strongly object to the fact that this stupid operation in the Ardennes is sometimes called the 'Rundstedt offensive,' ... That is a complete misnomer. I had nothing to do with it. It came to me as an order complete to the last detail. ...
>
> When I was first told about the proposed offensive in the Ardennes, I protested against it as vigorously as I could. The forces

2. 'The Watch on the Rhine'. It was later renamed *Herbstnebel*, or 'Autumn Mist'.
3. ISUM (First Canadian Army Intelligence Summary) 203, 19 January 1944, from SHAEF.
4. MacDonald, *A Time for Trumpets*, 38.

> at our disposal were much, much too weak for such far-reaching objectives. I suggested that my plan against the Aachen salient be used instead, but the suggestion was turned down, as were all my other objections. It was only up to me to obey. It was a nonsensical operation, and the most stupid part of it was the setting of Antwerp as the target. If we reached the Meuse we should have got down on our knees and thanked God – let alone try to reach Antwerp.[5]

Oberstgruppenführer Sepp Dietrich, commanding Sixth Panzer Army, which was to play a major role in the forthcoming attack, later complained that

> All I had to do was to cross a river, capture Brussels and then go on and take the port of Antwerp. And all this in December, January and February, the worst three months of the year; through the Ardennes where snow was waist deep and there wasn't room to deploy four tanks abreast, let alone six armoured divisions; when it didn't get light until eight in the morning and was dark again at four in the afternoon and my tanks can't fight at night; with divisions that had just been reformed and were composed chiefly of raw, untrained recruits; and at Christmas time.[6]

Orders were orders, however, and senior German officers prepared to carry out Hitler's wishes.

There was much concern that the Allied opponent would learn of the preparations for the forthcoming offensive and security was drastically tightened (see Document 8/1). All radio code names, call signs and code keys were changed. Only picked signal personnel were permitted to use land line telephones and, wherever possible, messengers were preferred. All major troop movements were made at night and road signs with unit names were sparingly used. Officers were only informed of the operation at the last possible moment and, even then, the information they received was restricted to the sector with which they were directly concerned. *Generalleutnant* Fritz Bayerlein, commanding the Panzer Lehr Division, learned about the forthcoming attack when he and several other senior officers were called to von Rundstedt's headquarters on 11 December, four days before the offensive was to commence. He recalled that

5. Milton Schulman, *Defeat in the West* (London, 1948), 228
6. Schulman, *Defeat in the West*, 229.

> After dinner we were told to attend a special briefing. We were all stripped of our weapons and brief-cases, loaded into buses and then driven about the countryside for half an hour. Finally we were led into a large room which was surrounded by SS guards who watched our every move. Then Hitler arrived accompanied by Field-Marshal Keitel and General Jodl.
>
> Hitler looked sick and broken, and began to read from a long prepared manuscript. The speech lasted for two hours, during which I felt most uneasy. The suspicious looks of the SS guards made me afraid even to reach into my pocket for a handkerchief. Hitler started off this briefing as if he were delivering one of his birthday speeches. For about an hour he told us what he and the Nazi party had done for Germany during the past twelve years.
>
> He then went into the details of the Ardennes offensive, telling us what formations were involved and what they were to do. The object of the attack was to capture Antwerp in fourteen days and at the same time trap Montgomery's Twenty-first Army Group in Holland. The loss of so large a force would cause Canada to withdraw from the war, and thoroughly discourage the United States about continuing the struggle. Hitler also impressed us with the fact that if this offensive did not succeed, things would then be extremely difficult for Germany. At this statement, Keitel and Jodl, who were sitting at the front table, nodded their heads approvingly. The Führer also promised us sufficient petrol, and a fighter support of 3000 planes which would keep the Allies out of the sky. When Hitler had finished, von Rundstedt expressed his loyalty to the Führer on behalf of the generals, and assured him that this time they would not fail him.[7]

The massive preparations and the tight security, however, alerted all ranks that something big was in the works and there was a feeling of exhilaration. The 116th Panzer Division only moved to its jumping-off point on 8 December but it was clear to all ranks that a major operation was going to take place. 'Everything is rolling!' enthused an officer of that formation,

> We almost feel the way we did in France during the offensive in France in 1940, weeks that seem to have been an eternity ago! All preparations are completed, but everything is still very secretive.

7. Schulman, *Defeat in the West*, 230.

> Many good and familiar divisions are starting their march. A certain anticipation has gripped even the most grizzled fighters.[8]

But many of those about to take part in the offensive were aware that *Wacht am Rhein* was – as one veteran NCO put it – 'the last push we can make,' otherwise, 'we will soon have had it'.[9] That push began at 0530 on 16 December when the German artillery opened fire and then the assault troops moved forward. In a letter to his sister, one of the attackers exhalted: 'Ruth! Ruth! Ruth! We MARCH!'[10]

One of the interesting aspects of the German offensive – and certainly one that has attracted much attention from authors and filmmakers – was the use of what today would be termed 'special forces'. This was Operation *Greiff*, undertaken by *Standartenführer* Otto Skorzeny's 150th Panzer Brigade, which included English-speaking recon teams wearing American uniforms and riding in American vehicles. Although they did little actual harm, these saboteurs caused disruption in the Allied rear areas as keen military police and sentries arrested anyone who could not answer knowledge questions or spoke with a funny accent.[11] Allied intelligence sources were forewarned of the existence of this special unit when the German order asking for volunteers and giving details of the new entity was captured – something that Skorzeny feared.[12] Although Allied intelligence officers noted that the 'potential threat' of such 'infiltration units needs no stressing', their belief was that it was doubtful that enough personnel with the 'necessary qualifications to form two battalions of the type envisaged' in the order 'would be available to the Wehrmacht at this time'.[13] Less than two weeks after these words were written, jeeps full of Germans dressed as GIs were travelling through the American rear areas.

A second 'special force' was *Kampfgruppe* Peiper, the advance guard of the 1st SS Panzer Division, named after its leader, *Standartenführer*

---

8. Diary of *Major* Fritz Vogelsang, 116th Panzer Division, 14 December 1944, quoted in Heinz Günther Guderian, *From Normandy to the Ruhr. With the 116th Panzer Division in World War II* (Bedford, 2001), 296.
9. Document 7/2, Diary of *Obergefreiter* Singer, 2nd Panzer Division, 16 December 1944.
10. Letter contained in 1st U.S. Division G-2 After Action Report, December 1944, quoted in MacDonald, *A Time for Trumpets*, 90.
11. In fact, Canadian provosts arrested and jailed a U.S. Army Air Force officer because they thought he spoke English with a funny accent. The man turned out to be from Alabama.
12. Otto Skorzeny, *Skorzeny's Secret Missions: War Memoirs of the Most Dangerous Man in Europe* (New York, 1950), 145.
13. ISUM 152, 29 November 1944.

Joachim Peiper. This force, the spearhead of the Sixth Panzer Army's attack, has also been a popular subject of study although Peiper failed in his mission because of a fuel shortage and his men irreparably damaged their record as soldiers by murdering prisoners and civilians. Chapter 3 contains two interesting eyewitness accounts from men who moved with *Kampfgruppe* Peiper – although not willingly. The first, Major Hal McCown of the 119th U.S. Infantry Division, went with the *Kampfgruppe* as a prisoner. McCown, however, was a perceptive man and his observations (Document 3/1) about Peiper and his subordinates, and their tactics, make for interesting reading. The second eyewitness account of *Kampfgruppe* Peiper is the diary (Document 3/2) of *Feldwebel* Karl Laun of the Luftwaffe, whose mobile light flak battalion had been attached to Peiper to provide anti-aircraft protection. Laun was a married 27-year-old Austrian with a child, who had some university education and was a devout Catholic. Having fought for nearly five years he was heartily sick of the war. He despised the Waffen SS and was very unhappy about having to serve with these 'bastards' who did not have 'the slightest inkling of international law, or for that matter, of humanity'.[14] Laun's diary from December 1944 to March 1945, which has been included in full below, is a fascinating panorama of the sunset of the Third Reich. During his unauthorized travels in the rear areas he catalogues the difficulties of everyday life: the shortages of food, fuel and transport and the constant interference and bullying of civilians by minor officials of the Nazi Party.

The third German 'special force' deployed during the Ardennes offensive is less well known than those commanded by Peiper and Skorzeny. This was a parachute *kampfgruppe* of about battalion size led by *Oberstleutnant* Friedrich, *Freiherr* von der Heydte, a distinguished veteran of the airborne forces. Chapter 4 contains interrogation reports of members of this force, including von der Heydte himself, which reveal a seemingly unending succession of problems: inadequate training, poor planning and preparations, last minute changes, incompetent leadership – and plain bad luck. These problems were not offset by the arrogance of von der Heydte who informed his captors (Document 4/4) that his nation would win the war because Germans were smarter than Americans!

Chapter 5 provides brief glimpses into the organization and experience of some of the German formations that participated in the Ardennes fighting. It reveals that, while they had received their share of weapons and equipment, the overall problems concerned lack of personnel and lack

14. Document 3/2, Laun Diary, 20 December 1944.

of time to adequately train them. We learn (Document 5/3) that nearly two-thirds of the men of the 9th SS Panzer Division came from outside Germany, including a sizeable number of Ukrainians, and many new recruits had never fired a rifle. A young officer of the paratroops confesses (Document 5/9) that he does not know which division his regiment belongs to. The popularity of captured American clothing and rations (Document 5/4) is an indication of the German army's supply problems in the last year of the war.

The letters and diaries of German soldiers who participated in the offensive will be found in Chapters 6 and 7. As the operation continues and it becomes clear that it will not succeed, the mood of the writers change. *Leutnant* Martin Opitz of the 18th *Volksgrenadier* Division, who confides (Document 7/1) to his diary, his 'feeling of elation' on 15 December, believes a month later that 'Everything looks hopeless'.

Chapter 8 contains documents relating to German tactics and methods and includes information on forest fighting, winter clothing, evaluating the Allies as enemies and comparing German and Allied armoured vehicles. During the Ardennes offensive, the Wehrmacht captured more than 20,000 American prisoners, some of whom revealed valuable information when questioned by skilled German interrogators. The dissemination of information about German interrogation techniques therefore became vitally important for all Allied armies and were included in the Intelligence Summaries.

At the outset, Josef Goebbels, the Reichsminister for Propaganda, made much of the Ardennes offensive, asserting that

> the present attack was the answer to those who asked 'Where is the Führer? What exactly has become of the Luftwaffe? What is happening to our industries in the Saar and Ruhr areas?' The Führer, it was claimed, was safe and well, and had spent days and nights during the past few weeks in working out plans for the present offensive in the minutest detail.[15]

When the operation began to bog down as a result of weather, terrain and determined American resistance, Goebbels changed his tune. By the end of December, the propaganda ministry was referring to it as 'the winter battle' and by the middle of that month, orders were issued that

> Soldiers are to be informed during the indoctrination period,

15. Document 10/1, ISUM 173, 20 December 1944.

> that our offensive in the west was not launched for the purpose of gaining territory. The main purpose was to eliminate the direct threat by the great masses of American armoured units to the Ruhr District, the Saar District, and the Palatinate, and thus force the enemy to regroup his units along the entire front.[16]

As German morale – so high in December 1944 – began to plummet in January 1945, the incidence of desertion – despite the harshest penalties – began to rise. The documents in Chapter 11 reveal the Wehrmacht's methods of trying to eradicate desertion, which by this time had become a serious problem. The diary of *Feldwebel* Karl Laun (Document 3/2) reveals that many German soldiers absented themselves from their units and were roaming the rear areas, waiting for either a chance to surrender or for the end of the war, and Laun was one of them. After a nearly month-long unauthorized absence from his unit, he returned to it for a few weeks but then departed on spurious medical grounds to disappear into the straggler's underworld until he could surrender to American forces in the first week of March.

No man is a hero to his wife and it would appear that the same holds true for field marshals. Chapter 12 contains two mildly humorous documents (mildly humorous because there really was not much to laugh about) including a telephone conversation (Document 12/1) during which Mrs. Model tells her husband, *Feldmarschall* Walter Model, to 'Stop playing soldier and come home', much the amusement of the German signals personnel listening in to the exchange.

Chapter 13 contains miscellaneous documents that do not fit easily into any other category but which are of themselves very interesting. We see a German officer (Document 13/2) trying to use the 'old boy' network to get promotion for a friend and another officer asking (13/3) the civilian police to vet the social and political reliability of a young women engaged to one of his subordinates. Document 13/1 (and 5/20) contain chilling descriptions of the murder of civilians carried out by men of the 1st SS Panzer Division in the Stavelot area. In this last chapter we also meet (13/5) another arrogant paratroop general, *Generalmajor* Richard Schimpf, who boasts to his captors that 'Everybody in the American Army knows me'.

When the Ardennes offensive had ended and four German armies had been pushed back almost to their start lines, *Feldmarschall* von Rundstedt issued an Order of the Day. He praised his men for having 'beaten the enemy

16. Document 10/4, ISUM 217, 2 February 1945.

in the great battles of the fall and the winter,' but warned them that Allies were now 'on the march for a general attack on the Rhine and the Ruhr' to 'try with all the means in his power to break into the Reich in the west'.[17] The next volume of *Blood and Steel: The Wehrmacht Archive* will document the German army's desperate attempts to prevent that happening.

Donald E. Graves
'Maple Cottage',
Valley of the Mississippi,
Upper Canada

17. Document 1/4, ISUM 237, 22 February 1945.

A Note to the Reader

The First Canadian Army Daily Intelligence Summaries, from which most of the documents below were taken, were the product of many different hands working under extreme pressure (and perhaps the occasional artillery round or aerial bomb). The result is that there was little consistency in format and terminology from one summary to the next. Some translators and typists retained the original German document format; others simply transcribed everything as they thought best. Even the translations of words or titles can vary from document and, thus, the 12th Waffen SS Panzer Division can be referred to as the *Hitlerjugend*, *Hitler Jugend* or Hitler Youth Division.

This lack of consistency made the task of editing the following manuscript not only laborious but also very difficult. There was also the consideration that the imposition of a strict but artificial consistency on the documents would have, in some cases, adversely affected their period 'flavour'. Therefore, editorial work was kept as minimal as possible. Obvious mistakes in times, names and dates were silently corrected. The titles and identifications of formations and units were anglicized in the document titles and preliminary comments but left as they appeared in the text of the original document. German words and phrases that appear in the text were italicized except for such words as Luftwaffe, Panzer and Wehrmacht that have become so common in English that they are near part of the language. I should mention that Wehrmacht is used below – as, indeed, it often was during the war – to indicate German land forces although it actually encompassed all three German services.

Editorial or prefatory comments by wartime intelligence officers have been put in italics as have comments by the present editor – the latter being titled 'Editor's Comments'. Wartime editorial intrusions are enclosed within round brackets () while those of the present editor have been placed within square brackets [].

One final point is that the Wehrmacht identified corps by Roman numerals, divisions and regiments by Arabic numerals, battalions by Roman numerals and companies by Arabic numerals. Thus, the 5th Company of the II Battalion of the 979th Infantry Regiment of the 271st Infantry Division was part of the LVIII Panzer Corps.

D. E. G.

Acknowledgements

I must acknowledge the assistance given to me by John Grodzinski, Christopher Johnson, Brian Reid, Patrick Wilder, Glenn Williams and, as always, special thanks to my wife, Dianne, my editor and translator.

D. E. G.

German Ranks and their Equivalents

German Army	Waffen SS	British/American
Generalfeldmarschall		Field Marshal/ General of the Army
Generaloberst	*Oberstgruppenführer*	General
*General der Infanterie**	*Obergruppenführer*	Lieutenant-General
Generalleutnant	*Gruppenführer*	Major-General
Generalmajor	*Brigadeführer*	Brigadier/ Brigadier-General
Oberst	*Oberführer*	Colonel
	Standartenführer	Colonel
Oberstleutnant	*Obersturmbannführer*	Lieutenant-Colonel
Major	*Sturmbannführer*	Major
Hauptmann	*Hauptsturmführer*	Captain
Oberleutnant	*Obersturmführer*	First Lieutenant
Leutnant	*Untersturmführer*	Second Lieutenant
Stabsfeldwebel	*Sturmscharführer*	Sergeant-Major Master Sergeant
Oberfeldwebel	*Hauptscharführer*	Technical Sergeant
Feldwebel	*Oberscharführer*	Staff Sergeant/
Unterfeldwebel	*Unterscharführer*	Sergeant
Unteroffizier	*Rottenführer*	Corporal
Stabsgefreiter	*Sturmmann*	Lance-Corporal/PFC
Obergefreiter	*Sturmmann*	Lance-Corporal/PFC
Gefreiter	*Sturmmann*	Lance-Corporal/PFC
Obersoldat/Obergrenadier	*SS-Oberschütze*	Private
Soldat/Grenadier	*SS-Schütze*	Private

* Or *der Artillerie, der Panzertruppen* etc.

Source: War Department, *Handbook on German Military Forces* (Washington, 1945).

List of Abbreviations and Acronyms Used in Text and Notes

AA	anti-aircraft
ADMS	Assistant Director, Medical Services
AP	armour-piercing
APCBC	armour-piercing, capped ballistic cap (shell)
AV (Tech)	Armoured Fighting Vehicles (Technical)
BDM	*Bund Deutscher Mädel* (League of German Maidens)
C of S	Chief of Staff
CG	Commanding General
CGS	Chief of the General Staff
CO	Commanding Officer
COS	*See* C of S
Coy	Company
CP	Command Post
CRA	Commander Royal Artillery
DAAG	Deputy Assistant Adjutant General
DAF	*Deutsche Arbeitsfront* (German Workers' Front)
DAQMG	Deputy Assistant Quartermaster General
DF (SOS)	Defensive Fire (SOS)
DSD	Director, Staff Duties
DTD	Directorate of Technical Development
FAO	Forward Artillery Observer (US)
FEB	*Feld Ersatz Bataillon* (Field Replacement Battalion)
FDL	Forward Defence Line
flak	anti-aircraft
FOO	Forward Observation Officer (UK)

FPN	*Feldpostnummer* (Field Post Number)
GAF	German Air Force, *Luftwaffe*
GHQ	General Head Quarters
GS 1 (A)	General Staff Officer 1 (Armour)
G.v.H.	*Garnisonsverwendungsfähig Heimat* (a soldier only physically capable of garrison duty)
HE	high explosive
HF	harassing fire
HJ	*Hitlerjugend* (Hitler Youth)
HKL	*Hauptkampflinie* (*see* MLR, q.v.)
i/c	in charge or in command, depending on context
Int	Intelligence
ISUM	First Canadian Army Intelligence Summary
KIA	Killed in action
MDS	Main Dressing Station
MG	Machine-gun
MLR	Main Line of Resistance
MT	Motor Transport
NAAFI	Navy, Army and Air Force Institutes
NSF	*Nationalsozialistischer Führungsstab des Heeres* (National Socialist Leadership Staff of the Army)
NSFO	*Nationalsozialistischer Führungsoffizier* (Nazi Indoctrination Officer)
NSKK	*Nationalsozialistisches Kraftfahrkorps* (Nazi Motoring Organization)
OB West	*Oberbefehlshaber West* (Commander-in-Chief West)
OC	Officer Commanding
OKH	*Oberkommando des Heeres* (army high command)
OKL	*Oberkommando der Luftwaffe* (air force high command)
OKW	*Oberkommando der Wehrmacht* (armed forces high command)
OP	observation post
ORs	Other Ranks (i.e. NCOs and enlisted men)
pdr.	pounder
pdv	Probability Directional Value

PIAT	Projector, Infantry, Anti-Tank
POL	Petrol, Oil and Lubricants
PW	Prisoner of War, both singular and plural
Q.	Quartermaster
RAD	*Reichsarbeitsdienst* (State Labour Service)
RdF	*Reichs-Rundfunk-Gesellschaft* (German Radio Broadcasting Service)
REME	Royal Electrical and Mechanical Engineers
RM	Reichsmark
RP	rocket projectile
RSO	*Raupenschlepper Ost* (a tracked truck)
R/T	Radio/Telephone
SA	*Sturmabteilung*
SD	*Sicherheitsdienst* (Nazi Party Security and Intelligence Agency)
SFH	*Selbsfahrlett-Feld-Haubitze* (self-propelled gun)
SHAEF	Supreme Headquarters Allied Expeditionary Force
SMG	submachine-gun
SP	self-propelled
SS	*Schutzstaffel*
VD	Venereal Disease
WIA	Wounded in action
WO	Warrant Officer or War Office, in context
WT	Wireless Telegraphy
z.b.V.	*zur besonderen Verwendung* (for special purpose or special employment)

Chapter 1

Orders

December 1944 to February 1945

Document 1/1[1]

Order of the Day, C in C West, 15 December 1944

Soldiers of the West Front!
Your great hour has arrived! Large attacking armies have started against the Anglo-Americans. I do not have to tell you anything more than that. You feel it yourself. WE GAMBLE EVERYTHING! You carry with you the holy obligation to achieve things beyond human possibilities for our Fatherland and our Führer!

von Rundstedt[2]
Generalfeldmarschall
C in C West

---

1. *Kriegestagebuch* (War Diary), XLVIII Panzer Corps, 15–16 December 1944, quoted in Guderian, *From Normandy to the Ruhr*, 298.
2. *Feldmarschall* Gerd von Rundstedt (1875–1953), the German commander in the West. Nominally, he was in charge of the Ardennes offensive, but was actually just a figurehead.

Document 1/2[3]

Orders, 66 Corps, December 1944

GHQ 66 Corps HQ 15 December 1944
Abteilung[4] Ia

Enclosed order of the Commander in Chief West and addendum of Army Group 'B' Commander as well as that of *Feldjägerkommando*[5] Commander, for special attention, will be made public shortly before beginning of attack.

For the GHQ
The Chief of General Staff
(Signed) Siebert[6]

Distribution for draft

62nd Volksgrenadier Division HQ, 15 December 1944
Abteilung Ia

The enclosed orders are to be made known to troops just before the beginning of the attack

For the Divisional Commander
The 1st General Staff Officer
(Signed) Troitzsch[7]

3. ISUM 172, 19 December 1944.
4. Section, in this case the chief of staff.
5. *Feldjägerkommando* was the meaningless codename given for Manteuffel's Fifth Panzer Army.
6. Probably *Oberst* Alfred Siebert, b. 1903.
7. Possibly *Oberstleutnant* Johannes Troitzsch, b. 1910.

Commanding Officer
Feldjägerkommando zbv[8] **HQ, 17 December 1944**

Nothing can be added to the address of the Führer and Commander-in-Chief of the Wehrmacht made on 11 and 12 December 44. I expect that all Regimental and Battalion commanders be informed.

The following is to be especially emphasized.

(1) We will march day and night, if necessary, fight all the time. All armoured vehicles and even the tanks themselves will roll at night. The founder of our arm, General Guderian, says to each tank commander, 'night is the tanker's friend!'

(2) Anyone, whether with the infantry, armoured infantry, reconnaissance or engineers, who has trouble with his vehicle, will march on foot toward his objective. What we are going to lose on sweat during the following weeks, we will save on blood during the next few months!

(3) The super-sensitivity as far as enemy aircraft is concerned, must be overcome. Remedy: Employ vehicles in width and depth, active AA defence by every soldier, camouflage, digging in of vehicles, weapons, and men.

Our ground mission must be continuous. Otherwise, we will not achieve our goal.

(4) No tank officer, no tank man dare disappoint us, they must all be clear in their minds as to their mission.

'On towards the enemy and go through him.'

Regulate your supplies; don't leave anything to chance.

(Signed) von Manteuffel[9]
Generalderpanzertruppen

Addition to Daily Order of C in C West

We will not disappoint the Führer and the Fatherland, who created the word of retribution.

Forward in the spirit of Leuthen.[10]

---

8. Z.b.v or *zur besonderen Verwendung* meaning 'Special Purpose'. It was usually used to designate temporary formations or units.
9. *General der Panzertruppen* Hasso-Eccord, *Freiherr* von Manteuffel (1897–1978), commanding Fifth Panzer Army.
10. The Battle of Leuthen, fought between the Prussian and Austrian armies in December 1757, was one of Frederick the Great's most famous victories.

Our motto is especially now:

No soldier in the world must be better than we soldiers of the Eiffel and of Aachen.

(Signed) Model[11]
Generalfeldmarschall

Forward, march, march! In remembrance of our dead comrades, and therefore on their orders, and in remembrance of the tradition of our proud Wehrmacht!!

v. Manteuffel
General

Document 1/3[12]

Order of the Day for Christmas 1944

COMRADES OF THE ARMY GROUP!
FIGHTERS FROM AACHEN AND THE EIFEL!

For the sixth time in this war we are celebrating Christmas at the front.

Christmas is the nicest holiday of the German family. The deep sentiment and miraculous strength of our nation appears in its proper light under the Christmas tree. During these days our thoughts are with the beloved ones at home more than at any other time. Our hearts are with them, even though the mail brings their greetings and good wishes rather late, because ammunition and battle supplies are more important.

Christmas is the day of 'peace on earth'. Our enemies do not want peace. The British and Americans, the allies of Bolshevism, desire the destruction and doom of our nation. They hate our German Christmas. For this reason we must enforce peace by the sword. For this reason we dedicate all our efforts to the utmost to the winning of the war.

---

11. *Generalfeldmarschall* Walter Model (1897–1945), commanding Army Group B and the actual senior commander of the Ardennes Offensive.
12. ISUM 193, 9 January 1945, from 82nd Airborne Division.

During this month of December we have drawn the sword of revenge in order to fight the great winter battle in the west. The young *Volksgrenadier* Divisions, the veteran infantry divisions, and the Panzer divisions of the Army and the Waffen SS, remarkably well supported by strong units of Army and Flak Artillery and other units committed, have broken through the deeply defended front of the First American Army and have penetrated into the territory of our surprised enemy. Numerous squadrons of the Luftwaffe have heroically fought against a numerically superior enemy in order to provide a protective umbrella for the ground forces which are attacking with great bravery.

We have seen the joy of the population in the Eifel when our armies rolled forward to the attack, armed with new weapons forged by the home front despite the terror of bombing. We have seen the happy faces of the people in the liberated German towns. We know that all of Germany looks upon us with pride and expectation. Their hopes were never greater.

Therefore, we must fight with undiminishing bravery during the Christmas days of 1944. We shall give the happiest Christmas present to Germany and our Führer, Adolf Hitler: A GERMAN VICTORY. What the fighters of Aachen prepared as a shield of defence must be finished by the fighters from the Eifel as a sword of revenge.

Christmas is also the day of Yuletide, the day of the rising light. The turn of fate is in our hands. If Germany continues to fight and work, the light of victory will shine for us. Soldiers of the Eifel and of Aachen! We have attacked the enemy in the spirit of Leuthen. We shall defeat him in the spirit of Leuthen. And then, some day, there will be the peace of Christmas over Germany again.

(signed) Model
Generalfeldmarschall

Document 1/4[13]

Order of the Day from C in C West, 13 February 1945

15th Panzergrenadier Division
Divisional HQ National Socialist Political Education Branch
13 February 1945

Soldiers of the Western Front!

The enemy is on the march for a general attack on the Rhine and the Ruhr. He is going to try with all the means in his power to break into the Reich in the west and gain control of the Ruhr industry. You know what that signifies so soon after the loss of Upper Silesia. The Wehrmacht would be without weapons, and the home country without coal.

Soldiers, you have beaten the enemy in the great battles of the fall and the winter. Protect now your German homeland which has worked faithfully for you, for our wives and our children in the face of the threat of foreign tyranny. Keep away the menace to the rear of the struggling Eastern front, so that it can break the Bolshevist onslaught and liberate again the German territory to the east.

My valiant fellow-combatants: The coming battles are going to be very hard but they demand that we stake our utmost. Through your perseverance the general attack of the enemy must be shattered. With unshakeable confidence we gather round our Führer to guard our people and our state from a destiny of horror.

Distribution as for
The C in C West Wehrmacht report

Signed v Rundstedt
Generalfeldmarschall

13. ISUM 237, 22 February 1945.

Chapter 2

Special Forces (1)

150th Panzer Brigade and Operation Greiff

Document 2/1[1]

Special English-Speaking Units in the German Army

Wartime Intelligence Officer's Comments

The following document discovered by XII Corps is a copy of a letter dated 30 October 1944 sent by HQ LXXXVI Corps to Parachute Regiment Hubner. It is doubtful that sufficient personnel with the necessary qualifications to form two battalions of the type envisaged here would be available to the Wehrmacht at this time. If, however, such formations are being organised, their potential threat as infiltration units needs no stressing.

The Führer has ordered the formation of a special unit of a strength of about two battalions for employment on reconnaissance and special tasks on the Western Front. The personnel will be assembled from volunteers of all arms of the Army and Waffen SS, who must fulfill the following requirements:

(1) Physically A1, suitable for special tasks, mentally keen, strong personality
(2) Fully trained in single combat
(3) Knowledge of the English language and also the American dialect. Especially important is a knowledge of military technical terms.

1. ISUM 152, 29 November 1944.

This order is to be made known immediately to all units and HQs. Volunteers may not be retained on military grounds, but are to be sent immediately to Friedenthal near Oranienburg (HQ Skorzeny) for a test of suitability, but a value will be put on fighting spirit and temperament.

Captured US clothing, equipment, weapons and vehicles are to be collected and reported for the equipping of the above special troops. Personal wishes of the troops to make use of this kind of captured equipment must take second priority. Details will be notified later.

Divisional Commanders are asked to take a personal interest in the formation of the above organisation. Rank, surname, christian name, unit (HQ) and date of departure of volunteer officers, NCOs and men who fulfill the conditions and are sent to Friedenthal, are to be reported to G Ops by 2000 hours on 31 October 1944.

Divisional Q staffs are entirely responsible for the collection of the captured equipment and will render a report by 1 November 1944 to Corps Q Branch.

(Signed) Wissman[2]
Chief of Staff

Document 2/2[3]

Orders Regarding Special Units

Subject: Operation 'Greiff'[4]

(1) Higher HQ planned to include in the attack the operation 'Greiff'.
(2) Undertaking 'Grieff' will be made by our forces with American equipment, American weapons, American vehicles, American insignias – especially the 5-pointed yellow or white star may be painted on the vehicles.

2. Possibly *Oberst* Helmuth von Wissman.
3. ISUM 171, 18 December 1944.
4. Griffon or gryphon. The griffon was a mythical creature, a powerful entity that was part eagle and part lion.

(3) To avoid confusion with enemy troops, the forces employed in undertaking 'Greiff' will identify themselves to our own troops:
   (a) During the day – by taking off their steel helmets.
   (b) At night – by red-blue light signals with flashlights.

(4) Forces of the undertaking 'Greiff' will also identify themselves to friendly troops by painting white dots on houses, trees, and roads used by them.

(5) Employment of forces of undertaking 'Greiff' will also identify themselves to friendly troops by painting white dots on houses, trees, and roads used by them.
   (a) Trois Ponts (5 km SW Stevelot). Bass Bodeux, Vilettes, Bra, La Fourche, Haarrs, Deux Ryn, Roche a Freus.
   (b) Right (8.5 km NW St Vith), Et. Thier, Ville du Bois, Vielsalm, Salmchateau, Road crossing at Point 444 (0.5 km North Joubienal), Hebronval, Rogne, Road crossing at Point 538 (2 km SW Malempre), Monhay, Road fork at Point 430 (eastern edge of Grandmenil), Road crossing Okt. 200 (1 km north Mormont) Roche a Frone.
   (c) Roche a Frone, Aisne, Juzaine, Domal Road fork 2 km SW Bomal, Tchigne, Oneux, Amas, Ocquier, Vervox.

(6) Publication of the above orders through Division down to companies. Written distribution of this order is forbidden. Only Company Commanders are to be informed of this order, except in the case of forward battalions, where platoon leaders will also be informed.

(7) Publication below battalion level may only be made after the objectives mentioned in the operations order under Para. 3 – objective area St Vith – high ground west and southwest have been reached.

For the General Commanding
Siebert, C of S

---

66 Corps
G-3 HQ, 14 December, 1944

In regard to: Operation Greiff

Following further identifications will be used by our troops. Wearing of Swastika armband. White verey-pistol shots, partial head-bandages.

For the General Staff
Chief of Staff. Signed: Siebert

Document 2/3[5]

Germans Disguised as US Troops

The following is an interrogation report of three Germans disguised as US troops who were captured by First US Army in the Ardennes.

PW: PW officer candidate Günther Billing (*Oberfähnrich* 'N. N.' Naval Signal Service) 21 years

Corporal Wilhelm Schmidt. (Formerly with 5 Company 223 Luftwaffe Signal Regiment) 24 years

Sergeant Manfred Permass (formerly with 3 Company 4 Signal Replacement Battalion in Chemnitz) 23 years

Unit: *Einheit Stielau*, (HQ (*Stab*) Solar

FPN: 32397 (This FPN was given only as temporary FPN 'for Chrismas parcels')

Captured: 18 December at Aywaille K51

Preamble: A soldier, a sailor, a Luftwaffe man, prepared to pay the price[6]

Information on Stab *Solar*

In the beginning of November 1944, recruiting for *Stab* Solar started. Men belonging to all armed forces and known to speak English, preferably with an American accent, were commanded to this *Stab* by their superior officers but Corporal Schmidt states he volunteered 'for a mission where linguistic knowledge was desired'.

PW Billing and Schmidt had to report to an SS camp (strength 1 Coy) in Friedenthal. Schmidt was examined as to his linguistic abilities by a board consisting of one SS, one GAF and one Naval officer. He and 20–30 other men including officers were told that the outcome of the examination would decide whether they were to go to the Interpreters' School in Grafenwöhr or Nürnberg or Oranienburg or whether they were to return to their respective units. Schmidt passed the examination but was ordered to refresh his English and for this purpose served three weeks in the PW camps in Küstrin (2000 US PW) and Limburg/Lahn (1000 US PW). Then he was sent to Grafenwöhr. PW Billing was sent there from Friedenthal without interview and PW Permass (obviously because he

5. ISUM 174, 22 December 1944, from First U.S. Army G-2 Report, 19 December 1944.
6. All three men were found guilty of being spies and executed by firing squad.

was considered for driver's duties only) was sent directly to Grafenwöhr without reporting to the board in Friedenthal.

The following troops were in the training centre in Grafenwöhr according to PW: parachutists, soldiers of armoured units, signalmen and linguists. PW estimate the entire strength at 700–1000. Of these 150 were linguists. There are strong indications that all these men were controlled by the 150 Panzer Brigade which trained in Grafenwöhr and to which most of the above 700–1000 men belonged. The commander of the 150 Panzer Brigade (not an SS Brigade) was SS Obersturmbannführer (Major) Hardie. PW claim they do not know much about the composition of their Brigade except that it is equipped with Panther tanks.

The 150 linguists were formed into a unit '*Einheit* Stielau' by name. The title was taken from 1st Lieutenant Stielau, the Company Commander. The real commander, however, was OSF (SS Lieutenant-Colonel) Solar, commanding *Stab* Solar (four other officers belonged to the HQ). PW Billing, who was admitted to the Officers' Mess, stated 40 officers (Army, Navy, GAF) were in the group of 150 linguists. Only two came from the SS. One of the officers was Major Loren. All others were company officers.

The linguists were trained in Grafenwöhr up to 15 November and then in the neighbouring camp Vilseck until 6 or 7 December. At first they were divided into three groups according to their linguistic abilities. Then they were formed into an engineer group, a communications destroyer group (*Nachrichtenzerstörgruppe*), and a radio group. Within these three groups small squads consisting of four officers or other ranks were eventually formed. PW state some of these squads had no officers and some even 2 or 3. Their training consisted of American Army organization, identification, close order drill and linguistic exercises. In addition, there were demolition and radio exercises for the different groups. At the beginning of December the first US weapons and uniforms arrived together with 30 jeeps, bearing arbitrary markings. The destination of the groups became clear. None of the men protested. On 5 or 6 December the 150 Panzer Brigade moved to Münstereifel. *Einheit* Stielau left on 8 December and arrived in Münstereifel during the night of 12/13. The group camped in tents near the gamekeeper's house 1 km from Münstereifel. There, additional US clothing and documents (driver's licences and pay books) were distributed. On 14 December, 29 jeeps, one with each squad of four men, departed heading for Hallschlag P09 and Stadtkyll P99 where *Stab* Solar was located. PW who overslept followed one day later. All men were dressed in American uniforms and had American weapons. For secrecy's sake, however, they were told to wear German parachute overalls while on the German side of the line.

Mission

PW state that it was the mission of *Einheit* Stielau to spearhead the German armoured attack. All jeeps were supposed to operate independently in the rear of our lines. The ten Engineers (Pionier) squads were to act as commandos and to destroy HQs and HQ personnel, the ten communications destroyer squads were to eliminate message centres, radio stations and communications lines in order to create confusion and to make the German advance easier. The radio squads were to reconnoitre behind our lines and to keep the approaching German armoured columns informed about our intentions and dispositions. PW who belong to the radio group state that they were to cooperate with the 150 Panzer Brigade via a message centre (*Leitstelle*). They believe that other squads of *Einheit* Stielau were to collaborate with other armoured units. PW were unable to identify these. They identified the parachutists of the 150 Panzer Brigade, employed as infantrymen, near Stevelot K60.

German Intentions

PW's squad consisting of the three PW (the fourth man of the squad became all of a sudden 'sick') left Münstereifel 15 December and moved to Hallschlag P09. The jeep broke down and PW were not able to spearhead the armoured attack. They reported therefore to *Stab* Solar in Stadtkyll P99 and received another US jeep plus the following mission: to infiltrate through our lines and to reconnoitre the conditions of the Meuse bridges and that of the roads leading to these bridges (Huy K21 to Givet O97). PW were to radio their reports to the previously mentioned *Leitstelle*. In addition PW were told to remain near the Meuse and to expect the arrival of German troops.

How PW were captured

PW penetrated our lines at Stoumont K60 and proceeded to Aywaille K51. PW were behind our lines only one half hour when they were stopped at the bridge at Aywaille by MP. They were asked for the password, and not knowing it, they were arrested.

Equipment of PW

PW, in addition to their American uniform, had German paybooks and dog tags plus the parachutists' overalls (which they didn't wear), two German maps and other smaller pieces of German equipment. The American uniform consisted of steel helmets, overcoats, OD shirts, trousers, US GI shoes and overshoes. PW did not wear leggings or field jackets and only one had a belt. They had American soldiers' individual 'pay records' and various forms including trip tickets and clothing authorizations, and were furnished with details about the 5th US Armd Div in order to be able to answer questions concerning this unit. (PW claim not to know why this unit was selected). PW in their jeep (not seen by the interrogator) had two radios with antenna. They claimed the radio is German but has US nomenclature stamped on it. The weapons were two machine pistols supposedly of the 'Sten' British type. One of them, PW claim, is soundless. Further, they had two 45 cal US pistols and one German Walther pistol, and six German egg hand grenades. PW state that they had 50 rounds ammunition for each pistol and 100 rounds for each machine pistol. PW had 10 rations and German hard tack.

The commando squads did not carry demolition charges heavier than three kilos according to PW.

Greiff

PW were asked by German troops whether they belonged to the '*Greiff*' enterprise. One PW claimed he was given the code word '*Rabenhügel*' (Note: this is the medieval name for the hill where the gallows stand).

Morale

OC Billing: 'I did not have any other choice. I had to obey orders or they would have shot me.' Corporal Schmidt: 'I admit that what I did was unfair.' Sergeant Permass: 'I could have avoided our capture by the MP but I wanted to sabotage our sabotage mission because I want the Americans to win.'

Document 2/4[7]

German Deception

Wartime Intelligence Officer's Comments

An officer prisoner from a group of English-speaking Germans who have infiltrated our lines in American uniform, driving in American jeeps and carrying American identification papers, was captured in Liège last night. Following is a preliminary report and contains only the highlights of the interrogation:

The leader of a German group, who specialises in the kidnapping and assassinating of higher personages and is named Skorzeny,[8] passed through our lines one or two days ago together with 55 to 60 of his men with the mission of killing General Eisenhower. This individual and his cohorts are the ones responsible for the rescue of Mussolini and for the recent kidnapping of Admiral Horthy, Regent of Hungary. Skorzeny and his men will be wearing American uniforms and have American identification papers, weapons, etc. The majority will be disguised as officers. One of their rendezvous points is said to be the Cafe De La Paix in Paris where Germans stay behind agents, and collaborators will meet them to furnish all the necessary information regarding General Eisenhower's whereabouts, security guard, etc. These men are completely ruthless and are prepared to sacrifice their lives in order to carry out their mission of assassinating the Supreme Allied Commander.

The PW states emphatically that the main effort of the German drive is to the Meuse River betweeen Namur and Liège. He states that the three bridges, which were of principal interest to the German Command, were between these two towns and located at Onbre-Rausa, Engis and Huy. PW claims that he heard the town of Liège mentioned several times in connection with dropping of a parachute regiment at a critical time when German SS columns were pushing toward that place. Further, he states that the two main efforts of all the SS Divisions are to be along the roads Stavelot–Laglaze–Lorce–Ayweiler–Liège and the parallel road Malmedy–

7. ISUM 175, 22 December 1944, from First U.S. Army G-2 Periodic Report, 20 December 1944.

8. *Standartenführer* Otto Skorzeny (1908–75), commander of 150th Panzer Brigade and the most prominent German special forces leader of the Second World War.

Spa–Theux–Liège. His story is that the three bridges mentioned above were not to be blown up but were to be reconnoitred and the infiltrators prepared to seize these bridges at the appropriate time. The maximum number of German parachutists who could be dropped in any one operation, he states, is approximately 1,000, owing to the shortage of transport aircraft.

The prisoner states that approximately 70 tanks, some American and some German camouflaged to appear as American tanks, were given the mission of exploiting a breakthrough, moving at night, going into the woods during the day, while English-speaking soldiers reconnoitred our positions in preparation for an attack late the following afternoon. These tactics have, in fact, been confirmed by reports received during the past three days. Another use which is made of American equipment and American-clad German soldiers is to infiltrate during a battle and then at the climax of the conflict start surrendering, thereby causing panic and confusion.

The tanks mentioned above form the 150 Panzer Brigade. This is a special armoured unit also used deeply behind our lines. All vehicles, tanks, half-tracks, scout cars, etc. are either captured American vehicles complete with our marking, or German tanks built up with wooden structures and much camouflaging to resemble US tanks from a distance or at night. The mission of this Brigade is, at a critical time during the present operations, to cause chaos, confusion, and panic in our rear areas as well as seizing certain key points, such as bridges over the Meuse River. Units of the Brigade, operating in small groups, hide in forests during the day and carry out their movements at night or just at last light. In some cases, they operate with advancing spearheads of armoured divisions, and it is believed that this has already happened in the VIII Corps sector. Another form of 'panic' procedure is for units to 'retreat' along our vital main roads blocking traffic by turning around or simulating breakdowns on the road; spreading wild stories to our units as they speed past, shouting that the Germans are only a few thousand yards behind them, etc. These tanks also operate in conjunction with the 'jeep parties' of *Einheit* Stielau.

IMPORTANT NOTE: It is definitely known, however, that these troops identify themselves to each other by the use of a blue flashlight and/or raising the right arm in the air. The answer to this challenge is the left arm raised to the head and/or red light.

Interrogator's Comments:

Like most Germans this man claims that his only desire is to help us and that he is willing to go along the roads to help us identify members of this group if we will agree to give him a gun with which to commit suicide and so retain his 'Officer's Honour'. Undoubtedly he has told us the truth regarding the tactics which this group is to use, the number who have infiltrated and the general scheme of the entire project. It also fits in very well with a captured document outlining operation 'Greiff'. From other sources we have most reliable indications that the attempt on General Eisenhower's life is planned. Whether his statements regarding the enemy's tactical intentions are correct or not will require further examination, which is being made at this time.

Document 2/5[9]

Germans in US Uniforms

120 English-speaking Germans in US uniforms operating in 30 captured jeeps were to precede the columns of German armour in the present attack. These German jeep teams were to be of three types:

(i) 10 radio reconnaissance patrols to report on approaches to Meuse bridges and condition of bridges.

(ii) 10 communications and headquarters destroyers. These teams are reported to comprise a CO (usually an officer), a linguist, a driver and a killer.

(iii) 10 sabotage units to destroy dumps and bridges.

Personnel will all speak English although generally only one in each team is fluent. They will impersonate enlisted and officer rank. US uniforms and equipment are used. Some have dog tags and AGO cards although not necessarily of the same name.

Many of the jeeps may be distinguished by some of the following characteristics:

(i) No windshield or top

9. ISUM 178, 25 December 1944, from First U.S. Army G-2 Report, 22 December 1944.

(ii) No tail light (one headlight)
(iii) A star without a white circle around it
(iv) Pieces of pine branches used for camouflage
(v) Markings on bumper; 7K and 9K with Headquarters numbers from 1 to 40

Any of the following means of identification may be used by GI-clad Germans to identify themselves to one another and to German troops:

(i) Wear pink or blue scarves
(ii) Overcoat or jacket open at second button
(iii) Blue and red flashlights at night
(iv) Knocking twice on helmet
(v) Lift helmet
(vi) Right arm up asking for identification; in answer the left arm is raised to the head

Among special devices reported are:

(i) Ampules of sulphuric acid which can be hidden in match boxes, etc. This is to be thrown into the face of a guard or sentry in order to escape.
(ii) American canteens fixed as time bombs, presumably to be left in or near Headquarters or vital signal installations.

Simple questions of the following type may be employed to establish identity:

(i) Password – reply?
(ii) Show dog tags
(iii) Give serial number
(iv) What is capital of home state?
(v) Who won the World Series?
(vi) Who had the best football team in the USA?
(vii) What is Dewey's first name?
(viii) Pronounce the following words:
Wreath; With nothing; Rather
(ix) What is the name of the 'Windy City'? (Few Germans can pronounce Chicago correctly).

These are sample questions but others should be used as a copy of this document might fall into enemy hands.

In addition to jeeps the enemy's plans call for the use of all types of captured vehicles and tanks marked as nearly as possible in accordance with US systems. These vehicles will be identified to Germans by letters on the front or sides. Letters which have been reported as used are: c, b, k, y and z. Occupants of these vehicles will not necessarily speak English or even wear US uniforms. These vehicles will be used for spearheading columns and attempting to form road blocks and obtain information on our dispositions and defensive positions.

Some of these parties are known to have large sums of American currency in their possession. One man captured on 22 December had approximately $900 and £1000.

Document 2/6[10]

Account of Wilhelm Schmidt, *Einheit* Stielau

Early in November 1944 I reported to an SS camp at Friedenthal where I was examined as to my linguistic ability by a board consisting of an SS, Luftwaffe and a naval officer. I passed this test but was ordered to refresh my English. For this purpose I spent three weeks at prisoner-of-war camps in Küstrin and Limburg, where large numbers of American troops were being held. I was then sent to Grafenwohr where the training of 150 Panzer Brigade was being carried on. The linguists of whom forty were officers, were then organized into a separate unit and given a special course.

Our training consisted of studying the organization of the American army, identification of American insignia, American drill and linguistic exercises. We were given courses in demolitions and radio technique. Then our unit was divided into an engineer group, a communications destroyer group and a radio group. The task of the engineer was to destroy headquarters and headquarters personnel, the communications destroyers were to eliminate message centres, radio stations and communication routes, and the radio group was to reconnoitre behind the American lines and keep the advancing Germans informed of Allied intentions and dispositions.

10. Schulman, *Defeat in the West*, 240–1. Schulman was an intelligence officer in the First Canadian Army and this account is probably from First U.S. Army G-2 Report, 19 December 1944 – see Document 2/3 above.

At the beginning of December the first weapons and uniforms arrived together with about thirty American jeeps. This was our first indication of what our job was to be. To my knowledge none of the men protested. On 12 December we arrived at Münstereifel, east of Monschau, where we were all given American uniforms, drivers licences and paybooks. I was told a number of details about the 5 U.S. Armoured Division which I was to use in answering questions. The mission of 150 Panzer Brigade was to create confusion and disorder in the American rear areas, thereby aiding the advance of the main German forces.

Our jeep, which only contained three men instead of the normal four since one of the crew had gone sick at the last moment, was given the task of infiltrating through the American lines and reporting the condition of the Meuse bridges and of the roads leading to these bridges. We were to make our reports by radio, and to remain near the Meuse until German troops had arrived. We had no difficulty penetrating the American line and reached the bridge at Aywaille, about twenty-five miles behind the front, in just over half an hour. Here we were stopped by an American military policeman who asked us for the password. Not knowing it we were arrested.

Document 2/7[11]

German Soldiers in American Uniform Department – Appeals and Apologies

Wartime Intelligence Officer's Comments

Seven Germans caught in American uniforms in First US Army territory after having been sentenced to death, addressed the following appeal for reprieve to the Commanding General:

This morning, the undersigned were notified of their death sentence for having entered the American zone of operations in American uniforms, in contravention of the Geneva Convention. The undersigned beg to be allowed to present this appeal for reprieve to the Commanding General

11. ISUM 199, 19 January 1945, from 12 Army Group.

with the request for mercy and re-examination of the motives for the act. It may be repeated that the act was not voluntarily committed but on higher orders, and that the undersigned, in the truest sense of the word, were driven into certain death. The personal ambition of a single man is responsible for this criminal action. We were taken out of our old units because we knew English and with the understanding that we would be interpreters, which is an honourable assignment. Only shortly before our commitment were we informed of the criminal background of the whole enterprise. One of my comrades who refused to obey the order, was court martialled and undoubtedly sentenced to death. Therefore we could no longer escape death. We were captured by American troops without having fired a shot because we did not want to become murderers. We were sentenced to death and are now dying for some criminals who have not only us, but also – and that is worse – our families on their conscience. Therefore, we beg mercy of the Commanding General: we have not been unjustly sentenced, but we are *de facto* innocent.[12]

12. This appeal failed and the three men were executed as spies.

Chapter 3

Special Forces (2)

Kampfgruppe Peiper

Document 3/1[1]

An American Officer with *Kampfgruppe* Peiper

Wartime Intelligence Officer's Comments

The following is an account, in his own words, of the experiences of Major Hal D. McCowan,[2] Commanding Officer of the 2nd Battalion, 119th Infantry Regiment, 30th Infantry Division, who was captured by the armoured spearhead of the Leibstandarte Adolf Hitler in the vicinity of Stoumont on 21 December 1944.

On the afternoon of 21 December about 1600, I, my radio operator and orderly were captured by a German patrol which had us covered from all sides in a trap; a machine gun fired over our heads and individuals from another patrol closed in on us from three directions. At that time I was moving away from the front lines where I had inspected the front line positions of my Battalion which was flanking Stoumont from the German's rear. I was taken back to the German HQ at Stoumont and as I passed through the town, I observed preparations everywhere for departure among the Germans. The German commander later told me that it was

1. ISUM 182, 29 December 1944, from First U.S. Army G-2 Report, 28 December 1944.
2. Hal D. McCowan (1916–99) was a professional U.S. Army officer who retired in 1971 as a major-general.

the appearance of my troops on his rear in Stoumont that caused him to evacuate the town that night. I was taken back to the main headquarters at La Gleize, passing through several areas where fire fights were going on between my men and the surrounded Germans.

Knowing my own plans for the capture of Stoumont were put into effect at that time I was half expecting to be recaptured before I reached La Gleize. This was not the case, however. In La Gleize I was taken to the cellar containing the commander of the German troops whose name I later found out was Lieutenant-Colonel Föder Pieper,[3] 1 Regiment, 1 Panzer SS Adolf Hitler Division. A man named Joseph Becker, who had spent ten years in Chicago, USA, served as interpreter. I later found out that the majority of German officers speak English fairly well. The Colonel spent a few minutes trying to get tactical information from me but seeing the attempt was worthless, sent me away again.

I was then taken to a cellar containing a German 2nd Lieutenant and several high-ranking NCOs; they were dressed very faultlessly in their black Panzer uniforms, each with several decorations. I mentally noted at the time that this would probably turn out to be one of their 'bluff' attempts to get information. All of the added effects were there – I was placed in a chair apart from the other occupants of the cellar where the light of a small electric bulb would fall mainly upon my face leaving the rest of the room in semi-darkness. One of the NCOs drew his Luger, examined his clip, reloaded the weapon and laid on the table in front of him. It was with difficulty that I managed to suppress a smile at these obviously studied and rehearsed preparations in a place so identical with what intelligence officers back in the States teach our troops to expect in the hands of the enemy. The only distracting feature to an otherwise perfect setting, as far as they were concerned, was the frequent crashing of an American artillery concentration sometimes quite uncomfortably close. The next thirty minutes were spent in an attempt to extract from me the information I had refused to give the commander earlier in the afternoon. I was surprised to see that as my failure to respond to their threatenings continued they grew no angrier but instead seemed to lose interest in the procedure. Finally I was taken to another cellar where a warrant officer searched me thoroughly, taking my flashlight and knife but leaving me my wrist watch, ring, a little food I was carrying, and my personal papers. I was conducted to a very small cellar

3. SS *Standartenführer* Joachim Peiper (1915–76), commanding officer of 1st SS Panzer Regiment. Peiper was convicted of war crimes and spent twelve years in prison. He later moved to France where he was murdered in 1976.

which contained four other American officers, all Lieutenants of my own regiment. We exchanged information about our present situation.

During the entire time I was in this town I gathered all the information I could from other captives as well as German officers and men (who talked to a surprising degree) about the strength, disposition and condition of the Germans in that area. The Germans in the La Gleize pocket were part of the 1st Panzer SS Division Adolf Hitler. Lieutenant-Colonel Pieper – normally a regimental commander – commanded this column which consisted of more than his normal command. I learned later that the La Gleize pocket consisted of only a portion of his column, a considerable portion being near Stavelot, the remainder near Trois Ponts and further back on the route of the breakthrough.

Initial order to Colonel Pieper contained the information that he could not expect supplies from the rear during the attack, that he would capture both petrol and food for subsistence. Extra ammunition was carried and strict orders against wastage of ammunition was emphasized.

I did my best to determine the objectives of this unit and gained from several sources among the German officers and men that this Division would be the first element in Liège and Maastricht. Colonel Pieper questioned me fruitlessly several times about road and bridge conditions in the Maastricht area.

An amazing fact to me was the youth of the members of this organization – the bulk of the enlisted men were 18 or 19 years of age, recently recruited but from my observations thoroughly trained. There was a good sprinkling of both Privates and NCOs from the years of Russian fighting. The officers for the most part were veterans but were also very young. Colonel Peiper was 29 years old, his tank battalion commander was 30; his captains and lieutenants ran from 19 years to 27 years of age. The morale was high throughout the entire period I was with them despite the extremely trying conditions. The discipline was very good. The noise discipline on the night movements – which I will mention later – was so perfect that I could hardly believe that they could accomplish it. The physical condition of all personnel was good, except for a lack of proper food which was apparent more strongly just before I escaped from the unit. The equipment was good and complete with the exception of some reconditioned half-tracks among the motorized equipment. All men wore practically new boots and had adequate clothing. Some of them wore parts of American uniforms, mainly the knit cap, gloves, sweaters, overshoes, and one or two overcoats. I saw no one, however, in American uniforms or in civilian clothes. The relationship between the officers and men, particularly the commanding officer, Colonel Pieper, was closer and more friendly than I would have expected. On several occasions Colonel Pieper visited his wounded and many times I saw him give a slap of encouragement on the back of heavily loaded men as we were climbing the steep hills, and speak a couple of cheering words.

Later on during the night of 21 December at approximately 2300 I was again taken to the cellar headquarters of Colonel Pieper. I found him in a very much different mood than the cold impersonal attitude which he used formerly. He and I talked together from 2300 to 0500 the next morning – our subject being mainly his defence of Nazism and why Germany was fighting. I have met few men who impressed me in as short a space of time as did this German officer. He was approximately 5 feet 8 inches in height, 140 lbs in weight, long dark hair combed straight back, straight well-shaped features, with a remarkable facial resemblance to the actor Ray Milland. He is the holder of the Iron Cross with oak leaves and had fought in Russia for a long period of time and briefly at Mortain and Caen. He was completely confident of Germany's ability to whip the Allies. He spoke of Hitler's new reserve army quite at length, saying that it contained so many new divisions, both armoured and otherwise, that our IOs would wonder where they all came from. He did his best to find out from me details of the success V-1 and V-2 were having and told me that more secret weapons like those would be unloosed. He said a new submarine campaign is also opening up and that they had been told that there had been considerable tonnage sunk in the English Channel just recently by the new underwater attack. The German Air Force, he said, would now come forth with many new types and which – although inferior in number to the Allies – would be superior in quality and would suffice their needs to cover their breakthough in Belgium and Holland and later to the French coast.

Concerning treatment of prisoners by the SS, I can state that at no time were the prisoners of this organization mistreated. Food was scarce but it was nearly as good as that used by the Germans themselves. The American prisoners were always given cellar space to protect them from the exceedingly heavy American artillery barrages. I was taken for a brief period to the main prison enclosure which was a large two-room, well-constructed cellar quite superior to any I saw in La Gleize. The men were considerably overcrowded and were allowing the guards to bully them a little. I organized the entire group of some 130 into sections, appointed a First Sergeant and laid down a few rules concerning rotation sleeping, urinating, equality and distribution of food, and got the German warrant officer in charge of the prisoners settled upon a fairer method of giving water to prisoners and providing ventilation.

Late in the afternoon of 23 December I was called once more to Colonel Pieper's headquarters. He told me that he had received orders from the commanding general to give up his position and withdraw to the east to the nearest German troops. He said that he knew it to be impossible to save any of his vehicles, – that it would have to be a foot withdrawal. His immediate concern was what to do with the American prisoners of which he had nearly 150, as well as his own wounded. He dictated to me a plan of exchange whereby he would leave all American prisoners under the command of the senior PW, a Captain, to be turned over to the American commander as the Americans entered the town the next day. He said that his wounded would also be left in the cellars of La Gleize and that he would leave a German medical officer in charge of them. He had previously left a considerable number of wounded in the chateau at Stoumont, which had already been captured by the Americans. In exchange for the American prisoners, all German wounded would be turned over to the 1st SS Panzer Division wherever they might be when the wounded were assembled. I would then be released back to the American lines as I would be the only prisoner retained during the foot movement of the Germans east from La Gleize. I told Colonel Pieper that I could not give him any assurance that the exchange would be carried out as it was a matter for higher headquarters. He said that he fully understood and all of the plan concerning the American prisoners was carried out as already stated.

All during the night of 23–24 December plans were laid for the evacuation of La Gleize. At 0300 on 24 December the foot column began to move. Colonel Pieper and I moved immediately behind the point, the remainder of his depleted regiment following in single file. Colonel Pieper told me that he had 800 men to evacuate. I later watched the column pass three separate times and this number was correct according to my own estimate.

We crossed the Ambleve River near La Gleize on a small highway bridge immediately underneath the railway bridge and moved generally south, climbing higher and higher on the ridge line. At 0500 we heard the first tank blow up and inside of thirty minutes the entire area formerly occupied by Colonel Pieper's command was a sea of fiercely burning vehicles, the work of the small detachment he had left behind to complete the destruction of all of his equipment. He told me later that there were a few vehicles he had not destroyed. I could not ascertain the exact reason why.

The foot column was closed into a thickly wooded slope on a very high hill. Colonel Pieper, his staff and myself with my two guards spent all day of the 24th reconnoitring for a route to rejoin other German forces. No food was available at any time after we left La Gleize; the only subsistence I received was four small pieces of dried biscuit and two swallows of cognac which one of the junior officers gave me. The German regimental surgeon later gave me one piece of Charms candy, the sugar of which did me lots of good during the later long march. At 1700, just before dark, the column started moving again on the selected route; we pushed down into a valley in single column with a heavily armed point out ahead. The noise made by the entire 800-man group was so little that I believe we could have passed within 200 yards of an outpost without detection. As the point neared the base of the hill I could hear quite clearly an American voice call out 'Halt! Who is there?' The challenge was repeated three times, then the American sentry fired three shots. A moment later the order came along the column to turn around and move back up the hill. The entire column was halfway back up the hillside in a very few minutes. A German passed by me limping who was undoubtedly leading the point as he had just received a bullet through the leg. The Colonel spoke briefly to him but would not permit the medicos to put on a dressing; he fell in the column and continued moving along without first aid. The point moved along the side of the hill for a distance of a half mile, then again turned down into the valley, this time passing undetected through the valley and the paved road which ran along the base. Several American vehicles 'chopped' the column but at no time was its presence detected.

The entire 800 men were closed into the trees on the other side of the valley in an amazingly short period of time. I could tell then that Colonel Pieper was basing his direction of movement on the explosion of American artillery fire as the probable location of his friendly forces. His information as to the present front lines of both sides was a meagre as my own and he had no radio and no other outside contact. He continuously consulted his map, thus proving that he was quite thoroughly lost. We moved from that time continuously up and down the rugged hills, crossing small streams, pushing through thick undergrowth and staying off and away from roads and villages. At around 2200 Colonel Pieper, his adjutant and his second in command disappeared from the forward command group. I and my two guards were placed in charge of the regimental surgeon whose familiar Red Cross bundle on his back made it easy for me to walk behind. I tried in vain to find out where Colonel Pieper went; one friendly enlisted man of Colonel Pieper's headquarters told me that Colonel Pieper was very much tired out and I believe that he and a few selected members of his staff must have holed up in some isolated house for food and rest, – to be sent for from the main body after they had located friendly forces.

The change of command of the unit also wrought a change in the method of handling the men. A young Captain in charge of the leading company operated very close to me and my knowledge of Latin as well as the German I had picked up enabled me to understand to some degree practically every order he issued. I heard him tell my guards to shoot me if I showed the slightest intention of escaping, particularly when we neared Americans; whereas Colonel Pieper had given a rest 'break' every hour or so, there were no 'breaks' given under the new command from that time until I escaped. The country we were now passing through was the most rugged we had yet encountered. All of the officers were continuously exhorting the men to greater effort and to laugh at weakness. I was not carrying anything except my canteen, which was empty, but knew from my own physical reaction how tired the men with heavy weapons load must have been.

I heard repeated again and again the warning that if any man fell behind the tail of the column he would be shot. I saw some men crawling on hands and knees. I saw others who were wounded but who were being supported by comrades on either side up the steep slopes; there were fully two dozen wounded in the column, the majority of whom were going along quite well by themselves. There was one Captain who was rather severely wounded, the Colonel had told me, who moved along supported by another officer and a medical NCO and was still with the unit the last I saw of him.

We approached very close to where artillery fire was landing and the point pushed into American lines three times and turned back. I believe the Germans had several killed in these attempts. Finally the commander decided to swing over the ridge and come down in the next valley and try to reach their lines. I was firmly convinced by this time that they did not know where they were on the map as there were continuous arguments from among the junior officers as they held their conferences. At around midnight the condition of the men was such that a halt would have to be given as well as warmth and food provided. I heard the Captain say that he would attempt to locate a small village where the unit could hole up for the rest of the night. At approximately 0100 I believe I heard word come back that a small town was to the front which would suffice. At this time I was not forward near the point – my guards held me back near the position which was occupied by the covering force between the village and the west – that is to say, towards the American rear.

The outpost had already moved into position before firing broke out not very far from where I was standing. My guards and I hit the ground, tracer bullets flashed all around us and we could hear the machine gun bullets cutting the trees very close over us. The American unit, which I later found out was a company, drove forward again to clear what it obviously thought was a stray patrol, this time using mortar fire as well. The mortar fire fell all around on the German position. I do not know if my guards were injured or not – shrapnel cut the trees all around us. The American machine gun and rifle fire was very superior to that of the covering force. I could hear commands being shouted in both German and English with the latter predominating. There was considerable movement around me in the darkness. I lay still for some time waiting for one of my guards to give me a command. After some time I arose cautiously and began to move at right angles from the direction of the American attack, watching carefully to my rear to see if anyone was covering me or following me. After moving approximately 100 yards I turned and moved directly toward the direction from which the American attack had come. I can remember that I whistled some American tune but I have forgotten which one it was. I had not gone over 200 yards before I was challenged by an American outpost of the 82nd Airborne Division.

Document 3/2

From the Bulge to the Rhine: An Unhappy Austrian Flak Sergeant with *Kampfgruppe* Peiper and Afterward

Wartime Intelligence Officer's Comments

Feldwebel Karl Laun participated in the Rundstedt offensive with 84 Flak Sturm Abteilung,[4] *then attached to KG Peiper. He saw the initial successes of the do-or-die campaign, its slowing down, and its inevitable consequences.*

4. *84 Flak Sturm Abeilung* was a light mobile anti-aircraft unit of the Luftwaffe, which accompanied the army. It comprised about 500 officers and men and 30 light anti-aircraft guns of 20mm and 37mm caliber, some self-propelled and some towed.

Deserting to US troops on 6 March 1945, he brought along his diary which shows some very interesting sidelights on the history of the past three months.

Laun is 27 years old, a former university student in Vienna, an intelligent fellow with a wide perspective. He disavows Nazism out of religious reasons.

15 December 1944[5]

Since the last few days a marked activity again prevails in the Battery. The displacement from Grevenbroick to all the way up here into the Eifel is not accidental. Why, there has not been a day of idleness in the Battery since I can remember – and now it has been already eight days that we are hiding in this thicket. To excuse this, the Old Man names us a pious fable of the big bad British paratroopers who – of all things – have chosen to descend in the Eifel wilderness.

Tonight, at last, the veil is lifted: every crack Division in the Wehrmacht has been alerted and is now gathered here in the Eifel. Our marshalling area is in Dahlen. The Old Man addresses us as follows:

> Tomorrow is Der Tag. Remember the 16 December, the turning point of the war. Germany's fate for the next 100 years will be in the balance. Thousands of airplanes (German planes – it goes without saying) will appear in the skies, bursts from thousands of artillery pieces will pave the way for our infantry, as a matter of fact, even German soldiers dressed in American uniforms will participate in the fight – in order to assure an even speedier success.

That did really happen? Everything was idle talk again. No special concentration if airplanes, a few solitary artillery missions, otherwise nothing new on the Western Front. Once more they were able to drive the dumb German Heinie forward, perhaps for the last time.

16 December 1944

Last night the platoon leaders received their march orders, but march orders notwithstanding, H-hour (0500) still finds us lying fitfully in an air raid shelter. Something must have gone hay-wire. Finally at 1700 we see *Kampfgruppe* Peiper approaching. My platoon and I stand at a street crossing west of the town (Dahlen) ready to join the convoy. The Tiger Royals present an imposing picture as they thunder past us, their exhaust pipes aglow. This is an example of the machine age being directed into a fiendish path. And it is significant that it was the Germans who gave birth to this spirit of wanton destruction.

5. ISUM 269, 26 March 1945, from First U.S. Army.

It is a long night, but the difficulties of convoy driving are keeping me awake. Dead silence permeates Kronenburg – not a soul in sight. The silence is only broken by columns trying to join the convoy. We reach Stadtkyll and the first American PW are marched past my vehicle. They look dead-tired; most have probably already marched a hell of a long way. The battery comes to a halt, and I try to catch a few winks, but the doodle-bug,[6] or as the population calls it, 'the Eifel terror' always rudely awakens me. Like a cyclops it rages through the night – a truly heinous weapon.

17 December 1944

We approach Losheim at dawn. Just before we get to the town, a battle group turns off to the left – and it suddenly becomes ominously quiet. No one of us knows at this time that we have now become the advanced tank column, everybody still deceives himself into believing that we are still secure in the second echelon. The typical fate of the *Landser*:[7] to stumble around in a blackout of ignorance until suddenly a cruel streak of lightning lights up the darkness and in its harsh clarity shows his position of utter hopelessness.

Another halt is called before Losheim. Suddenly an intense artillery fire breaks loose and everybody crouches into some ditch. Nobody knows what to do, till finally somebody has enough sense to order 'Dig in'. That sort of thing for advance parties was frowned upon in earlier stages of the war, but '*tempora mutantur nos et mutantur in illis*'.[8] When we have finished digging our fox holes, the command comes through 'Mount your vehicles'. In the meanwhile the German artillery on both sides of the streets fires a total of 2 rounds as 'counter-battery mission'. We advance 500 metres and then stop again, no doubt in order to await noon or rather the *Jabos*.[9]

There they are already, those Thunderbolts and Lightnings. Their flying order is perfect, with only the 2 Mustangs, those Katzenjammer kids, diving in and out of formation and generally indulging in gymnastic horseplay. They are always there where there is something interesting to dive on.

Now the first wave of Thunderbolts starts diving at us. Our quadruple Flak platoon opens up and succeeds in setting the last plane on fire. However, our positions here along the highway are so unfortunate that a series of

6. Slang term for the V-1 flying bomb.
7. *Landser* was the German slang term for the common or private soldier, equivalent to the British 'Tommy' or the American 'G.I.'.
8. A Latin phrase usually translated as 'Times change and we change with them'. It is clear that Karl Laun was an educated man.
9. *Jabos*, German military slang and a corruption of *Jagdbombers*, i.e. fighter-bombers.

prematurely bursting flak shells makes 7 men of our Battery candidates for the *Verwundeten* medal.[10]

Instead of the advertised 1000 planes, approximately 50 ME and FW finally arrive, who are evidently very reluctant to enter into dogfights. One can easily sense it from down here how they wriggle and turn to get out of the *Jabos*' field of vision. In the evening the proportion of airplanes shot down is 3:1, in favour of the US. In the late afternoon we continue our advance. All of a sudden, there is a tremendous din followed by stifled cheering. Herr Major Sacken has graciously condescended to drive over a mine. We have two regrets: one that nice Volkswagen, secondly – Herr Major, outside of his aerial acrobatics, has sustained no damage. We drive on, accompanied by the constant pounding of American Artillery. At dawn we get a thin and cold pea soup. Past an abandoned Flak position we advance direction Honsfeld. Stretched on the road lie the first *Landser* victims. They obviously died a horribly painful death. A silent accusation of those – war criminals. The brass know they had better give us a pep talk. Those Michaels [Austrian nickname for Germans] always were suckers for pretty speeches. The latter are not long in coming: Peiper issues an order of the day – Aachen and Metz retaken by German troops; German Panzers have penetrated the American lines in all sectors; our Blitz-bombers were committed in other areas.

After having been given that shot in the arm, we await nightfall. Two of my pieces alternately have to draw each other out of the mud while moving into the bivouac area. Other gun crews were smarter and just stayed behind, marooned in the mud. I start to settle down when a Tiger wakes me up, dangerously close to me. We might have had mincemeat there.

18 December 1944

There has got to be some 'fun' – even for the *Landser*. Therefore, as 'comic relief', we are allowed to participate in the organized looting of the shop of an escaped Frenchman. The SS have already been at work here before us. I'm glad to notice though, that the German civilian population does not take in this form of barbarism.

The retreat route of a US Panzer Army is said to lead over Ligneuville and Vaymonville. But we see no evidence of disorder on this route. Marking our route of advance off both sides of the roads are immobile Tigers,

10. The *Verwundeten Abzeichen* or Wound Badge was a German decoration awarded to soldiers wounded in action. It came in three classes: Black (1 or 2 wounds), Silver (3 or 4 times) or suffering the loss of a hand foot or eye; and Gold (5 or more times) and loss of vision, brain damage or similar serious injury.

Panthers, and even Panther Royals.[11] Everywhere a frantic search for petrol; they even approach the Flak with a solicitation for a few gallons of petrol. The gentlemen from above 'solve the problem' by merely ordering [them] to capture petrol.

Before Stavelot the masses of SS concentrate. Obviously there is trouble brewing in town. And, yes indeed, our AA outfit receives the honour of being allowed to advance into this purgatory. My vehicle is the last one to be given this dubious honour. There is small arms fire, and mortar barrages aimed directly at us. I miraculously escape being hit by shrapnel. A few splinters got into my eye and I can't see a thing as we advance into town. A few knocked-out Panthers stand by the road side. It is said that Belgian patriots took care of them by applying *Panzerfausts*.[12]

There is a giant crater in the road. All men go on a pick-shovel detail. A few arrive in time to witness another example of SS heroism. Three civilians, among them a woman and a girl, are 'vanquished' by a burst from the automatic pistol. Reason smilingly proffered by the SS: 'They did not know the password.'

After crossing the railway tracks the last three pieces regain contact with the first three. The six in between either get stuck or beat it; at any rate we never saw them again. Mercifully the night settles over the impending drama.

19 December 1944[13]

We continue driving for a little while, till at dawn we come to a halt. Nobody knows why we stop, furthermore nobody gives a damn; for our bellies are empty and won't get filled by contemplations over offensive strategy. At day light, there are a few nice bursts and then our Hows open fire on a couple of Shermans which dodge into a forest. Mortar fire proves to us that we constitute the forward lines. Later on, 200 Americans come out of town (Staumont). They gave up. But still I don't think we'll gain our objectives; the tanks are down to their last few gallons of gas.

At last we find some grub. They are 'US field rations'.[14] Like animals we wolve down these delicacies. Unfortunately, artillery fire curtails our mealtime, and we have to dig in – only to change positions as usual just

11. This is clearly an error as there was no such tank. Laun probably meant to write 'Tiger Royals' or Tiger II tanks.
12. The German hand-held, recoilless, hollow-charge anti-tank weapon, which was deadly at close range.
13. ISUM 270, 27 March 1945, from First U.S. Army.
14. Probably American C or K Rations.

when we have finished our entrenchments. This time we take new positions in La Gleize. Behind a school building, at the worst bivouac area in the neighbourhood, we dig in. We are supposed to surround the area with guards; the order came from the SS – the all-knowing SS who certainly know better how to run a Flak outfit than we do ourselves. Another night follows, a night such as I have never experienced before. I dive under our prime mover, but not even the devil could endure this, and I run in long spurs for the cover of the school walls. Apparently, the artillery is shooting at us from three different directions. Without closing an eye I live through this night. During the entire 24-hour period, no supply vehicle reaches us. And I would not mind if they would provide some hot chow for a change. Latrine rumours from SS latrines have it that we are encircled.

20 December 1944

With dawn I return to our positions. I can't believe it, but miraculously only one prime mover became scrap metal. Our bivouac area is punctured by artillery craters.

Without warning, a monstrous, abhorrent picture presents itself to me. Its horror slaps me in the face. Corpses of murdered soldiers. Soldiers, who after an honest fight, had surrendered to our paratroopers. They were then turned over to the SS who organized them into small groups of 6–8 men each for the purpose of the slaughter. Who of these SS bastards has even the slightest inkling of international law, or for that matter, of humanity? Nothing, absolutely nothing, is sacred to them. there they lie, those seven or eight US soldiers, without weapons or helmets, about three paces apart; evidently shot from behind, mute witnesses against a system of murder. They are the witnesses, but where is the prosecutor and where the judge? I know that up above there is a higher tribunal, and I'm certain if we down here don't punish them, that a just Lord will do it unfailingly.

In the afternoon we advance in forced march tempo to a bridge in the direction of Cheneux. In the beginning, our mission is defined as 'bridge protection'. But hardly have we reached our destination, when Peiper requisitions one of our platoons for infantry commitment. To an ever-increasing degree does the SS rely on the prowess of the Flak units, probably to refill their badly decimated ranks.

The din in the village (Cheneux) is maddening, a fact to which I personally testify as I am selected to stay at the bridge. In vain do I try to point out to Herr Major Sacken that an employment of our pieces near the bridge is plain and simple suicide. For an incessant artillery and mortar fire seems to be zoomed in on this point. I inspect the first piece and already find one man of the crew wounded. He is evacuated. I return and hear that another man has disappeared without leaving a trace; probably was expedited into the murky river by a hit. And then I find Lt Porep severely wounded. When I place the unfortunate guy at the Major's feet, Sacken becomes concerned over his own safety. In the meantime, I have already taken it upon myself to order the survivors of my platoon to retreat.

In the meantime, the SS was cajoled into new positions behind Cheneux by threats, kicks, and curses of their officers. At night, American infantry counter-attacks twice. We suffer heavy casualties, while the *Herrenmenschen*[15] sit in bunkers and basements. Prior to taking cover, they displayed their courage by ordering the herding together of all civilians in Staumont. Somewhere in the night we hear the anguished screams of women.

21 December 1944

A German counter-attack at dawn is stifled by enemy fire. Nobody shows any inclination to fight – not even the SS. As a matter of fact, they are the first ones to withdraw. Suddenly one of our tanks makes an appearance near the bridge. Again a frantic solicitation for gasoline. Draining all vehicles, including the Volkswagen, and the wrecked prime movers, we scrape 30 gallons together. The Tiger continues towards Cheneux.

I am darned glad that I don't have to be in the inferno prevailing in that village. Down here the enemy artillery bursts have somewhat subsided. In the morning hours two of my best comrades and I are selected to form a *Panzervernichtungstrupp* (Anti-tank squad). Six *Panzerfausts*, one machine pistol – and now we constitute a formidable force which will be able to stop all enemy tanks. Our battle plans concentrate around the selection of the most favourable route of withdrawal.

Everything at our old AA position is quiet now. The piece lies by the roadside nearly segmented. I am just about to inspect one of my platoon's quadruple guns, when all of a sudden twelve Americans, shouting continuously, their rifles and MPs raised above their heads, break out of a thicket. They shout '*Nicht schiessen*' [Don't shoot]. At first I think this is a ruse and tell my men to go into firing position, but then I recollect the [Operation] *Greiff* boys. Yes, indeed, it's these lads who have returned, accompanied by some sizzling hot farewell messages from the Americans. They posed as the 88th HQ Coy, but the Yankees refused to swallow it. The 'gangs' as they call themselves, at once change uniforms and the gangsters continue fighting as harmless anti-aircraft boys.

15. *Herrenmenschen* or 'master race', was German soldiers' slang for officers.

I don't know how it came about, certainly nobody gave orders to this effect, but suddenly everything on the Cheneux highway is making a dash for our bridge. There is no more stopping; the situation has become hopeless. I swing aboard the first vehicle that comes along and we make a mad dash for La Gleize. In front of a bridge, the SP gun, overloaded with its human cargo, starts sliding and I pick myself out of a ditch. In the meantime the Americans have been able to occupy the heights to the right (east) of the road and their guns pay careful attention to all vehicular movement. I barely succeed in clamping myself onto a passing truck to escape towards La Gleize.

The town has changed since we passed through here on our way to the grand attack. The old burg is aflame on all corners. I run into old acquaintances. Even the action *Greiff*, those scalped Indians, who I already saw at Losheim, make another appearance here. Nobody thinks of placing a gun into position although this constitutes a direct violation of the orders of Herr Major Sacken. Fortunately for us, the American artillery seems to be taking a break too. There is a cold drizzle and if somebody would have tapped me on the shoulder and said 'Hands up, come along', I think there would not have been a happier person in the world.

22 December 1944

This morning we get new orders: to throw a perimeter defence around La Gleize. With this order the *Landsers* begin to realize that we are cut off and encircled. I had a premonition of this. Like a flash, I realize the deadly seriousness of the situation. Should the Yanks catch us here together with the SS – caught together, hung together. And those SS madmen may want to fight to the last man – including us . . .

The boys of my platoon have become taciturn; passively they have accepted their ate. Like robots they go through the motions of carrying out the orders which I pass down from the Battery CO. I know darn well that only utmost alertness and interest could see the men through in this critical moment, but these qualities are lacking as much as the motor fuel in the gas tanks.

We occupy the SE side of La Gleize, facing the railway bridge. Everybody digs and claws to gain the slight cover mother earth can afford. With a woodsaw we fell a few trees and roll them over our foxholes as protection against shrapnel. We add a few shovelfuls of dirt and place a prime mover right over a 4-man slit trench. This improved bunker serves only as inadequate shelter against those Yank mortars.

On the other side of the river we spot American infantry. Our propaganda machine at once starts to work: 'You see, boys, the Americans are retreating ...' In the evening the American artillery cuts loose. We crawl into our trenches like moles. Hunger overpowers me, but in spite of this, I don't dare to get one of my booty US rations only about 30 yards away. The artillery shells fall as quick as hail into our positions.

During the night a plump JU 52 [transport aircraft] hums above us and throws down barrels with gasoline. Many of them land on the American side – where there is an over-abundance of this juice without our involuntary contribution.

In the distance, behind our lines, we hear the grumbling of *Werfers* [mortars]; again a gala occasion for the *Herrenmenschen* to feed us a good line. 'Hooray, they are coming!' But nothing came. Another morale booster is not long in coming. The SS Divs *Hitlerjugend* and *Hohenstaufen* will 'box' their way through to us. But nothing came. Only the monotonous whine of the enemy artillery assumes an even more intense tone.

In the small hours of the morning I find my blanket which I had stuffed into the foxhole. It is frozen board-stiff. But our American comrades sympathize with us and obligingly send over a few phosphorus grenades to make it sufficiently hot for us.

23 December 1944[16]

For breakfast we get a double helping of artillery and mortar fire. We helplessly stand by as an anti-tank gun is jockeyed into position. Just a few moments later it broadcasts its overtures for our benefit. And already the fourth round dissects one of our cannons. Then we become cognizant of the fact that only two of our tanks are still manoeuverable, while just about 18 Shermans race around, firing relentlessly once from one, then from another direction.

I straighten out my accounts with the forces above, for I have given up all hope of escaping this hell alive. Herr Major Sacken stages an appearance among us in the afternoon. The boys wink at each other knowingly; the good Major is really scared stiff. Verbose though he likes to be, he now keeps his trap shut and silently cowers in his hole. Nobody in his vicinity may utter a loud word – 'The enemy is listening'.

Out of the 2000 men who so proudly advanced through La Gleize on 19 December 198454, approximately 700 dejected souls remained. Under these conditions and in the face of the pleasant prospect of an impending

16. ISUM 271-11, 30 March 1945, from First U.S. Army

bomber attack, about which we learn through interrogation of a captured US Major,[17] Peiper decides to beat a retreat (*Absatzmanoever*). But perhaps his prime consideration is that his valuable person has to be saved for his admiring Nazi contemporaries. If he could leave this trap by himself, I don't doubt for a minute that he would gladly leave us in the lurch.

My comrade Heissner is assigned the mission of destroying all secret orders and, after carrying out these instructions, to rejoin our ranks. Only too late do we learn that the charge had an instantaneous fuze. If the poor guy has carried out the order, and I don't think he is the type that could, he has become a victim of the SS murderers.

'On the command "X-mas present" we will fight our way back to the MLR'.[18] Those are the instructions which I get from the Old Man at 2000 hours. Is it possible that we will escape this inferno? Tense minutes crawl by. They add up to hours. Shortly before midnight I awake from my semi-slumber. It has quieted down somewhat. I try to go to the SP gun to get my field pack which I have stowed behind the steel plating, but all I can find are the ragged remnants. It looks as if mice have gnawed on it. So I charge my underwear, toilet articles etc to the account of the Yank artillery boys. At the same moment the din of a dozen death- splitting mortars breaks loose. I make a dive for my fox hole.

24 December 1944

A starlit night sky hangs over La Gleize. It has grown bitter cold. The flames, still bursting forth from the ruins, flicker spookily. In between, as if demonstrating that the end is at hand, the American artillery punctuates the death-sentence of this town. Since last night the impacts lie exclusively within this small place. The field hospital has to be moved to the comparative safety of cellars.

We start out again at 0200. The once so arrogant SS battle group Peiper collects its sad-looking remnants. In single file we march over the road bridge south of the town. Objective: to regain the MLR at Trois Ponts. The Tigers, Panthers, a large number of vehicles, SP guns, weapons, now become booty of the Americans, providing they haven't been knocked out by Yank artillery already. I even forego the destruction of my 2 cm AA pieces, although I had orders to do so.

17. This is Major Hal McCowan; see Document 3/1 for his account of his time with *Kampfgruppe* Peiper.
18. The MLR, Main Line of Resistance, was the line designated to be held at all costs and if any part was taken by the enemy, it was to be recaptured by an immediate counter-attack. The German term was the *Hauptkampflinie* or HKL.

The way leads over cliffs and through swampy bayous, which often look deceptively as if they were frozen. The *Panzerfausts* load us down; nobody knows why he drags these bothersome gadgets with him. Slyly and cautiously these toys are discarded. A few machine pistols and carbines follow suit.

Our password is 'Christmas Present' – and we get it. When we reach the mountain top at daybreak, the surprise parcel already awaits us. It comes in the form of a column of troops marching down a newly constructed forest road. At first we don't know whether we have Germans or Yanks in front of us. However, that characteristic US steel helmet soon dispels all doubts. All discipline breaks as everybody scrambles for cover. The danger passes, they don't see us. But the long chain of 700 men has irrevocably been broken. I am fortunate in having my lensatic compass with me and I take it upon myself to select the escape route for my small group. The lengthy detour around Bodeux appears safer to me than the direct road over the bridges at Trois Ponts. Noontime finds us exhausted, and with empty stomachs. Nobody has a bite to eat with him; orders were to carry along the small arms and nothing but the small arms. A burning thirst, which is caused by the dry cold, bothers us most. The men tear the ice-covered snow from the trees and suck on it. Others, animal-like, throw themselves over each puddle and drink the muck.

We have to cross one more stretch before we get to Bodeux. In packs of 20 men each, we dash over the road. With our steel helmets in our hand, with our ragged camouflage suits we look more like hobos than soldiers.

Dejectedly, through a fog-curtain, does the sun sink on our mad antics down here. We stumble along, but then our troubles start multiplying, for the *Jabos* circle above and apparently take an interest in us. We perspire profusely in our heavy camouflage suits. At last I get myself to stoop over a murky creek, but my thirst becomes only more painful.

The forest seems to be without end. Under the curtain of darkness we cross a busy highway. In the meantime 200 men have gathered again and this group tries to reach the German lines south of Wanke.

Hunger forces me to eat my carefully hoarded chocolate bar. But the thirst become insufferable; our lips are chapped and start cracking. I don't give a damn any more about the cleanliness of the puddles over which I throw myself, but the mucky moisture begins to nauseate me.

The men are becoming more and more exhausted. Here one falls by the roadside, there another breaks formation – probably to stay behind and spend the rest of the war in a prison camp. When we take a 5-minute break, some fall asleep on their feet, don't wake up when we resume march – and in the darkness we don't see them again. Morale as well as the thermometer seems to be reaching the zero point. We stumble over rocks, get stuck in the moors, tear our hides on the primeval underbrush. At last we reach a good road. We follow it and then find a giant castle. Perhaps it is an abbey. But our dream castle all of a sudden turns into a bastion as only 100 metres away we see parked American vehicles. An American sentry challenges us.

We have been challenged – and like a bunch of cornered rats we scatter back into the forest. One of the *Greiff* boys gets orders to approach the sentry. An argument between the real and the pseudo-American ensues. And the incredible insolence of the *Greiff* man succeeds! He manages to deceive the sentry. But still we take the precaution of making a wide circle around the castle.

We reach a railroad overpass; after that the Salm, a small river – but at a temperature of 10 below zero (Celsius), a crossing of even this creek does not constitute one of the niceties of life. Two men stumble and disappear in the whirlpool of the swollen river. I am icy wet as I reach the opposite shore. The reception committee already awaits us – one of our SS friends. One can't recognize his rank in the darkness, but he shows his superiority by dealing out curses and kicks to the stragglers. On the other side of the river these courageous gentlemen were very quiet and subdued; but now, knowing the last American sentries are safely behind them, they at once assume again the typical SS arrogance.

25 December 1944[19]

So that was my Christmas! A merry Christmas indeed. At dawn, around 0400 hours, I reach the town of Ville de Bois, where we at last see German outposts again . . .

That the long detour we took over Bodeux paid dividends we learn in the morning. Other groups of stragglers who tried to cross the Salm at Trois Ponts got entangled with American platoons in which entanglement the KG suffered some casualties, among them Peiper, who stopped a bullet with his hand. Oh hell, why couldn't that Yankee take better aim?

I am overjoyed to be out of this action. To have fought with the SS sure isn't a recommendation for the visit I intend to pay. Perhaps there'll soon be a better chance to surrender. But it was just out of the question to get myself caught in the company of those SS criminals.

19. ISUM 272, 31 March 1945, from First U.S. Army.

In the afternoon we resume our march, direction Recht. I notice with horror that my feet fail me. They are frozen. My friend 'organizes' a bicycle – and like a piece of baggage I hang onto the rear wheel. In Recht we at last have a night of rest, but we have to loot from the abandoned houses. In Ville du Bois the army had not even provided us with as much as a dry crust of bread, an example of the Fatherland's gratitude which Herr Goebbels so glibly has promised us.

26 December 1944

Looking for the rest area of my battery, I become from afar witness of the US bomber attack on St. Vith. The forest forms a sound-proof wall against the rumbling detonation of the bombs, but thick smoke indicates that 6 km in front of me a town is dying by being disemboweled. A never ceasing array of airplanes flies in loose formation over St Vith. The thunder of the motors resounds in my body. How often have I witnessed such a modern Pompeii, but here the causes are not natural but are brought about by a few power-mad individuals who were seized by the mania to rule the whole world.

Early in the afternoon, much too early to suit me, I regain contact with the mad *Sackenhaufen* [this approximates to 'bunch of bags' – a pun on the Battalion CO, Major Sacken], the 84th squirrel cage as we 'proudly' call ourselves. I make my way through the kitchen of a neighbouring battery. A limping bomber appears overhead, returning from the St Vith show. All of a sudden, the damned thing, evidently trying to get rid of its eggs, starts diving towards that nearby field kitchen . . .

And now the bombs start dropping. I throw myself down. When I dare to rise again I look over to the field kitchen. It's gone; the cook and mess personnel are dead or severely wounded. Well, there went our supper.

Captain Koch (Battery CO) puts in an appearance. I scarcely recognize him – he has become so quiet since La Gleize. Has he too come to the realization that one can't conduct a war with inadequate supplies staring one in the face at every turn? In Wiederemmels I make an interesting discovery. The lice are about to devour me. Of course, in La Gleize I had no time to take care of such 'minor details'. I don't even mention the nice l'il scabies[20] which also have attacked me. This illness is apparently quite fashionable in our battery.

20. Scabies is a skin disease caused by the presence of a tiny parasite, which moves from human to human in crowded and unhygenic conditions. The afflicted person would experience skin rashes and skin irritation and itching. It was common in all armies during the war but was treatable.

27 December 1944

The remnants of the battery are scraped together and Captain Koch counts heads and lo and behold a few heads and their owners are among the missing.

The bitter pill which is in the coming is being sugar coated by a few bars of chocolate (Scho-ka-kola)[21] which are distributed. And here it comes. General Pickert addresses 'his boys' of the 84th – 'You men fought heroically – I know you are just itching for another chance to oppose the enemy with new weapons.' Hell, the only itching I can feel is caused by scabies.

The ire of the men knows no limits. That . . . bastard General, what a slick, contemptuous way to cheat us out of our 14 days furlough, which, according to the Führer's orders, is to be given to men 'who fought their way back to the lines after being surrounded.' The *Landsers* look at each other, uncomprehendingly. Miserable, beaten, licked, ill and no equipment except what we wear on our itching bodies – and we are supposed to go back into the line. The venom of the men is unmitigated by the generous distribution of decorations ('E.K'[22]).

During the night I toil over two prime movers with US artillery fire spurring us to greatest haste. The two motors alternately go on strike, and we try to get them under cover before the Thunderbolts start their daily parade again. We drive all night to reach our destination.

28 December 1944

To change radiators at a temperature of 10 below zero (Celsius) is a time-consuming and unpleasant task. It's already late afternoon when I reach Blindert. Blindert is an infinitely small hamlet. In spite of this fact, our billeting officer succeeds in quartering the entire battery here. Space per man: about 3/4 of a square metre. That, without saying, doesn't apply to the Herrenmenschen.

29 December 1944

Tonight we are packed so tightly that lice can travel freely from one host to the other and enjoy their progenitive processes. But the mating season is in full swing somewhere else too. The officers are privately billeted – and among others, baby-faced Lieutenant Kratzenberg has a crease in his pants and a fat village wench in his comfortably heated room. He entertains

21. 'Scho-Ka-Kola' was the brand name of a chocolate and caffeine combination that was often found in German military rations as it was a mild stimulant and increased alertness. It is still being sold today.
22. 'E.K.' *Eisernes Kreuz* or Iron Cross.

the young lady by dramatizing his courageous exploits at St Vith, as his orderly tells us. What a laugh! This dauntless crusader heard of the St Vith operation only in the *Wehrmachtbericht*.[23] He joined our unit when we came to the Niederemmels 'rest' area . . .

In the next village we get the inevitable pep talk. New weapons and equipment are on the way. They cautiously omit the mention of clothing. We know thereby that we will stay in the lousy, mud-caked, tattered and punctured uniforms in which we 'celebrated' Xmas Eve at La Gleize.

30 December 1944

My pal Heinz and I are determined to go to the hospital; our urge for cleanliness and physical restoration has become so imperative that it is actually a matter of self-preservation. Our medic is stone-hearted and states that he can cure such trifles himself without the benefit of a doctor. Our battalion surgeon became a PW at La Gleize. Well, we've both decided to resort to trickery. We tell the medic that the First Sergeant thinks we should go to a hospital. Then we turn around and tell the First Sergeant that the medic considers our hospitalization unavoidable. Result: the *Spiess* (First Sergeant) has the orders typed out and sends us over to the Old Man to get them signed.

I present the orders. Sacken scrutinizes them; then looks us over. This creature might go and check our story – and I wonder whether our ruse instead of getting us into the soft beds at hospital Bad Neuenahr might not land us in the misery of a Penal Company . . .

'What's the trouble', growls the Old Man. 'Lice, fleas, and scabies', I begin. He interrupts me and reluctantly affixes his signature to the document.

We are on our way to the hospital. The Ahr valley, once known for its excellent vineyards, now looks as if a volcano has erupted here. The battered ruins from Schuld to Ahrweiler show only too clearly what a toll Germany is and will be paying for the folly of allowing the Nazi war machine to develop. The once thriving little town of Schuld – 2000 inhabitants before the war – is now a rubble heap in which 60 people find cave-like shelters.

At the fall of dusk a snowfall sets in. Like magic the scenery changes. Bad Neuenahr stands out like an oasis in the desert of utter destruction. A hospital zone – and the Allied bombers have painstakingly refrained from visiting this town. The Nazis, too, know what's good for them. At the city

23. The *Wehrmachtbericht* or armed forces report was the official German military communique broadcast daily on the radio. It was known to be full of exaggerations, mistruths, half-truths and downright lies.

limits a sign announces that the town is 'Off limits to all troops'. We enter as patients.

The hospital has been lavishly installed in a former summer resort Casino – in stark contrast to the personified misery that is sheltered in those marble plated halls. An endless convoy of *Sankas*[24] rolls up to the hospital. The severely wounded are lined up everywhere and their constant begging for water accompanies us through the reception rooms. In one ward severe cases have already been waiting twelve hours for medical attention. But the surgeons are overburdened as it is and the sawbones grind night and day. A call for volunteers to give out a special diet of cereal to the 'semi-dead'. We pitch in. In the face of such suffering our scabies and frozen feet appear rather insignificant. We also help to carry the litter patients out of the ambulances. The new arrivals are packed into the air raid shelters. There is a smell of freshly spilled human blood in the air, of sweat and of feces. Heinz is overcome by this pestilence-like odour and I have to take him into the courtyard. While we are recuperating out there, a new transport of severely wounded arrives. A group of lightly wounded which hobbled all the way from St Vith to Bad Neuenahr is at once directed to a hospital further to the rear, a fate which we are to share somewhat later. We are allowed to spend the night in the hospital.

I go on the hunt for some extra food – and have the luck to run into a nice gal, a nurse, from home. She takes me to a storage room and supplies me with some extra chow. It's very quiet in this part of the hospital. In a kitchenette I find a young lieutenant, severely wounded – one fingernail was torn off – together with a Red Cross nurse. Tonight he forgets his physical pain and finds solace for his spiritual ills in the company of this patriotic nurse. The young lady is on duty now, as my girlfriend tells me. I think of the rows upon rows of beds and litters where pain-crazed men whimper for water . . .

31 December 1944[25]

This morning I undergo the novel experience of a delousing cure. Clad in bathing trunks I watch my clothes being steamed and gloat over the death of my animal friends. Other *Landsers* join me. Their bodies look like mine – gnawed, fleabitten and infected.

We are ordered to report to another hospital in Niederbreisig. Rumours have it that this hospital is as overcrowded as the one we are coming from.

24. *Sanka*, slang for *Sanitatskraftwagen* or military ambulance.
25. ISUM 273, 30 March 1945, from First U.S. Army.

So we dump our baggage somewhere in Niederbreisig and make our minds up first to ring in the new year appropriately. We walk down the streets of this village. The moon transforms the lazily flowing Rhine into a stream of silver. The peacefulness of this scene compared with the excitement of the past few weeks leaves me with a dissonance of emotions.

We make for the nearest tavern. For New Year's Eve the sale of wine has been authorized. At 2300 hours sharp the first bottle is allowed to be opened. A First Sergeant has established his HQ right in the tavern. He has a liberal amount of liquor and everybody sponges on him. I too frequently go over to the corner where he and a waitress are imbibing. The liquor lies heavy in our empty stomachs and in the rendition of the Rhenish folksongs, beauty is sacrificed for loudness. At 2400 hours a toast: to a speedy peace. Then a few political jokes follow. Even in my alcoholic daze I notice a bull of a man, who has scarcely touched his glass, but acts as drunk and as boisterous as the rest. And glancing behind the bar I notice that the innkeeper is sharing my concern. That guy hasn't cracked a joke yet, but he seems to be quite interested in that political brand of humour. And it is a well-known fact that the Gestapo is everywhere.

1 January 1945

The innkeeper's concern grows visibly. Heinz and I decide to leave the tavern. The fat guy says nothing as we go out. So I guess we'll never know whether one of Hitler's bloodhounds was present at the New Year's Eve party in Niederbreisig.

The hospital is located in the Rheinhotel. We get there late and slightly drunk. The reception clerk doesn't take much trouble with us, and puts us in the nearest ward.

The New Year brings its first surprise. The clerk has placed us in the VD ward! My neighbour solicitously asks me whether I already had my second injection. I shudder when I recall this episode . . .

I am promptly transferred to the skin disease ward. There is no physician available – 70 to 80 severely wounded are still awaiting medical attention. An elderly soldier sits among the *Landsers*. Monosyllabically he joins in the conversation. Grey hair and a drawn face are indicative of long suffering. We get kind of chummy and he confides in me. He was wounded on 23 December when shrapnel punctured his arm and chest. He was shuffled from one aid station to the other; from one hospital to the other; and today, ten days later, he is still wearing the same bandage that some company aid man slapped on his wounds. The latter, of course, are now completely infected. I meet another patient. By contrast, this cripple is a child, 17 years old. He arouses my interest by his loud complaints. He is sitting on the staircase swathed in blood-soaked bandages. A *Jabo* bullet pierced his arm. He suspects that a bone has been shattered. With the tardy treatment he is receiving, it is almost a certainty that this youngster will lose his arm. He doesn't know this, as he aggressively makes speeches against the war, the army and everything military in general. His vehemence draws a circle of patients of like opinion around him. They are carried away by their bitterness, and I remind the fellow that caution is necessary, even here in the hospital. '*Zersetzung der Wehrmacht*'[26] is the usual charge . . .

Dinner consists of a thin one-pot dish without meat. Supper is simulated by giving us a small bowl of milk-soup.

Later I run into the grey-haired soldier again. He received a new bandage which is a farce; a small piece of gauze with paper wrappings on the outside.

2 January 1945

For the time being we are undergoing medical treatment, we are billeted in Haus Mühle, a small boarding house. We sleep well on two stolen mattresses. There is no drinking water, so the waters of the swollen Rhine have to serve. Electric light in this town is out for the duration. But who gives a damn if we are compensated today by a treat rare in this area. We get three slices of bread!

We try to obtain another rare item for our room: a candle. I find a can of pork loaf in my baggage, left over from the booty we took in La Gleize. Just in front of our boarding house we meet two urchins. When we ask about candles and mention 'American rations' they take off and return within 30 seconds with a long, brand-new wax candle. Our joy is short-lived, however, for a little later the sirens start screaming. We head for the nearest air raid shelter and are engulfed in a human tidal wave. The civilian population is preparing for a night in the shelters. Perambulators, blanket rolls, laundry, bags, and babies-in-arms – a torrent of human confusion. In between run stray dogs and children. At last the stream stows itself in a courtyard. Step by step we work ourselves towards the shelter. And there already are the first waves of planes, flying direction: Rhine . . .

Now the flak cuts loose. The air battle is some distance away, but despite this, the civilians present a picture of turbulent fright. Children are crying, and their mothers are themselves too terrified to be able to calm them.

26. 'Undermining the Wehrmacht'. The penalties were severe and might result in execution or transfer to a penal company.

At last everybody is inside the shelter. The soldiers enter as the last ones. Before I go down I see the first flares which bathe the town in unreal clarity. Then the coloured flares follow, dropped to set off the area which is to 'get it' tonight. The thuds start now – the planes are unloading. Thousands of tons of explosives are coming down on a neighbouring town. In between phosphorus rains from the skies, as if to forebode the last Judgement Day. The fires surge skyward and are mirrored in blood-red colour by the black clouds. The first squadrons turn back. I want to see what goes on in the shelter. I stumble down a dark hallway, climb down a narrow wooden ladder into the dungeon-like room. The scene that presents itself here could have been deliberately posed for a painting of the Roman catacombs. Two smoky, tired oil lamps give just light enough to accentuate the utter pandemonium of baggage and bodies. The continuous crying of small children mixes with the grunting of pigs whose stable is in the building next door. The odour coming out of this sweatbox is unbearable.

At last the air raid warden appears at the door and bellows 'End of Alarm!' As we file out I recognize the *Kreisleiter*[27] and his staff of *Goldfasanen*.[28] These yellow swine just emerge out of a 300-metre distant 'Command Bunker'. These command bunkers I remember from former days. They are comfortable concrete shelters, adequately supplied with cigars and a well-stocked bar.

3 January 1945[29]

We don't know yet whether the medicine we have been consuming in copious quantities will be effective. So far we don't notice any signs of progress. Our empty stomachs persuade us to visit the town. With the help of a few 'organized' cigarettes we try to do some black marketing. We go to a bakery, and the barter is accepted by the store-keeper. The baker tells us his troubles. It is well-nigh impossible to keep a bake-shop running without electricity. And for about a week now he has been unable to obtain salt. He tells of the queues of hungry people who are begging him for bread. My mention of the abundance of US rations – evidenced during the Ardennes offensive – evokes a tirade of invectives against the Hitler regime. 'Mark my words,' he concludes, 'the Nazi *schweine* will be driven from the banks of the Rhine. Just remember what Churchill said in November 1944 in Paris.'

27. *Kreisleiter* or County Leader was a local Nazi party official who wielded considerable power in his area.
28. *Goldfasenen* or 'golden pheasants' was a derogatory term for Nazi Party officials derived from the light yellow-brown uniforms that they wore.
29. ISUM 274, 31 March 1945, from First U.S. Army.

It looks as if the BBC, despite the vigil of the Gestapo, is still popular in these parts.

Back in our boarding house the sharp competition for the few pieces of soup-meat ensues. But we are to get something special for dessert. A misguided youngster supplements our frugal meal with a reading of the *Wehrmachtbericht*. '562 enemy aircraft destroyed on the ground by the Luftwaffe.' 'Well, well,' some of the incurable optimists gloat, 'tomorrow we'll bag another 1000.' But, alas, their castles-in-the-air are blasted out of existence by the shrill whistle of the air raid siren, and the harsh reality of a thousand Allied planes destroys any illusion my fellow boarders might have had . . .

We are again in the medical examination room. The chief surgeon himself, a Major, has stooped down to examining bedraggled *Landsers*. He gives everybody a cursory diagnosis – and then declares that 70% of the patients are, in his judgement, healthy specimens and fit for immediate front-line duty (*kv*[30]). The men who return from his examination show clearly three different reactions: one group in a fit of blind rage is so overwrought that they don't give a damn who knows it. 'That idiotic swine; that Nazi s.o.b.; you bastard, come out into the trenches some time and I'll put a bullet through your damned skull.' The other group starts talking to a nurse, desperately trying to convince someone that cripples cannot do combat duty. The third group is submissively silent, but the faces reflect a contained rage, an animal-like hate, a bridled fury that is even more dangerous than the vociferous curses of the first group. I personally belong to the second group and bring up enough courage to voice a faint objection to the Major. 'My frozen toes, my scabies . . .' He interrupts me with a roar comparable to that of a circus lion. I'm a saboteur, a goldbrick. And then he threatens to investigate my whole case history . . .

The major calls me a few more complimentary names, before we manage to beat a hasty retreat. The hospital becomes empty after this radical 'cure'. Cripples are transformed into fighting men by order of this medical miracle-man.

As we dejectedly file out, another endless line already crowds the entrance to the hospital. I'm sure that this human wreckage will have no better luck than the thousands of other groups that came here before them. They will find their hopes for some medical attention and rest shattered by a well-groomed Nazi doctor who has not even the slightest conception of what life 'out there' means. There's a Viennese kid among the new arrivals.

30. *Kampfverpflicht* or 'fit for service'.

I start talking to him. He was wounded in Poland, shuffled from one hospital to the other, till he finally landed here on the Western Front. When he hears of the quack who officiates inside this slaughter house he betakes himself out of range of this surgical voodooist. He is going to try another hospital . . .

4 January 1945

The nice days have passed, but the itchy feeling underneath my skin remains. I hold my travelling orders in my hand. They read 'returned to duty'. My reasoning tells me to comply, but the flesh is weak. Heinz seconds the motion of voting ourselves a short convalescence furlough. We decide to visit his home town. Wehrmacht transportation will be utilized. Therefore we pile into an Army truck as stowaways. In pitch-black darkness we arrive in Koblenz. We feel our way through the ruins. There is a stench of phosphorus and fire. Small flickering flames dance up and down like Northern lights. Deathly silence. Here and there a foreign worker stealthily makes his way along half crumbled walls – looking for fuel and food stores. The death sentence is involved, should he be caught in his nocturnal work. With our red light we impersonate a traffic cop. The driver inspects us with distrust, but this feeling is reciprocal – for this 4-F is proudly displaying the SS insignia. Heinz plays it safe and greets the SS bus driver with 'Heil Hitler'. That breaks the ice. During the rapid trip we learn that we have the rare and dubious privilege of riding in a Party-carrier bus. In Bacharach, Boppard, St Goar and Bingen propaganda material and secret orders are unloaded. In turn, the bus is loaded down with wine and schnapps. Here, incidentally, lies the reason why looting has been prohibited. The gentlemen from the Party receive the privilege of first pick.

The driver's final destination is to be the post office in Bad Kreuznach, but to the consternation of my SS friend, this building is now non-existent. Only a small fire palely illuminates the site of the building which has disappeared through the magic of Allied bombers. A pyre of rolling stock tells the story of past events at the close-by freight station. We double-time through this ghost town . . .

5 January 1945

The large railway bridge between Bad Kreuznach and Bad Münster is among the missing. This prolongs our journey by 6 km. While walking over to the Bad Münster railway station, we are joined by a column of boys carrying bag and baggage. We talk to two boys and learn that this sorry-looking aggregation is the newest edition of the RAD[31] unit in Hermeskeil. These kids gripe and curse like veteran *Landsers*. Their induction notices ordered them to bring sufficient rations for six days. That, one youngster maintains, is like ordering a lame man to lower the world record for the 100-yard dash. Where in Germany can you buy bread, butter and sausage sufficient for even one day? Now these boys have been en route for three days and they are weak with hunger. In the crowded train we meet a pretty and apparently intelligent girl, the fiancee of a first lieutenant. The *Oberleutnant* has obviously left his imprint. She is one of the few civilians firmly convinced Germany will win the war. I ask her whether she ever listened to Radio Luxembourg.[32] She shies away from me as if I were Public Enemy No. 1.

The trip is a nightmare. Compartments are stuffed with a compressed mass of bodies. The night is black and cold, and the closet-like compartment lacks light and heat as well as windows. Civilians make this hellish trip without the benefit of railway tickets. Nobody has a chance to check. We arrive at Türkismühle frozen to the marrow. We leave the train by a door leading to the wrong platform in order to slip through the net of MPs. We cross the square opposite the station, just get ready to turn a corner when all of a sudden an MP towers in front of us. We know there is no getting away from this MP. So we try it with insolence. Heinz at once asks his directions. The joker feels himself flattered and officiously describes the route. We rejoice in having outsmarted this *Kettenhund*[33] . . .

We resume our trip to the Saar valley where my friend lives. It's peaceful along the highway here. The sun shines from a steel-blue sky and snow reflects the beams, bathing all the scenery in an ocean of light. Why did these loons have to start this war? The murmuring forest and the gay song of the Nahe River symbolize the frustration of a world born to live in peace. In my imagination I still hear the thud of bombs, the screaming of artillery shells, and the detonation of mortars . . . The thought that I will soon have to return to this symphony of death nearly drives me mad. But for the moment I listen to the lullaby of the Nahe.

---

31. *Reichsarbeitsdienst* or German Labour Service. In the Third Reich all young Germans had to perform compulsory labour service, the men usually working on construction projects or agriculture, the women more often involved in domestic matters.
32. Radio Luxembourg was a pre-war commercial station in Luxembourg, which broadcast into Britain and Ireland. It was taken over by the Germans in 1940 and used for propaganda broadcasts. Captured by American troops in 1944, it was put back into service as a 'black' station to broadcast propaganda into Germany.
33. Military Police, called *Kettenhunde* or 'Chain Dogs', because of their shield of authority, which was suspended around their neck by a chain.

We hike around a corner – and there it happens. A *Feldgendarme*[34] stands on the bridge and checks all vehicles and all soldiers. He has seen us – so we can't back away from him. He asks us for our travelling order. We play a desperate game. We pull out or march orders and tell him that Blindert is in the vicinity of Saarlouis. And our luck holds. The dumb flatfoot apparently is ignorant of the geography of the Saar Valley. As a matter of fact, his gullibility is so complete that he stops the next truck and asks the driver to take us along. It is dangerous these days to travel in these large trucks. The *Jabos* swoop down on all vehicular traffic and usually hit their target. What would I do now if those Lightnings would appear. The *Reichsführer* gave orders to shoot at them with machine pistols.[35] Soon they'll tell us to fight *Jabos* with pocket-knives!

Around noon we arrive in Ottweiler and therewith in comparative safety. Heinz's parents are splendid people. They, like many of their neighbours, are more than fed up with the Nazis and try to do 'their share' to shorten the war. They at once comprehend that we kind of have to go underground . . .

7 January 1945[36]

It's 0300 hours. I have woken up in a spasm of fright. And then I know why. Overhead I hear that terribly familiar roar of airplanes. The Yanks or Tommies must be returning from a mission. I try to go back to sleep, but my nerves as well as my body are war-weary – a condition not conducive to slumber. Furthermore I'm no longer used to the comforts of a real feather bed. I toss for hours.

I open the black-outs and light a war time quality, evil-smelling cigarette. The dawn rises on a frost-clear winter day. I look over at Heinz and in the half light watch the regular breathing of his fatigue-ridden body. Warm friendship has sprung up between the two of us. I curse under my breath. For no damned good reason whatsoever I'll soon be shouting once more at him 'Man that gun' when those death-delivering *Jabos* are overhead.

I wake Heinz up by roughly poking him in the ribs. His folks set the best obtainable breakfast in front of us. The hearty meal consists of saw-dust like bread, synthetic marmalade, and Ersatz coffee. I sullenly make comparisons between this and those US cans we 'captured' in the Ardennes. Mrs. Lehnert (Heinz's mother), Heinz, and I discuss the impending visit

34. Military Policeman.
35. *Reichsführer SS* Heinrich Himmler, commander of the Home Army ordered all soldiers to engage Allied aircraft with submachine guns, which was practically useless.
36. ISUM 275, 1 April 1945, from First U.S. Army.

of the *Kultusministerium*[37]-disciple, Heinz's ex-teacher. If we never see this fellow, it will be too soon. An excursion to the family of a friend of Heinz will provide the necessary excuse to avoid this unpleasant encounter.

The family owns a farm in a neighbouring village. We hike over there. Mrs. K gives us a hearty welcome. She tells us that Joachim, Heinz's friend, is on the Eastern Front. They haven't heard from him in months. During the conversation she breaks down and starts crying. Joachim, it seems, was running the farm after his father died in an accident five years ago. He was given an occupational deferment until ten months ago, but was drafted into the infantry. The only male member of the family left at home is Joachim's grandfather. Joachim's mother is complaining bitterly. She talks of the unwilling foreign farm-hands; grandfather, she claims, is already infirm and is unable to help her in keeping the farm going. 'All he does is grumble and complain of his rheumatism,' she goes on, 'and now he's being enrolled in the *Volkssturm* . . .' At this point, this ancient worthy hobbles into view. We talk to him and learn that grandfather was an *Unteroffizier* in the last war, by virtue of which fact he has now been appointed a squad leader in the second *Aufgebot*[38] of the local Volkssturm – And this is Germany's 'last hope' . . .

We eat an old-fashioned honest-to-goodness *Bauernessen* [farmer's meal]. Our hostess has especially prepared a smoked ham, which she had a tough time hiding from the *Ortsbauernführer.*[39] The latter 'inspects' the farms at least once every two weeks. He stays strangely corpulent in these trying times, our hostess tells us.

After having been persuaded to stay for dinner, we are also coaxed to stay overnight.

8 January 1945

We leave this hospitable family around 10 o'clock. We start to hike, but decide to take advantage of the Wehrmacht, as we see an Army vehicle approach. The truck stops and we pile on. We find ourselves among *Volksgrenadiere* of the 167 Div – and, of all things, a *Blitzmädel*[40] – but not of the usual variety. She is not clad in the standard grey-blue of the Luftwaffe but wears the green uniform of the Army with SS insignia on her cap and blouse. Her round, chubby face appears bloated, her body is buxom, but firm. The buttons of her tight-fitting jacket close only with difficulty over

37. Ministry of Education.
38. Contingent.
39. Nazi Party leader of local farmers.
40. *Blitzmadel* or 'Blitz girl', was a member of the women's auxiliary forces.

her over-substantial bosom. So that's what she looks like, the SS maiden. The appearance of this furlough-bound female is in stark contrast to the drawn faces of the lean women in the bombed-out towns. This is the first time that I saw such a representative of SS ideals.

Heinz tells me more of the 'functions' of these harlots in uniform. There is, for example, a camp for these girls. High ranking SS officers, supposedly particularly valuable specimens of the German race, visit this camp from time to time to have the girl of their choice 'delivered' to them, as the technical term describes it.

With a shudder I turn away from this stray example of womanhood. I wonder what the generation born out of this 'selective breeding' will look like . . .

8 January 1945[41]

We are back in Ottweiler – the little town in the vicinity of Neunkirchen. There is no heavy industry in this district, but the same organization of women for labour commitment has taken place. Every day they hitchhike to work which is often miles out of town. The streetcars have long since ceased to run – the bomb attack on Neunkirchen and Saarbrücken took care of that. It frequently happens that key-workers come late to work. The threatened penalties can only rouse a man or woman out of bed two hours earlier, but against the vicissitudes of wartime living they are still powerless. While the women wait for transportation for hours, the *Kreispropagandaleiter*[42] drives a luxurious car in which he distributes documents and leaflets and in turn 'receives' eggs, bacon and tobacco. One has long ceased to even discuss these petty racketeers.

Heinz's parents are residents of Ottweiler for many years and their favourite talk centres around conditions as they were before 1935. The people call themselves *Saarochsen* [stupid oxen of the Saar] for having allowed themselves to be fooled into voting for an *Anschluss*.[43] But during that time before elections everybody lost his head in the deluge of promises and veiled intimidations. After the election the rude awakening came step by step. Now another turning point for the Saar valley seems to be approaching. Three weeks ago, when the first artillery shells started to rain on Saarbrücken, the Nazi 'bigshots' received orders to prepare themselves

41. ISUM 276, 2 April 1945.
42. District propaganda leader.
43. Under the terms of the 1919 Treaty of Versailles, the Saarland was administered by France. In 1935, the people of the Saar voted in a plebiscite for a return to German control.

for an evacuation to the Westerwald and Mittelfranken. Most of them have already sent their wives and children away, while they stay behind for the time being in order to convince the population that there is no danger impending – a fact which they demonstrate by still parading up and down in their brown uniforms and by making life miserable for the old *Volkssturm* men who they drill relentlessly every Sunday.

9 January 1945

Yesterday, we were talking of the *Parteiweiber* [wives of party men]. Today we hear that those Nazi b[itche]s have returned. The danger seems not to be acute at present and these ladies return to their husbands. It doesn't matter that the trains are overcrowded with war workers or that people are awaiting evacuation from their bombed-out towns . . . these Nazis still get travelling permits for 100 km long luxury trips. *Quod licet Jovi non licet bovi.*[44]

Heinz's mother is plagued by gall bladder trouble, but her trip to the specialist in Bad Bertrich has been disallowed as non-essential to the war effort.

Today we had a visitor. Heinz's prospective brother-in-law comes over. He has managed by some incredible trickery to get himself stationed at the local hospital. But he tells us a tale of woe today. A 'deadly enemy' of his has arrived in the hospital – a *Stabsartzt*[45] of the Nazi variety. Peter had some political arguments with him while he was serving under this man in Bad Godesberg.

We are comfortably seated around the dinner table when there is a knock at the door. Automatically we dive into the sleeping room, while Mrs Lehnert throws our plates into the nearest closet. We hear male voices at the door. Has our battery already missed us? Are they now making inquiries at Heinz's home through the local Wehrmacht commander? Through the keyhole we see two soldiers.

But a little later, Heinz's sister gives the 'all clear'. The interruption was unfortunately directed against Peter. He is to report to his CO at once.

Peter returns later in the evening and brings with him renewed evidence that the Nazi denouncers not only rule the civilians but also the Wehrmacht with an iron rod. His CO was quite satisfied with Peter, but when this Nazi *Stabsartzt* told him a few things . . .

44. *Quod licet Jovi non licet bovi* – a Roman proverb which translated means 'What is permitted to Jove is not permitted to an ox' or 'Do as I say, not as I do'.
45. A staff doctor attached to a hospital rather than a unit.

At midnight Peter already holds his travelling orders in his hand, ordering him to report to a *Volksgrenadier* Division fighting in the east.

10 January 1945

We don't want to share the fate that overtook Peter – so we two keep ourselves well underneath the surface – like submerged submarines. Our recovery is progressing nicely.

11 January 1945

Every once in a while I am seized by a certain fear of returning to our old man. I don't give a damn any more. If the old monkey catches on to our little tricks, we'll beat it to St Vith and try to reach the American lines.

12 January 1945

We now make up our battle-plan; we'll visit a farmer in Niederemmels, a good friend of Heinz's. We'll keep under cover there till the Americans arrive. We'll take a certain amount of food along and hope for a speedy delivery. And it seems that once again world events are playing into our hands: Radio Luxembourg announces that the Americans are advancing in the direction of St Vith. In our exuberance and enthusiasm we slap each other heartily on the back.

13 January 1945

We have some painstaking details to take care of. First of all, our travelling orders from the hospital acquire a new date. The 4 January now reads the 14 January, a change which is also duly entered in our *Soldbuchs.* I have no scruples as I commit the first forgery of my life. I am on the road to becoming a professional criminal, but I have no trouble in rationalizing my crime: 'I am first, last and always an Austrian and don't owe those German Nazi swine a farthing's worth of allegiance.' My 'combat pack' is made ready. Heinz is bidding one of his many fiancées a tender farewell . . .

14 January 1945

At 0400 we creep along the railway dam towards the station. A train is scheduled for 0500. They only drive by night, for during the daytime Johnny Thunderbolt and Jimmy Marauder hold session. There is no MP patrol at the little station of Ottweiler. Therefore with our forged travelling orders as identification papers we have no difficulties in reaching the platform. While Heinz hums a sad tune, we enter the train which carries us into the uncertainty of the future.

We change trains after two stations – for the railways in this area run a shuttle service now. One shuttle train runs between Neunkirchen – St Wendel; the next from St Wendel to Türkismühle. Then there is one from Türkismühle to Kirn – and if one's luck still hasn't given out in this game of chance, one may even catch a train to Bad Münster.

There is a change of trains at every larger station. Hundreds of fellow travellers wait at each station. This game of running after trains is catch-as-catch-can; and we are firmly pinned to the mat in Türkismühle where we wait for a train – in vain.

Thus it becomes imperative to take to our feet. It's a clear day – and that means the *Jabos* will engage in the frolics.

We know the favourite beat of the MP patrols in Nohfelden and skilfully play hide-and-seek with the flatfoots. Then we turn in direction Heimbach where a train for Bad Münster is scheduled in the evening. We make a sharp right after Hohfelden, walk towards the viaduct when all of a sudden the clear blue sky is speckled with glistening aircraft. We just pass the Neubrück freight yard – or rather the site where this freight yard once stood, when with demonic speed and an eerie whine the first *Jabos* start diving. Everybody is dashing for the shafts and shelters. Heinz glances quickly towards the skies and shouts: 'Watch it, bombs.' We have just about ten seconds to get into the dead angle of the bomb-fall. The competitive dash which we now start has our lives as prize . . .

14 January 1945 (continued)[46]

Like mad we race for the first house of Hoppstädten. As we practically break down the door, a series of thirty bombs burst only 100 metres away from us. The Lightnings lay their eggs with precision work exactly on the railway line and the main highway. Five minutes later everything is over. It'll take a lot of unscrambling to fix that rail line again. Dead and wounded civilians litter the highway . . .

Today is one of those days when one just can't venture out without the risk of having one's skull split by a present from the Tommies. We are preparing for darkness so we can finally get going again. Around 1700 hours, a horse and wagon hobbles into sight. Our decision to utilize this 'army vehicle' proves profitable. While Heinz engages the 'groom' in a fascinating conversation about the merits of horse manure I – out of pure boredom – start investigating the contents of the wagon. This is a piece of good luck – the wagon is loaded with about 200 loaves of *Kommisbrot* [army

46. ISUM 277, 3 April 1945.

issue bread]. I decide that there are two loaves too many and I appropriate them for my rucksack.

There is little danger in boarding the train in Heimbach; this station is fortunately not endowed with an MP patrol. If it weren't for the constant transferring from train to train, we could even feel comfortable now. As a matter of fact, our worst experience on this trip is the small matter of two broken window panes in our compartment. In Bad Münster, however, a new surprise awaits us. In former days, it could happen that one got to the station and the train was gone. Nowadays, one gets to the train and the station is gone . . . With loud curses we hike to the next station, Bad Kreuznach.

The station here can even boast of an as yet undamaged canteen. We intend to drink a cup of acorn coffee and sit down – when the door opens. A conglomeration of officers plus one *Bluthund* [blood hound – nickname for rear-echelon MP] strut into the room. 'Present your identification papers and travelling orders!' Hot and cold chills alternately run down my vertebra. But it looks as if we have allies. They come to our rescue in the strength of whole swarms. The sirens start whining and bring the entire room into an upheaval of confusion. We make ourselves scarce. After two hours we stealthily approach the train. We bypass the MP patrol in front of the station by making our way between two burnt-out trains.

15 January 1945

Our hard-fought-for train only travels a few kilometres. Then we start hiking again till Bingenbrück. The explanation for our enforced hike is simple: 24 bombing carpets were laid in this area. At 0500 hours we at last catch a direct train for Koblenz. It is getting lighter and a snowfall promises that we may have an undisturbed journey for a change . . .

In Koblenz we start hitchhiking. We mount a truck and find among other civilians a pretty girl as travelling companion. Heinz, my Don Juan-like friend, starts a conversation. The young lady confides in Heinz. She lives in Regensburg and is already six days en route. Twice during the trip she underwent the ordeal of a bomb attack. One was a heavy night attack by RAF bombers on Mainz. The girls tells us more during the trip. She is married and is trying to visit her husband, stationed in Dormagen, without the benefit of a travelling permit. Though there is no longer anybody else on the truck we catch ourselves whispering. Significant and symbolic of the behaviour of people in Hitler's War Germany. In Sinsig the truck stops. It will be hard to find quarters and we certainly want to stay clear of the *Ortskommandatur* [local CO]. We venture forth to the only hotel in town.

The lobby is incredibly packed with soldiers. Conversation is conducted here in a half-tone. As we learn later most of the boys are in the same fix as we are, which is to say without travelling permits. After a long wait, a parlour maid silently heads us to an unheated room. The room is filthy, the wallpaper is torn and a slight shudder overcomes one as we enter this spookish place. Suddenly the electric light goes out . . .

The room is swallowed up by darkness. The young parlour maid, who has escorted us, is still in the room.

Wartime Intelligence Officer's Comments

At this point Laun describes the ensuing episode in a realistic Hemingway-like style. The episode, for obvious reasons, had to be omitted.

There is no reason any more to moralize. There is such a shortage of men in combat-zone Germany that the female of the species has become the pursuer.

16 January 1945

We are off for a trip into the 'land of freedom' which we expect to be somewhere around St Vith. The thermometer has dropped and the bitter cold of ten degrees below zero (Celsius) adds to our hardships. A trip on an open truck just about finishes us. We rub our feet with snow and it takes a long time till the blood again circulates through our toes. The truck has dropped us off in Ahrhütte, a small village in the Ahrtal. We try our luck at the first farm and find out that soldiers have already been quartered there. There is a small motor pool too. A sentry halts us. It is apparent that this guard is very anxious to keep us out of the house. I pull rank and Heinz convinces the man that we can't stand out in the cold. As we enter I soon perceive the reason for the sentry's reluctance to let us in. Everybody is crowded around a heavy oak table and as we enter they all feverishly pretend to be doing something. There on the table stands a portable radio. Unhesitatingly I say: 'Don't let us keep you from listening to the news. It happens to us too that we turn the dial the wrong way.' In a matter of minutes all of us are listening in perfect harmony to the offerings of Radio Luxembourg. But the news broadcast tonight spells bad tidings for us. It becomes evident that we can't hide out in the St Vith area as we had planned. Those Yanks have anticipated us by a few hours.

17 January 1944[47]

We have to take the bitter consequences. There is no other alternative than to return to our battery. Blindert is quite a distance from here. I am toying with the idea of crossing the lines, but Heinz hasn't enough guts for such an undertaking and besides, our food supplies are insufficient. Well, we have one consolation: there is always a place for us at the bosom of mother Wehrmacht.

We could reach our destination by afternoon but our pace slows down considerably. In Wershofen our determination weakens. Perhaps it would be better to hike the remaining 4 km tomorrow. And so the rest of the day is spent in writing letters, reading and sleeping. We empty the cup of freedom to the last dregs.

18 January 1944

The Burgomeister has turned out to be a good egg. He puts me up overnight. The honourable Burgomeister is roused out of bed very early the next morning. A replacement battalion with 200 parachute troops wants to be billeted in his town. We can see him ponder this problem. 200 parachutists, fresh from the front, in his small community: that means 200 times 200 lice, 200 different sicknesses and Lord knows how many babies . . .

We complete the last 4 km of our Via Dolorosa.[48] We reluctantly invade the inner sanctum of the 'Old Man'. But it's a new Old Man who 'greets' us. My first glance sees only a *Ritterkreuz* [Knight's Cross] and behind it a fat little man with a stupid expression. A magnificent example of the *Herrenmensch*, presumptuous and arrogant. His large face and protruding eyes suggest brutality. In a short cross-examination we complain to him about our scabies which supposedly still plague us. Obviously disinterested he turns us over to the First Sergeant. This old soldier is very busy and this in addition to his limited mentality permits us to pull the wool over his eyes. 'We should be sent right back to the hospital' we tell him 'and we only returned to get some clean laundry.' With the usual distrust of all First Sergeants he sends us to see the battalion doctor. 'Surely now all is lost', I tell myself and Heinz stares terrified at our forged '*Marschbefehl*' [marching order]. The new doctor, whom we don't known, lives in the next village. It seems that our old doctor stayed with the Americans in Cheveux. Who will examine us now/ Misfortune seldom comes in small doses and a large dose appears in the form of Major Sacken. He mustn't see

47. ISUM 278, 4 April 1945, from First U.S. Army.
48. The Via Dolorosa or 'way of tears' is the route that Christ took in Jerusalem as he carried his cross to the crucifixion site.

us and instinctively I pull Heinz back around the street corner. Too late. Sacken is upon us . . .

But the unapproachable Sacken, lucky for us, does not even bother to talk to the black sheep who have returned to his fold. Against our better judgment we proceed to the hospital, where we have every reason to believe that at least some of our tricks of the last couple of weeks will be unearthed. But when we enter the hospital, we find that instead of the dreaded new battalion surgeon a friend of ours, Medical Sergeant Braun, is on duty. We unload our troubles on him and succeed in getting his assistance to execute the next AWL operation. As we get ready to leave, I take everything I want to keep with me. We have no intention of ever seeing Blindert again . . . For the time being we travel without travelling orders.

An icy snow storm clears our heads for the contemplation of the difficult future problems which we have to ponder. We both look like tramps. We are wearing our ragged camouflage suits. It's easier travelling in the rear areas if a guy looks as if he's just coming out of the trenches. We have also removed our rank insignia. As a non-com it is difficult to be accepted into the exclusive fraternity of buck-privates – and we foresee that we'll have to ask *Landsers* a lot of important questions in the future . . .

We take a break in a small inn and celebrate Lady Luck who has so far smiled on us. We open my two Christmas packages. They finally caught up with me in Blindert. That is a minor miracle. Most of the Christmas mail and packages got lost. In my battery only five men received their Christmas parcels. And I know that fourteen of my letters are missing, as my wife always numbers the letters.

19 January 1944[49]

We waited for two hours for a lift. We never considered a tractor a luxurious medium of transportation but when such a vehicle finally picks us up, a latest model of Mercedes, it could not be more welcome. We rattle towards Dümpelfeld. On the way we pass an Organization Todt detachment clearing the snow from the streets. All these workers are our Axis friends, but it appears as if the Fascist enthusiasm of these Italians has been considerably cooled as they stand there, looking like snowmen.

In Bad Neuenahr we change over to a truck on which other soldiers are also travelling. Unexpectedly a '*Goldfasan*' [Party official in uniform] joins us. This man had obviously tough luck in selecting his travelling companions. Quite openly an infantry Staff Sergeant, apparently just

49. ISUM 280, 6 April 1945, from First U.S. Army.

back from the front, advises this worthy man to have his shiny brown belt salvaged for some shoe-leather. 'You'll need it when you start running', he explains. Our Party friend fumes – in silence and when the butt of our verbal attacks leaves us in Sinzig, he is, despite the cold, close to boiling point.

Andernach is not very far from here and we reach this pretty little town towards evening. The farmer whom we ask for quarters shows anything but a friendly face, however, when we kind of intimate that we are fed up with the Nazis his face lightens up.

He gives us a nice room and here Heinz breaks the surprise about which he has made wisecracks ever since we left Blindert. That jack-of-all-trades pulls out a blank travelling order with the correct seal on it. He stole it in Headquarters while I was talking to the First Sergeant. With meticulous pains we make the necessary entries. Heinz is granted the privilege of assuming the role of our Battery CO as he affixes the signature to this document. The future begins to look decidedly rosier.

The farmer invites us for dinner. As we sit around the table, I notice that here is a typical example of the disintegration of an entire family through the ravages of war. The wife of the farmer died two years ago of shock, when she heard the news that her youngest son had been killed in action on the Russian Front. Another son was taken prisoner in Africa. Around the table sit a Polish servant girl, a Russian farmhand, and the farmer with a four-year-old daughter.

We listen to the news. Prime Minister Churchill spoke in the House of Commons: Unconditional surrender and the abolition of all Nazi institutions in Germany. We discuss events to come. It looks as if Germany will have to climb a steep hill after the war, but the way will be upward. And the slope the Germans have to ascend will by no means be as steep as the present decline.

I regret the fact that we so seldom get a chance to listen to the radio, and it is ever rarer that we can give the dial that wrong twist. Just a few days ago a sentence was pronounced here in Andernach. Two years in the penitentiary was given for listening to a foreign station.

Tonight, the farmer turns on *Soldatensender Calais*.[50] This station falls flat on its propaganda. 'Our troops succeeded in stopping the enemy at X'. For a moment the illusion is created that this is a German station. But after

50. *Soldatensender Calais* was a British propaganda radio station that operated under the cover of being a standard German armed forces radio station. Broadcasting from 6 pm to dawn, it interspersed real news with clever propaganda and the latest music. It was very popular in Germany.

a few bars of dance music a little item is transmitted which quickly shatters this illusion. 'The Party member Schulz could probably be enticed to make a small contribution to the garment collection drive. He holds numerous business conferences with his frequently changing secretaries and brings silk stockings back as trophies.' The latter is not even bad propaganda, but the contrast between the cleverly doctored news bulletins and these items is just too great.

20 January 1944

We need some darn good alibis for our stay in Andernach. Therefore, between two large-scale bombing attacks we visit the local delousing station. The clerk to whom we report is a nice chap. It is easy to engage him in a conversation and, thus, to gain his confidence.

He leaves the room for a moment. But a moment is all two habitual criminals like Heinz and I need. Like a flash we are over by the open safe, take out the unit stamp and endow a blank sheet of paper with an official seal. We have timed it perfectly. As Heinz puts the paper in his pocket, the door opens. The bath at the delousing station refreshes us and keeps our minds alert. We know only too well that we cannot afford one false step . . .

We make daring plans. We are going to get a bona fide travelling order. For this purpose we have to venture into the lion's den. With our forged travelling orders we report to the *Frontleitstelle* [Military Travel Office]. Though my knees are shaking, I audaciously demand a *Marschbefehl* to return to our unit. But this time the wine of good fortune turns into the vinegar of tough luck. The clerk, instead of making out a new order, merely puts a rubber-stamp endorsement on our forged document. But still we managed to 'get one over' on them. On the strength of the endorsement, we draw travelling rations for three days.

In spite of all hazards we spend the night in the local hotel in Jungbluth. We soon go to sleep, for tomorrow we will be facing a difficult decision . . .

21 January 1945[51]

We come to a decision! We won't go back to our unit. We'll go to Heinz's parents, or perhaps later on into the Hunsrück Mountains and there await the Yanks. We double-time to the next official hitch-hiking place. A queue of approximately 150 people including women and children, is already waiting for connections in this haphazard transportation net.

In vain I wrack my brain trying to find a way to 'buck this line'. All of a sudden my pal Heinz spies an MP. And he is off again on one of his eccentric

51. ISUM 281, 7 April 1945, from First U.S. Army.

ideas. 'Do you know the exact time?' he asks. The *Kettenhund* complies. Heinz casually starts a conversation, complains about the bad connections, tells him we missed our train – and that we are on a top priority courier trip from the front, and that flatfoot swallows it – hook, line, and sinker! Consequently, he stops the next Wehrmacht truck for us. The truck reaches Koblenz in no time at all. The large Mosel bridge has really changed its appearance since we were here the last time. A few gaping holes invite our truck to take a dive into the cold waters of the Mosel.

The truck stops outside Koblenz and we start using our thumb again. It looks as if our intention of making 100 kilometers today will scarcely be realized. As the sun breaks through the clouds at noon, we are still standing at the outskirts of Koblenz. It is as if we were jinxed. Again Heinz starts looking around. He returns with a large window frame. Within five minutes this contraption is converted into a sled and placing our heavy packs on it, we start pulling. No truck driver can withstand such a picture of hardship – and a little later the Wehrmacht obliges. We seem to have more luck than brains, for this truck is headed for Idar-Oberstein, right up our alley.

We pass St Goar. There has been comparatively little bombing around here, and yet a few burnt-out houses have toppled into the Rhine. In fact, there has scarcely been a sector in Germany untouched by the war. I ask myself – will those *Sau-Preussen* [Prussian swine] at long last learn their lesson? Or will that 5 month-old kid of mine – whom I haven't even seen yet – be raised only to serve as cannon fodder as soon as he is old enough to tote a rifle . . . There must be thousands of people who think like me – and yet the senseless slaughter of World War II is still in progress. Why? One of our travelling companions exemplifies the reasons. This idiot calls attention to a sign painted on a house 'Victory or Siberia'. 'We must win', he rattles on, 'and we will win, because our Führer says so.' The man to the left of me seems to be a bit more realistic. He is a *Volkssturm* man from Bad Kreuznach who received a furlough because his house was completely bombed out. This man tells of some of the rumours prevalent in the ranks of the *Volkssturm*. 'The *Volkssturm* is not recognized as soldiers by the British. You fellows know what that means . . .' I don't believe this rumour – but this clearly shows one fact once more! The *Landser* is the best medium for disseminating news inside isolated Germany. Both the anti-Nazis and the Nazis have recognized this – and both groups start veritable rumour campaigns.

We pass the scenic town of Bingerbrück. The trip is going too smoothly, so the RAF breaks the monotony by sending a few planes over.

We literally tumble out of the truck, which sharply pulls to a halt. But everything remains quiet. Those hunters must be out for bigger game today . . .

After this intermezzo of 'Planes Overhead', we continue our trip on the same truck. The truck rolls to a halt before a miniature railroad station. The 'Express' to Turkismühle is supposed to pass through here sometime around 1900 hours. When the train crawls into the station at 2100 hours, we retaliate for this delay by not paying our fare. In Turkismühle we make connections to Ottweiler. As we detrain in Ottweiler, we do our good deed of the day by not causing any difficulties for the railroad officials there. Therefore, we tactfully sneak from the platform via a gap in the fence. Then we undertake a masterly outflanking manoeuvre around the traffic MP at the station – and, for the time being, we are in comparative safety. As we breathe more freely, we reflect that we have probably established a new world record in hitch-hiking. The two tramps, Heinz and Karl, succeeded in covering a distance of 195 km on the 'racetrack' Andernach – Koblenz – Bad Kreuznach – Idar Oberstein – Ottweiler in the phenomenal time of 10 hours and 56 minutes.

22 January 1945

People one meets on the trip are generally a pretty accurate barometer of the sentiments in Germany. Here, under the cover of complete anonymity, the usually tight-lipped people become a bit more commital. 'When will the war be over?' This question, frequently discussed of late, evokes only a shake of the head. How different it was a few months ago, even as recently as the beginning of January. At that time, the beginning of the retreat from the Ardennes was still wrapped in the milky fog of German propaganda. Today, just about one out of two hopelessly asks: 'What is to become of us now?' Nobody has the courage to face the truth or the naked realities. But a time will come when everybody will have to discard the rosy red glasses which Dr Goebbels so liberally issued to the German nation.

The Party boys in Ottweiler are laying low at present. In the neighbouring town of Heunkirchen, the local population showed itself somewhat unfriendly. During a night raid in this town, the *Ortsgruppenleiter*,[52] upon leaving his private air-raid shelter, was administered several solid blows upon his brownish uniform. The example of this gentleman, recuperating in a nearby hospital, has served as a stimulant for his colleagues who, all of a sudden, show a marked improvement in their manners.

52. A regional Nazi Party official.

Mrs Lehnert invites us for a long stay before we, complete with white flag, pay a social call on the Americans. Heinz's girl friend even offers to hide us in an air-raid shelter, which her parents had erected on their property. A couple of days ago, a wave of excitement swept through the village for AWOL soldiers. Going from house to house, MPs literally dragged soldiers out of bedrooms, hay lofts, basements and clothes closets. 46 soldiers were rounded up. And we have no inclination whatsoever to wind up in a Penal Company.

23 January 1945[53]

The romantic life of pirates which we are leading at present, sooner or later, must come to an end and be exchanged for the more orderly conditions prevailing in a PW camp. When, oh when, will that large-scale Allied offensive come off? Is it a matter of days or of weeks? We are sweating it out . . .

24 January 1945

We really intended to leave today, but we think it over once more – in the wilds of the Hunsrück Mountains, where we intend to have our rendezvous with the Americans. There are very few comforts. Electric light, for instance, is an unknown term there. In Ottweiler itself, gas has given out since the last air raid.

25 January 1945

Our radio does not get a rest any more. The tubes don't get a chance to cool off. People are already secretly discussing the details of how to surrender individual houses. People are preparing white flags . . . There is a rumour that Ottweiler is to become a hospital town. Hospital town? Does that mean that a few violations of the Red Cross are to be committed here? In Normandy, as Heinz tells me, ambulances were used to haul ammunition and troops . . . Today it is exactly one month since we escaped from La Gleize. How fast things change. A month ago we were dodging bullets, now we are dodging MPs . . .

26 January 1945

According to the latest radio reports, there are no indications that a large scale offensive is in the making. Unfortunately we can't stretch our period of AWL in Ottweiler indefinitely. If our 'hospitalization' takes too long, we may come under the suspicion of desertion. What would happen if our battery would take a sudden interest in our well-being? However, for

53. ISUM 282, 8 April 1945, from First U.S. Army.

once we are glad that the Wehrmacht apparently does not give a damn what happens to its men. Today, I am dealt a hard blow. In spite of three delousing cures, I still find a little vermin on my body. But we haven't time now for a fourth cure. Our baggage is ready and tomorrow we are slated for a trip into the Hunsrück.

27 January 1945

That piece of paper with the stolen unit seal, which we deftly procured in Andernach, comes in handy now. With the help of a typewriter we fabricate a bona fide travelling order. This paper is sufficient to pass the MPs at the railway station. However, in Turkismühle, the dreaded *Streifendienst*[54] appears. We disappear into the waiting room. A train is due in a few hours. In the meantime, we try to secure some water for the trip. This is a most difficult feat – all the water pipes in town are shattered by Allied bombardments.

28 January 1945

Midnight has just passed, when the door opens and a *Kettenhund* enters. His face shows clearly that he is dissatisfied with the nightshift-work and is consequently in correspondingly bad humour. Heinz is out of the room – and I sneak out of the door by taking cover behind the broad backs of a few *Landsers*. But our baggage is still inside. I hold a war council with Heinz. At last the MP comes out of the waiting room and it is possible to pass him in the darkness of the hallway . . .

The train arrives and at 0400 we reach the station in Kirn. Heinz has some relatives some 16 kilometres away from here – and if everything goes smoothly the Americans will be here in a very short time. But right now we still have to cover 16 kilometres. However, it is a romantic night for a hike. By the light of the moon, we break a window frame out of a house and use it as a sled for our baggage. We act as dog team and draw the sleigh up into the Hunsrück. The road winds upwards in serpent lines. To add to our troubles, a furious snowstorm looses itself upon us at the break of dawn.

28 January 1945[55]

Our journey becomes more and more arduous. Often we are compelled to take a break and sit down in the wet snow. But Heinz proves himself to be invaluable as a travelling companion. His terrific sense of humour

54. The *Streifendienst* was an organization of the Hitler Youth, concerned with enforcing discipline among all German youth groups but later used as auxiliary police to watch out for deserters, escaped prisoners of war and foreign workers.
55. ISUM 284, 10 April 1945, from First U.S. Army.

and his constant wisecracks keep both of us going. When we finally reach Woppenroth, 16 km from Kirk around noontime, we are two dead-tired frost-bitten AWL'ers. We receive a hearty welcome and a splendid dinner. The farmers show little concern for their ration stamps. They rarely use these rather meaningless scraps of paper – on the strength of which one can usually receive nothing except the regrets of the merchants.

29–31 January 1945

Three days, filled with hoping and waiting . . . There is no sign of a major attack by the Americans. Radio Luxembourg announces that the last phase of the war is near. The Russian and Anglo-American offensive added together will bring the destruction of Germany as sum-total. We try to prepare ourselves both mentally and physically for this 'final phase'.

1 February 1945

Hans, an old acquaintance of our hostess, has just returned from the retreat out of the salient. He is a veteran of Bastogne and now is on the way to Saxony where his unit is to be reformed. He was to lead a convoy of three vehicles of his ordnance unit to the designated rest area, but one vehicle after the other fell prey to the ever watchful *Jabos*. Now he is bereft of all vehicles except the ordnance repair truck. There are no quarters given as the sad vestiges of SS glory attempt to withdraw into the recesses of the Eifel – and then even further east. Hans tells of hundreds of burnt-out vehicles lining the highways.

We take leave of our hostess. It appears as if the Americans refuse to cooperate with our desertion-manoeuvre, and we just can't afford to prolong our unauthorized furlough. There is always the danger that some SA swine or Party agent might denounce us. And even in this rural Hunsrück sector the manpower-starved Wehrmacht sends its MP patrols. The last time they found plenty. No barn, cow stable, attic room, basement remained unsearched, and over 20 freedom-loving *Landsers* found themselves on their way to the nearest Penal Company. I initiate Heinz into some daring plans of mine, but my pal does not approve of the inventions of my fertile imagination. Thus, the final decision rests with him – and that means 'back to the 84th Squirrel Cage'.[56]

However, we could not have wished for better accommodations for our return trip. Hans is taking his ordnance truck via Koblenz. It is nice travelling weather, which nowadays is equivalent to a cloudy and dark sky, preferably with some long-lasting showers thrown in. On these days our

56. Laun's unit was the 84th *Flak Sturm Abteilung*.

Allied 'fair-weather' friends do not visit us. However, his nice weather lasts only until about 1300 hours. Then the sun comes through. It is a hell of a feeling to sit in a closed trunk and to hear a sinister noise overhead. But we seem to stand under some special protection. (Heinz tells me that the Safe Conduct leaflets, tucked away in our pockets, 'protect us from all evils'). There are a lot of diving planes in the vicinity, but those boys up there ignore us completely. We don't feel snubbed, though. On the other hand, as we learn later, those planes erased the town of Simmern from the map.

It is already growing dark as we reach Koblenz. Our hostess in Woppenroth had given us a letter of introduction to a family in Koblenz. First, however, we take leave of Hans and wish him lots of luck in carrying out his conjuring trick which is to take place somewhere in the Westerwald. Our friend will make himself disappear . . .

En route to our social call, we have to walk over the railway bridge. A heavily armed sentry challenges us. But he is an old and time-worn gentleman from some *Landesschutzen*[57] battalion and in spite of being a walking armory, becomes very docile in the face of our bellicose attitude.

As we pass the tiny guardhouse we hear a radio playing. The voice of the announcer is not exactly unfamiliar. Well, I give these old home-guards credit for having enough guts to listen to Radio Luxembourg so openly. And those oldsters must know that the Koblenz *Standortältester* [local party commander] is a Nazi S.O.B. who likes to invoke the death penalty when he catches this type of radio fan.

After stopping in front of the guardhouse for a while to listen to the radio, we resume our walk to the Gebauer residence where we, on the strength of our letter of introduction, want to establish *Familienanschluss* [connections to a family]. But when we get there, we find nobody home. A neighbour tells us that Mrs. Gebauer has already gone on her nocturnal walk. It seems that our hostess-to-be no longer can endure the experience of an air raid and every night she walks about 6 km to Kappellen, a suburb of Koblenz, to spend the night with her sister-in-law. Her husband is on duty with the *Heimatsflak*,[58] and his post is located on the very bridge over which we just came. We have no quarters for the night, so we decide to go back to the bridge. Perhaps Mr. Gebauer can help us out. We tell the guard that we have a letter for Mr. Gebauer and this together with our Flak uniforms gains us entrance into the Flak tower. Mr. Gebauer, already an

57. The *Landesschutz* were territorial units, often composed of older veterans, used for rear duties such as prisoner guards.
58. *Heimatsflak* were regional anti-aircraft units.

elderly man, starts telling us his troubles after preliminary introductions are over. He works in a defence plant, has to devote his spare time to man an AA position and now the old men from the *Heimatsflak* have been pressed into service to put heavy boards on the bridge. The bridge sports so many holes that it is practically impossible for a heavy vehicle to negotiate it. We are told that the Sixth Panzer Army is to pass over this bridge – on its way to the Eastern front. We ask our friend how he receives such precise information. 'Oh,' he answers, 'Radio Luxembourg predicted this several days ago . . .' Mr. Gebauer is able to put us up overnight in the Flak tower.

2 February 1945

We try to make the 8 o'clock train from Koblenz to Hönningen, but for a change the eccentric German Railway has taken off prior to schedule. We start walking – across the punctured Koblenz-Ehrenbreitstein street bridge. There is something doing on this bridge. Vehicle after vehicle rolls across the bridge; column after column. It appears as if the staff cars of a high headquarters are on the move. Then come signal cars, tanks, staff cars again. A wild melee. Heinz throws me a knowing glance. The retreat in the west has started; no doubt this is the beginning of the end. As the Sixth SS Panzer Army floods backwards, it is clear that soon, very soon, the ocean of Allied might can no longer be dammed. As much as I welcome this event, now that it is so closely at hand, I can't but help having a slight attack of fear; a fear which is based not on fear of the Allies, but of the knowledge that the ringing in of this new era will cost blood, lots of it. And I have a wife and kid at home. But damn it; – better an end of bloody terror than this persistent, shiny, and vicious onslaught without ending. Using our slightly worn out thumbs again, we solicit transportation to catch a truck, already crowded with civilians. Heinz at once starts looking for a likely 'quail'. He finds one in the form of an RAD-girl. The girl apparently is one of the few remaining 'innocents' in the German labour service. She tells us that there is scarcely any food left in their camp in the Ahr valley. The site of the camp will soon be changed. They are moving to the right bank of the Rhine. This story supports my pet theory. All Germans will soon be crowded into Thuringia and the Harz Mountains and there proceed to starve to death. The girl in her uninhibited patter, also tells us that the Hospital Niederlahnstein burned down completely in the last raid. We file this bit of accidental intelligence for future reference.

The truck takes us to Schuld, convenient for us, because Heinz knows a farmhouse there where he was once billeted. Indeed, the farmer turns out to be a heck of a nice guy. He invites us to stay with him 'for a day or two'. We are in no hurry to get back to our unit . . .

4 February 1945[59]

The farmer's little daughter has her birthday today. As we partake of the birthday cake, I realize that I too have some sort of anniversary today. It has been exactly 75 months since I spent my birthday at home.

In the course of the afternoon someone knocks on the window, and a soldier demands to see the proprietor. When our host arrives, the caller is straight and to the point. 'I got a can of raw oil here – give me some bacon and we can do business'. But our farmer-friend explains that the soldier is obviously not informed of the latest rate of exchange. 'For a slice of bacon I can have a hell of a lot of Wehrmacht equipment,' he lectures. The soldier finally settles for a loaf of bread and half a pound of butter.

5 February 1945

The die has been cast – and we are on our way to Blindert to start once again a 'legal existence'. We form our battle plans. We heard on our trip that the hospital in Oberlahnstein was completely bombed out, so that is naturally the place where we were. We still have that one forged march order from the delousing station, and as far as our Soldbucher are concerned, well, you can't expect a bombed-out hospital to make entries into people's Soldbucher. We talk our plan over again and again. It has to work this way . . .

And it does! Everybody from the battery clerk up believes our story. Our joy, however, is short-lived! We make the closer acquaintance of our new battery CO. A typical Nazi first Looie whose only distinguishing mark is a *Ritterkreuz.* The pompous ass plants himself in front of us and opens his fat face to give us a welcoming speech upon our return. 'Gentlemen, sit down on your rear ends and start studying the new weapon. The battery is at present undergoing training to change from a 20 mm AA battery to a 37 mm battery. The 37 mm is the most modern and finest AA piece in the world and you two NCOs will have the honour to act as instructors in this training programme – Out of this room and to the guns.' I again find myself in front of the door and am conscientiously trying to diagnose the case of that man in there. With the help of Heinz I reach the conclusion that he is an absolute idiot. Well, before we go out to school men in firing the finest AA weapon in the world, we decide to partake of our noontime meal. But that proves to be a tactical error. Mr. Heydrich (name of the new CO) tells us that in this hour of need, there is no time in the Fatherland to miss

59. ISUM 285, 11 April 1945, from First U.S. Army.

a training period on account of such unimportant trifles as chow.

We run into the First Sergeant. This man is a bit more inquisitive about our past activities. We launch into an after-dinner speech in which we time and again repeat bombastic phrases such as 'bombings, emergency hospital, transportation and travelling orders'. At the weak spots of our story we become particularly garrulous. End result: The First Sergeant is so well taken in by our net of pretty phrases that he even forgets to check our travelling orders. The series of lucky coincidences has not broken yet – and we thank Providence that it has watched over us so well as we were treading our path of 'wrong-doing'.

The Mess Sergeant tells us of the large-scale disorganization in the ration depots. Cigarettes are unobtainable; bread rations are confined to one loaf per day for five men. The distribution of meat is disorganized and haphazard, and often he obtains meat rations on paper only. For being in a rear area, these conditions are the worst yet in this war of privation. Here, too, the end is casting its black shadows ahead.

The billeting officer sends us to a farmhouse. The people are rather unfriendly. They are sick and tired of having troops billeted in their home. The houses are all filled to the gills. We find an unpopulated spot on two benches in the kitchen. Too late, we learn that our old friend, baby-faced Lieutenant Kratzenberg, is also billeted in this house. The platoon of this gentleman is already back in the lines at the hot corner of Holzheim, but the Lieutenant, who does not enjoy danger, appoints himself an expert on the 37 mm gun and being such an authority, as he words it, 'he considers it his highest duty to assist the troops in the arduous training ahead.'

As we go to sleep tonight, we discuss baby-face. He has no love for us, in fact he more than suspects where all the nice stories in circulation about him originate. And as we sink back into the comfort of the stone-hard wood benches, we look forward with keenest anticipation to nip and tuck warfare in this peaceful little billet . . .

Lieutenant Kratzenberg shows his animosity to us the next morning. My platoon, which according to the Lieutenant shows not enough progress during the training, is restricted to the area. But we are always a step ahead of the Lieutenant. We tell the First Sergeant that we had to leave our rucksacks in an inn some distance from here. We take off, reach the inn and find two weary soldiers there. They belong to some QM unit. Their truck has run out of petrol at this very convenient spot. 'We are awaiting a shipment of petrol', they tell us. It seems as if they reported their status 14 days ago, but nobody has done anything about it yet. They are hoping and praying that the Americans will come before the petrol arrives. This sort of fighting spirit is further fortified by the 20-year-old daughter' of the innkeeper. This lass amply supplies us with wine, black market stuff, after having turned down some officers with the excuse that nothing, absolutely nothing, was available. We decide that it is impossible to find our way back to Blindert tonight – so we will stay in a nearby farmhouse. And we don't miss Lieutenant Kratzenberg in the least.

6 February 1945

The training programme is in full swing – and this is just about the most disgusting period of my Army career. Men with six years' service, owners of the *Verwundeten* Medal, soldiers just out of the trenches, they are all put through their paces by a Lieutenant who comes out of OCTU and whose combat experience is confined to commanding some AA unit at home. But all this is the spirit of Prussian militarism. Keeping the soldiers constantly occupied – so they don't have time to think or to contemplate the folly of this whole bloody war. Added to this is the fact that the 'men must snap out of their lethargy'. Lethargy, hell!! These men suffer from the most acute case of war-weariness which has ever befallen a unit. Today, during the training periods, I notice that even the NCOs are long past caring. They take frequent breaks, talk to each other, and the main subject of conversation is a fertile exchange of ideas on how to avoid dangerous duty. Nobody is in the least interested in dying some sort of heroic death so near to the end of the war. Anybody who can find some sort of legal pretext tries to leave the battery. Two men returned yesterday after having prolonged an emergency furlough by 14 days. A court martial is to take care of them . . .

Most of the boys openly state that they would rather return to the trenches than enjoy a course on the 37 mm AA gun given by Kratzenberg. The enthusiasm to listen to his explanations is tremendous. About every 15 minutes he has to send out a posse of NCOs to hunt some men who have sneaked away to enjoy a peaceful siesta in some quiet corner of the training grounds. As I become more acquainted with the most modern AA piece in the world, I can't help but burst out laughing. The construction is elementary – not too bad – but it is royally loused up by the ammunition. On an average, one shell in every ten has some sort of flaw.

Our training does not make the expected progress today. The *Jabos* are overhead and Lieutenant Baby-face's badinage is punctuated at frequent intervals by the air raid alarm. I don't mind this, though. In my opinion, a bomb concussion is still preferable to the hot air emanating from our youthful leader . . .

7 February 1945[60]

At 0630 fate shakes me up in the form of the CQMS [Company Quartermaster Sergeant] 'It's time.' Time for what, I ask myself. During this training period, my bad humour has reached its peak. Time for you Nazi blankety blanks to go to hell . . . We drag our weary bones to the parade grounds. There, at least one ray of light awaits us. Mail call. But there is nothing for me, and that means that I'll have to wait for at least a whole week for the next supply transport from Siegburg. And still, we never receive such a giant mail pouch as those of the Americans which we found at La Gleize.

This morning, I really have to start a more intensive training programme. Until today, I have suffered from chronic boredom during the training periods and have been very superficial in my examination of the 37 mm cannon. I am just simulating a feverish activity around the gun position, when Heydrich appears in the distance. The name of this joker nauseates me every time I hear it. It has the putrid SS stench.[61] The Old Man approaches with an inimitable arrogance; his best dress uniform is gleaming in the sun. He carefully skirts every little puddle on the training grounds, but while keeping his eyes on the ground, he still – out of general principle – passes out bouquets of reprimands wherever he goes. 'These field positions are not half good enough,' he let us know. 'The men from the supply trains, effective at once, will start on the construction of better positions.' He approaches me and informs me that although I have incurred the displeasure of Lieutenant Kratzenberg, he intends to leave me in my position as Platoon Sergeant. Not that he has anybody else to take my place – but at any rate, I thank him profusely. In the meantime, Heydrich stands in front of me like an overstuffed flour bag and only the swinging *Ritterkreuz* shows that there is life and motion in this prototype of a Prussian militarist. In leaving, he can't forego his duty of reprimanding, and therefore tells me that one of my buttons is open.

8 February 1945

One day passes much like another. Our private war against Kratzenberg continues. Tonight, Babyface invited two other officers to a round of Skat. In the absence of any games room they hold their session in the kitchen, where I am peacefully reclining on my bench. The gentlemen play more with their mouths than with the cards and I find it difficult to sleep through

60. ISUM 286, 12 April 1945, from First U.S. Army.
61. A reference to Reinhard Heydrich (1904–42), Himmler's chief deputy and nicknamed 'The Hangman'. Universally feared, Heydrich was assassinated by SOE operatives in 1942.

their din. 'Herr *Leutnant*', I start with politeness oozing through my words, 'would you be kind enough to tone down your conversation? I would like to sleep.' The *Leutnant* is speechless for a moment, but makes up for the silence by cramming enough expletives into the next three minutes which at the ordinary rate of speech could fill an hour. He terminates his forceful speech by telling me that I sleep all day on the training ground and that therefore I needn't go to sleep so early at night. After the gentleman has finished, I, without answer, turn around on my bench and start snoring, as if I were trying to imitate a whole company asleep. Herr *Leutnant* is learning his lesson and all of a sudden the conversation of the card players dies down to whispers.

9 February 1945

Heydrich evidently is wracking his Nazi brains how to put some pep into the battery, for this morning he announces that the best gunner will receive an extra portion of cigarettes. Heydrich's promises are interrupted by a loud detonation. We look overhead – no *Jabos* in the air. What on earth is going on?

Three seconds later another explosion breaks loose from a northerly direction. Two smoke columns rise at the place where the explosion apparently took place. A little later we learn the sensational news that V-1 sites as well as rockets around Falkenberg were blown up.

10 February 1945

We are beginning to be amazed by the constant change of uniform with which Heydrich parades around. His conceit seems to be without bounds. Yesterday he appeared in a parachuter's camouflage suit which he confiscated from a soldier of our battery. His phobia goes so far that he literally tears pieces of cloth from the bodies of some of those men to whose equipment he has taken a fancy . . .

The fat rations have been drastically cut. There is no more butter and we have to get along with that vile-smelling uniform mixture of two thirds margarine and one third butter. The bread, stretched by potatoes, has become unbearable of late. If one saves a slice for even a few hours, it dries out and becomes brittle. More and more water is added to the dried vegetables.

Today the CO tells us that the training is supposed to be brought to an end within five days. That is bad news, for such an announcement points to an early commitment.

11 February 1945

Today the fireworks start again. All around us explosions seem to take place. The V-1 sites are to be moved to the Westerwald. Well, does that mean that the left-Rhenish territory has already been written off as untenable. It is high time for my expedition. Today I walk for two hours to get to a radio: I must know the news. Our Signal Platoon is stationed in Marthel and there, under the privacy of earphones, I listen to Radio Luxembourg. The reception, as always, is good, and I learn that the Americans are pressing towards Prüm, while in the east one Silesian town after the other falls to the Russians. I sneak off to tell Heinz the latest news.

12 February 1945

Rumours have it that we'll soon be on the move again. There must be something to this rumour; for today our battalion CO, Major Sacken, as well as the Regimental CO, Major (now Lieutenant-Colonel) Franz holds an inspection. Franz is no longer the 'barking dog', the nickname under which he is known to the *Landsers*. Perhaps the rapidly deteriorating situation is improving the manners of these gentlemen. Their speeches of 'holding out to the last man' are becoming noticeably rarer . . .

13 February 1945

The rumours are further substantiated when the Old Man leaves on reconnaissance for new positions. Our platoon at once receives the final instructions with the 3.7 cm AA guns. It's my own. There are only four men left in the platoon who participated in the La Gleize engagement. All the others are a motley lot; mostly limited service men. But the emphasis has shifted from quality to quantity. And all of the men are undernourished.

The sun breaks through again and dries out our positions which in the last couple of days have been transformed into quagmires by the constant rain. In the afternoon, a thick swarm of two and four-motor bombers rolls over us, direction Rhine. It seems as if the two-motor bombers fly with double the ordinary speed. As I look closer, I see for the first time the new 'Invader'. In other words, something even more terrible has cropped up than the 'Marauder'.[62]

62. This is a reference to the A-26 Douglas Invader, a twin-engined aircraft introduced into service in late 1944. It is often confused with the Martin B-26 Marauder because the A-26 was later re-designated the B-26 Invader.

14 February 1945

The 3rd Platoon has been recalled from Holzheim. Something is in the air. Indeed, at around 1100 hours Heydrich appears with a lot of circulars in his hand. He calls the whole battery together and in his Russian voice starts reading a message of the radio: 'Soldiers of the west front! The enemy is preparing for an all-out offensive. After conquest of the Silesian industries the enemy will attempt also to get the Ruhr Valley into his hands. Soldiers of the west front! It is all up to you. Each foot of German soil must cost the enemy streams of blood, so that he sees the senselessness of his offensive.'

14 February 1945[63] (continued)

Heydrich adds a few official announcements and let us in on the open secret that we may expect a change in location in the near future. Nobody has any idea where we are going to! The Eifel has become my second home, because it is very easy here to stage a disappearing act. The others, however, seem to be happy to leave this rough country.

15 February 1945

There is high-tension activity in my platoon. 2nd Platoon is supposed to be fully ready for commitment within 48 hours. At the moment there are only seven places in the battery, but we are told that the others will not be long in arriving. There is considerable lack of machine pistols in the battery, but Heydrich has a beautiful 'out' for this minor problem. Each man receives two hand-grenades, which we are ordered to drag along with us at all times. Twelve cases of *Panzerfausts* complete our armoury. These cute gadgets have only one disadvantage: nobody ever received any training in how to play with these toys, but again miracle-man Heydrich solves a knotty problem. He distributes small leaflets which come in gaudy colours, and there one gets implicit instructions in the use of the *Panzerfaust*. Like a kindergarten jingle, we learn that

> 'Wie du hältst ist einerlei
> Die Panzerfaust schiesst rückstossfrei
> Nur eins bedenke: Rohrende frei
> Und nun Panzer Knacker Heil'
>
> (It does not matter how you hold her
> The Panzerfaust has no recoil

63. ISUM 287, 13 April 1945, from First U.S. Army.

Just remember to keep the barrel end free
And now happy tank hunting)

It's as easy as that . . .

In haste we draw ammunition. With concern we notice that there is a high percentage of anti-tank ammunition among the stock. That seems to point to some hard fighting ahead. I don't think that the best anti-aircraft weapon in the world will do very well against Shermans.

16 February 1945

We are undergoing training up to the last minute. Then comes the order 'Load up'. The Henschel and the Mercedes Diesel engines are loaded up to one ton above capacity. On top of all this, the men have to squeeze on the vehicles. And to complete the build-up for a breakdown, each vehicle is used as a prime mover for two guns each. The pieces are hooked up to the vehicles by an artful wood construction. The battery never received any additional vehicles after the Ardennes offensive and our mobile battery has now a grand total of six vehicles, a command car and four motorcycles. That's exactly one fifth of our former motor pool. During the whole day the weather is perfect as far as the *Jabos* are concerned. That means that the vehicles have to be driven into the forest and that we have to drag the equipment about three quarters of a mile from our position to the vehicles. I get our travelling orders as late as one hour before departure.

I get the responsible job of riding at the rear of the convoy. For this job I am placed on the back seat of a motorcycle and receive a motorcycle driver. An assignment like this – at least as the driver and I interpret it – is an open invitation to go on a little weekend spree. For this purpose, Maus, the driver, smuggles enough petrol sufficient for a 100 km trip.

The pieces for my platoon haven't arrived yet. That might mean that as soon as we get to the front we'll see a bit of infantry service . . . The hour for departure was to be 1800, but it is almost midnight when the battery is finally ready to take off. The packing was done with haste and a confusion that shows only too clearly that none of the men gives a damn any more. As I learn later, a substantial part of the ammunition was purposely left behind. the men got tired of carrying the heavy boxes to the trucks.

At last the convoy takes off and when after 200 metres our motorcycle gets stuck and we two take an involuntary mud-bath, I take it as a bad omen of the cumbersome road that lies ahead . . .

16 February 1945[64]

Maus and I zigzag after the convoy; shortly before Münster-Eifel we drive up to *Leutnant* Kratzenberg to show him that we are faithfully discharging our duties as shepherd dogs of the convoy, but when we reach the tail end, we make a sharp right turn. We have some friends around here. We visit this family and learn that the good people are already fully prepared for the American onrush. They built a shelter in some property outside of town, sufficiently equipped with eight days' food. So even if the fighting in the village lasts for a while, they'll be well supplied. They have even brought the goat to the cave.

17 February 1945

In the morning we resume our trip, but only to take a prolonged break in Türmich. We finally arrive at the HQ at 1700 hours. We offer the usual excuse – motor trouble. But the Old Man is too tired to care. He is worn out from his 'reconnaissance mission'. The old boy, as his driver tells us, had to start creeping and crawling. I can just see all the ludicrous positions which Heydrich must have undergone. We hear that Heydrich did not engage in this form of locomotion out of sport, but on urgent invitation of the *Jabos*. Seems our valiant commander showed himself too unconcerned when the planes blasted a horse and carriage in front of him all over creation. As he kept right on going, probably in the erroneous belief that the *Ritterkreuz* is a good luck charm, the planes also swooped down on his car and Mr Heydrich chose to get off the road by running on all fours. His car is at present in the repair shop.

We look around for our new AA positions. Well, if this is not a typical *Himmelfahrtskommando* [suicide mission] I don't know what is. We are supposed to protect the Erft bridges. The local population cheers us up by telling us that the dive bombers pay social calls here every day. The many many bomb craters around here bear out the good news. By moonlight we start constructing field positions. The site is ominously sown by bomb craters. 'The guns will arrive soon', Heydrich promises. 'And by the way you must drive the men mercilessly tonight. Everybody will have his foxhole ready in one hour. Then you'll dig in the trailers. Then you start camouflaging everything.' His voice trails off in a dozen more 'then's'. After these lengthy instructions he runs out of breath and turns away. I already breathe more freely when the *Saukopf* [pig head] comes back once more. 'Oh yes, avoid all movement during the daytime! And for the building of

64. ISUM 289, 15 April 1945, from First U.S. Army.

each of these positions have about 16 trees felled!' When I politely interject that the men of my platoon haven't eaten yet and that the assignment is a bit large, he hands me a lecture in human psychology: 'The greatest effort can still be improved by merciless pressure . . .'

The area is swampy and water is everywhere. When I tell the Old Man about the difficulties involved in digging here in this mudhole, he replies curtly: 'I get too much lip from you.' When our master leaves us, I put a guard on the position and start looking for half-way decent living quarters for my Platoon. I find a house which is only partially damaged. So at midnight we leave a skeleton guard and set up housekeeping in a damaged house in the vicinity of Mödrath. If the Old Man feels like playing soldier, let him live in a tent.

The kitchen hasn't arrived yet; perhaps the mess officer used the prime mover to pay a visit to his girlfriend. Finally, late at night the last vehicle of the convoy which fell out due to motor trouble limps into view. It bring with it the 3rd Platoon. The poor boys are ordered to unload late at night. To get even for this, the boys make so much noise, especially when they pass the tent, that the Old Man surely won't get much sleep tonight . . .

18 February 1945[65]

The nocturnal din, staged by the embittered 3rd Platoon for the benefit of the Old Man, has the result that our valiant CO flees his tent this morning and establishes his HQ in a private billet.

The guard whom I left at the gun position bring us some pleasant news. Due to the opening of the Erft dams, the ground water has risen to such a level that our tents are now complete with 20 cm-deep footbaths.

Today we resume the construction of our field positions with an enthusiasm that borders on mutiny. Instead of felling thick oak trees, we find it more expeditious to steal some Engineer bridging equipment which apparently is ownerless. We go to work with axe and saw; the heavy boards are soon disassembled and fashioned into the proper sizes. Of course, this bit of illegal work we do at top speed – and so much eagerness must have aroused the suspicions of the Old Man. After inspecting our work through field glasses, Roly-Poly comes towards us. As a morning greeting he starts cursing that the ammunition has not been dug in yet. But these introductory remarks are like a lullaby compared to what is to follow. Mr. Heydrich has seen the neatly-cut bridging equipment. My dear CO turns pale, then breathes heavily, inflates himself and would most likely have

65. ISUM 290, 16 April 1945, from First U.S. Army.

exploded due to internal combustion if First Lieutenant Schmidt had not arrived and dammed the white-heat rage of Heydrich somewhat. 'You saboteur, you imbecile, you moron, you idiot, you . . . you . . .' The smiling face of Lieutenant Schmidt finally calms him down a bit. 'Get that blankety-blank stuff back to where you got it,' he bellows. We carry the bridging equipment back. Schmidt keeps on smiling. One hour later, the men from his battery come to the place and triumphantly carry the ready boards away to their positions. Now it's my turn to get mad. I inform Heydrich that the bridging equipment is in the hands of 1 Battery and that First Lieutenant Schmidt evidently had not listened to him while he, Heydrich, explained that these boards were to be used for the retreat route Düren-Cologne in case the Erft bridges would be blown up. Heydrich puts himself in position as public speaker and lets me know that he didn't give a damn what the other batteries did, that Herr *Oberleutnant* Schmidt was an idiot anyway, and that it was none of my blankety-blank business what went on outside of my platoon . . . We start felling oak trees.

As we get back to our tumbled-down house, I find the *Ortsbauernführer* there. This gentlemen tells me that the men stole some straw from him. I tell him that I don't know about this incident, but if that were true, the straw would only serve to furnish a bit more comfort for some soldiers. But what does a Party leader care for some soldiers? He takes the straw back with him.

19 February 1945

Today two pieces arrive, fresh from the assembly-line. But it seems that on the transport *Jabos* must have been interested in them. The steel plating on one of them is already punctured while the other shows a few bends in the barrel. 20 men work like pack-mules to draw those two-ton heavy monsters into position. The flooded meadows don't make our work any easier. As soon as we have the pieces in position, we have to start camouflaging – or the *Jabos* will swoop down, our weapons will be gone, and then we'll play infantry soldiers for sure.

I now have a little leisure to examine the new pieces more closely. The one whose steel plating is still in order bears serial number 5. That means that it is an experimental piece. The construction is a bit peculiar. But that is not the worst. The damned thing has stoppages and the recoil fluid flows out like a fountain. I call my platoon together and we make a few little agreements. They all centre around our tactical deployment in case the first Sherman tanks should suddenly roll into our field of vision from direction Keppen. Our weapon for their reception is prepared. Out of a piece of bedsheet a white flag is carefully fabricated. Then I'll lead my platoon to the edge of the woods and we disappear. This plan sounds as simple as the American leaflets advising us on how to surrender. If they knew some of the 'light complications' that may set in while carrying out a project of this kind . . .

19 February 1945 (continued)[66]

I sound out my men on how they feel on the subject of waving a white bedsheet should the Americans appear. Staff Sergeant Mayer is solidly behind me – and Heinz I don't even have to ask. Only a solitary gunner tells me that a lot of things can yet change. Well, that is quite true, but I take a statement like that as a manifestation of Nazi spirit. In an undertaking of this kind, where one literally takes one's life into one's hands, one just can't be cautious enough.

I get a few twinges of fear as on this score the very same day, the 2nd Platoon gets an additional NCO. Does the Old Man distrust me?

20 February 1945

Since we arrived at our new location, the air raid sirens have almost constantly sung their eerie song. As a matter of fact, the periods of 'all clear' are now less frequent than the air raid alarms. We have just got up – and we notice that those pilots must have had an even earlier reveille. The sky is clear, visibility unlimited, and it looks as if another song-and-dance of Allied flying activity is in the making.

The first *Jabos* dive around 1000. Thunderous noise is heard from direction Kerpen. In the afternoon a few Thunderbolts fly over our territory on their return from the Reich. The first one is taken under fire. We miss. I suspect that our pieces shoot inaccurately and need adjusting. But I'm much too smart to tell my CO about this. However, this gentleman has to tell me a few things after this morning's intermezzo. He informs me that he gave implicit orders that while taking a fighter-bomber under fire only 48 rounds must be fired. And our platoon has committed the unpardonable crime of firing 52 rounds. Heydrich lets me know that he is saddened by the fact that such an irregularity occurred in his battery. And I, responsible for all this, am an outright traitor to the cause of the Fatherland.

In the evening an Allied dive-bomber swoops down on us. We don't know yet whether he is after our bridge. We open fire. The pilot ignores us. He pulls out of his dive – the bombs start falling. A few seconds later the railway station which was in a shambles already, is practically pulverized.

66. ISUM 296, 22 April 1945, from First U.S. Army.

Evidently this plane had some eggs to get rid of before flying home. And those eggs came home to roost . . .

Heydrich again has something to say. He is mad that we missed. From now on he is going to direct the fire himself. I'm happy about this. At long last I am relieved of some of my most unpleasant duties. The excitement just does not stop today. The Allies stage a bit of a firework display tonight. Flares magically light up the scene. A few seconds later the fighters attack the street. The Lord have mercy on anybody who is on this road tonight! The attack is ferocious. We are scared out of our senses. Out of the town, let's get away from Mödrath. Like scared rabbits the men run towards the open country; stumble through the moonish meadows, get stuck, fall and finally just throw themselves down somewhere on the wet, cold ground.

21 February 1945

Again beautiful *Jabo* weather. The air resounds with motor noises. I'm anything but anxious to stay in this hot corner, therefore I venture forth to Heydrich's den and tell him that I need a new pair of glasses and have to go to the Battalion aid station. This time I really hand him a line. I tell him that in this time of need I would like to be in 'top fighting condition' and that a new pair of glasses is essential to this purpose. For once, Heydrich agrees with me. He adds that an AA-man who is shortsighted might shoot on German planes. With an effort I keep myself from saying, 'What German planes?'

After dinner, I start on my way to the Battalion aid station. But I have walked only 50 metres away from our position when a *Jabo*-attack on the heights west of Mödrath comes off. Dirt and smoke columns rise into the air. The planes turn back slowly and are only 300 metres above us. But nobody shoots! The Old Man is next to the pieces and is scared that if he starts shooting, the *Jabos* may consider that an unfriendly act and put a few MG slugs into Herr Heydrich's fat body.

21 February 1945 (continued)[67]

I get as far away from the pieces as possible. In Balkhausen where the Battalion aid station has been set up, I have to take cover between the railway tracks. Four *Jabos* dive and systematically start to make Swiss cheese out of a locomotive.

After leaving the hospital my humour is as sunny as the sky. Medical NCO Braun came once more to my rescue. Now I have an official permit in my pocket, signed by a battalion surgeon, allowing me to take a trip to a

67. ISUM 298, 24 April 1945, from First U.S. Army.

hospital in the rear to have some glasses made. Now, at the first sign of an American offensive, *Feldwebel* Karl Laun is going to take off with legitimate travelling orders – but not in the direction of a hospital.

As I get back to the vicinity of Mödrath I become witness to a major curiosity. From afar I notice someone who like an idiot jumps into a foxhole as four planes appear in the sky. I see no reason to take cover. A little later this scared rabbit comes out of the foxhole again, but only to disappear once more five minutes later like a flash when a few bombs start dropping on the distant Kerpen. The man has stayed on the same spot for five minutes now. I saw that the valiant man there is wearing officer's uniform so I step behind a tree to watch the show the gentleman is putting on. As he carefully sticks his head out of the foxhole once more, I notice that it is none other than the great Major Sacken himself. His face is smooth – the typical frown has disappeared. The good Major is evidently too scared to play the usual role of tough battalion CO. He is benevolence himself as I pass him. 'How are you, Laun? Hot today, in every respect. Ha Ha Ha . . . Where have you been?'

When I tell him that I went to the aid station – something he disapproves of wholeheartedly – a miracle happens. Sacken walks on without making any comment. I run into two boys of my platoon who tells me that Sacken has stood at the same spot for two hours watching his first and second batteries. Perhaps he is looking to make sure no ammunition is wasted . . .

22 February 1945

It's pitch dark – 0400. The guard wakes me up. 'Orders of the CO, everybody is alerted.' Within thirty minutes all guns are to be ready for firing. Like mad we rush over the Erft bridges to our positions. Nothing happens though. The Old Man calls his platoon leaders together. His words are worthy to be set down in the history of this war. 'In case the enemy succeeds in breaking through at Düren, he will most likely try to advance on the Kempen road. *Feldwebel* Laun, you will go on reconnaissance for likely positions for a *Panzer Vernichtungstrupp* [anti-tank squad].'

The position must be not more than 60 m off the road to be within the range of the new *Panzerfaust*. Furthermore, I have taken over the defence of the Erft bridges. We will defend the bridges to the last bullet. However, if necessary, we will go into position on the heights east of Müdrath and will destroy the enemy from there.' After having thus been briefed on the situation, we are dismissed. We go away with the feeling that Herr Heydrich knows as little as we do and what is more, does not know his own plans yet.

The boys in my platoon anxiously await the news. When I tell them of Heydrich's intended last stand, their faces show the disgust which they are afraid to voice. They know that if no general retreat order arrives, we'll soon be facing the Shermans. In the afternoon hours a giant formation appears on the horizon. Is this the overture to the concert to come?

23 February 1945[68]

Shortly before 0300 the artillery barrage breaks loose. The whole Roer front seems to be one giant wave of excitement. That must be the beginning of a large-scale attack. At the arrival of dawn, the artillery has left deep craters northwest of Müdrath. We leave our billet on the double and man the guns. I report to Herr Heydrich with an overlay showing him where I have selected positions for the 'AT squad' and then we beat it into the forest. The Old Man shows signs of being rather nervous. No doubt the situation has a bit to do with that. Around noon the artillery fire dies down somewhat. During this breathing spell I dash to the HQ, go up to the QM and ask him to fill out my travelling orders for Dormahen. Now I have a tussle with the Old Man in front of me. At this moment the courier comes down from Battalion and brings the new situation map along. Before he gets to the CO, I intercept him and take a quick look at the map. The Americans have succeeded in crossing the Roer in a wide sector below Julich and Düren, also in reaching the railway dam 1 kilometre further east. That means they have penetrated our line and that in turn means that we will probably move again. Now I have to act fast. I delay the courier by offering him some cigarettes and I step into Heydrich's tent, click my heels and ask him to affix his signature to the orders and that I'll be back the next morning. Heydrich signs . . . and tells me that I can leave as soon as I am off duty. But of course I can't wait that long. The reason is obvious: about two days ago I gave the boys of my platoon permission to slaughter a calf. Today rumours of my deed have already reached circles not too far away from Heydrich. We haven't even eaten all of the calf yet and the *corpus delicti* lies in the form of 10 kg steaks in the Platoon CP of the 2nd Platoon – my platoon. I double time the 200 metres back to our positions and turn the entire platoon, secret orders, verbal orders etc. over to Sergeant Meyer within two minutes, then say goodbye with the explanation that the Old Man is driving me to greatest speed. Quickly I pick up my haversack in my billet – my light field pack I always carry on me anyway.

As if hounded, I hurry along the road to Türmich, hiding occasionally in a slit trench to avoid being seen with my luggage. The latter consists of

68. ISUM 292, 18 April 1945, from First U.S. Army.

practically everything I own. I don't want to leave so much as a trouser button with my battery. My blanket and shelter half are the only two souvenirs which will remind Herr Heydrich of his former platoon leader. I am determined never to return to Army life.

I get a hearty reception from my acquaintances in Türmich and have the pleasure of sleeping in an honest-to-goodness feather bed. Before I turn in, we converse about the Nazis, and I hear that some of the local criminals are already preparing themselves for a hasty departure, and all through the conversation there runs the fear that before National Socialism, brain disease of the Twentieth Century, is stamped out, all Germany will be in rubble and ashes.

24 February 1945

To cover distance while it is still dark – that is the most important thing this morning. A light drizzle transforms the road into a gleaming band. The only transportation to 'speed' through this danger zone is a horse and wagon. The coachman is an Austrian and he at once comprehends what I am up to. He benevolently covers me with flour sacks (empty, luckily) and camouflaged like this, I pass the hot corner of Müdrath where an MP is on duty, and the HQ at Horrem. The cart stops just outside Horrem – and I note that, to my momentary horror, this is exactly the bivouac area of the company supply trains . . . One of the Sergeants sees me – talks to me – so I guess nothing has become known yet of my departure. So I might as well make the best of it – I walk over to the kitchen and ask for my travelling rations on the strength of Herr Heydrich's orders. The boys back here don't have the foggiest notion of the situation. These idiots can't even imagine that there can be anything like a retreat.

It's rather unpleasant to tramp the roads today. The *Jabos* are out to get the Fortuna Werke around here. I see myself compelled to await dusk and take cover in a house in town. We are listening to the radio when all of a sudden the *Jabos* swoop down, hit the power plant – and there is no more radio. In the neighbourhood of the house two bloodhounds [MPs] sniffle around. But they pass. I get a ride up to the street corner Commirskircheneckum. The night is pitch-dark, there is not a sound on the street and I, like a specimen of human misery, stand at the street corner. I don't feel like walking any further tonight, a vehicle won't come anyway and it is four kilometres to the next village. But my luck once more comes to my rescue. A nice villa still shows light, I knock – am given quarters and am even allowed to hear the latest news – the true version. The Allies are approaching Erkelenz and München-Gladbach . . .

25 February 1945

About 0800 I'm woken up by a terrific din. The *Jabos* are singing their song and see to it that no more traffic rolls over the highways and byways. One of those vehicles that does not pay heed to the *Jabos* is soon capered and as I look out of the window I see the car in flames. The AA positions around here are constantly singled out for attacks by Thunderbolts and Typhoons. My landlady comes upstairs and warns me to go down into the air raid shelter.

Clouds are slowly coming up and darken the sky, the airplanes disappear and everybody ventures out of his hiding place again. I stay for dinner, but then it's high time to get going once more. But once again, I'm delayed; the *Jabos* have returned in even stronger formations than before. I think the whole Allied air force has taken the communication centre of Eckum as its goal. One bomb carpet after the other is being laid here; I lie in the corridor of the house, flat on the ground. One detonation follows the other and all of a sudden I find myself sandwiched between the floor and a door which the concussion knocked out of its frame. The bombs stop falling and I rush out of the house. Practically the whole street is in ruins. A farmer stands in front of his wrecked house and cries. I try to console him by telling him that the main thing is that he is unhurt; houses can always be rebuilt. He turns around, points to the rubble and tells me that his wife and daughter lie underneath the ruins. I shout at him not to just stand there and grab a shovel. He snaps out of it too and feverishly we start working. Big mounds of earth form behind the house. Helpers join us and soon there are 30 shovels flying. While we are working, the local CO majestically walks past us. He is immaculately dressed and has emerged from his command bunker untouched by the bombardment. From a distance of 50 m he 'inspects' our work and after five minutes noiselessly disappears again. An acid hatred is vented against the pig.

In the former kitchen of the house I find the old woman and the daughter. They are squashed to death. Here all further work is useless. There are a few drops of blood on the fine dust of this ruin . . .

Out of a neighbouring shelter where the door has broken in, I rescue two children. Then I grab my haversack. These *Alltäglichkeites* [daily occurrences] must not stop me. I walk down the street and notice that half of Eckum has ceased to exist.

And as I leave the city limits I can only ask myself for whose sake these people died today. Can any group of human beings ever be sufficiently punished for having made the whole world miserable?

It is already 1700 hours when I catch a lift for Dormagen. There is a lot of activity at the local hospital. Pro forma I report here, to play a safe game. I'm ordered to report to the eye doctor the next day. In the dormitories there is an avalanche of wounded. They give me an idea of the most recent happenings in the front lines. Steinstrass fell! They are drawing closer, those Yanks.

During the night more ambulances arrive and we are woken up so we can help to carry this human wreckage to the wards . . .

26 February 1945[69]

At the designated hour I, together with a group of eye-sick people, report to the ward. The enormous rush means that the examination apparatus goes on strike. Thus, the verdict of the first day is as good as if I had given it myself – 'Report back tomorrow.' The front is rapidly becoming fluid. Already Garzweiler vicinity Grevenbroich is being mentioned. My job is plain: to let the American front lines reach me at the most opportune spot.

27 February 1945

The examination takes place during the morning hours and soon I hold orders reading 'back to your unit'. According to the latest reports, my unit must have already retreated or 'fought to the last bullet'. Now I'll approach the front lines on the look-out for an appropriate hiding place.

The first town on my way is Delhoven. It appears to be a highly unsuitable place for my purposes, for at the village entrance somebody is posted with a *Panzerfaust* and the community is in full swing. It might become dangerous around here. West of town is a lengthy forest. Alongside the forest a great number of gasoline wagons are parked, excellently camouflaged. Columns of supply trucks pass me, on their way east. They are trying to make the Rhine ferry in Zons.

In a forest clearing I find the old cloister Knechtsteden. It offers a picture of complete peace, a cloister like it is listed in Baedekker.[70] A hospital is located inside – and this looks like the ideal spot for me. How to get over these walls? I look through my pocket book and lot and behold – I find an order to have my stomach examined. It is dated 2 December 1944 – but those little discrepancies have long ceased to be any obstacle to me. I make the necessary changes and go inside.

The first examination goes according to plan. I'm to get an X-ray

69. ISUM 302, 28 April 1945, from First U.S. Army.
70. The Baedeker [*sic*] travel firm of Germany published a series of travel books which were detailed and reliable.

tomorrow. The *Landsers* just back from the front tell of fighting at Bercheim and Grevenbroich. All are tired and down to their last physical reserve. They are happy to have found a refuge in the last hospital which remains on the left bank of the Rhine.

28 February 1945

He who never suffered from a phony stomach disease does not know how to value it. First of all, they pump my stomach dry: one of those sensations as if one's guts are being sucked up one's throat. Around noon I have already reconnoitred all basement rooms. In the afternoon, the light cases are marched out of their wards. The hospital is in a state of dissolution. I draw rations once more and then disappear to a vantage point near a basement. More and more casualties arrive in the hospital . . . the Erft line must have been broken. A little later there is a formation of cripples. Evidently the hospital is now officially broken up.

I go on a little reconnaissance mission. The basement links up with the domain Knechtsteden. This little reconnaissance mission pays dividends, for I run into a Dutch forced labourer. I confide in him and he promises to help me.

1 March 1945

There is a lot of confusion in the hospital at around 0500 hours. They are packing. All severely wounded are placed on horse-drawn carriages; the lightly wounded have to hike. I now disappear in the catacombs of the wide cellars. With the aid of some matches I have just found a waterspout.

All of a sudden, a manhole opens above me and two persons come down.

1 March 1945 (continued)[71]

Two girls come down the staircase. They converse with each other in Russian. I beat it to one of the catacombs. Life here is unbearable. Although the *Jabos* circle above all day long, I would prefer to live in a barn or stable than down here among the rats. I remember my Dutch friend and under cover of darkness I visit him in the pigsty. He is surprised to find me still here. For, as he tells me, many a *Landser* asked him for refuge in the last couple of days, but I'm the first one to have actually remained. He tells me that the large barn of the domain could conceal a regiment. There are still medics in the courtyard – and a Gestapo agent.

71. ISUM 303, 29 April 1945, from First U.S. Army.

2 March 1945

Again the *Jabos*. They are having a game of hide-and-seek with everything on the road. The only thing is – these eagles up there are playing for keeps. I make the acquaintance of the boy who milks the cow. Well, that milk makes a welcome addition to my diet. And the boy even tells me that he can arrange it so I can listen to Radio Luxembourg. Towards evening, the Gestapo man leaves. There are a lot of his comrades who also pile on the truck which is loaded with rations. As they leave, I realize that the system of subjugation is gone from Knechtsteden. And they were in such a hurry that they could not even take the plunder away from the cloister which they had already 'confiscated'. Later at night, my Dutch friend brings me some good news: Neuss and München-Gladbach have fallen.

3 March 1945

Artillery fire can be heard very distinctly now. The impacts draw closer and some are not too far away from the domain. A unit is retreating right past the domain and I observe now the SS at once stops the retreat with machine pistols and relentlessly drives the men forward again. Radio Luxembourg just brings news that the Germans are evacuating Koblenz. In this sector events are not moving so fast yet.

4 March 1945

The US breakthrough columns must be approaching. I can already hear small-arms fire. All of a sudden, a terrific detonation shakes the earth. Smoke columns rise up from the nearby forest: an ammunition depot has been blown up. Halftracks rattle back to the Rhine, the symphony of the retreating Wehrmacht. A few *Landsers* are still running around the cloister walls. This time I have selected an OP at an attic knothole. A round of heavy artillery reminds me to be careful, but up to now no impacts have fallen within the walls of the cloister. The latter still bears the Red Cross. As a matter of fact, a few severely wounded, in too poor condition to be transported, have been left behind with a medic.

5 March 1945

The weather is very unfriendly and a cold drizzle is falling. Three German tanks roll past: the last three. The Americans are said to be only one half hour away. There is no *Landser* left to defend this sector. The story as to what happened to them is told by discarded rifles which lie outside the cloister walls. It has become incredibly quiet round here. *Niemandsland* [No Man's Land].

We are now between the two lines. At 1700 hours sharp there is a rumble on the road and someone shouts 'They are coming'.

The abbot of the cloister at once goes on the road to contact the first American officer in this area. He gets the order that all soldiers remaining in the vicinity of the cloister should keep themselves quiet until tomorrow.

In order to give up my period of inactivity, I participate in the general fun which consists of throwing all Hitler's pictures out of the window. This is one way to vent one's hatred, but I would prefer it if we had the man here in person.

6 March 1945

It is all over – I can walk around without the constant feeling of fear. I wait till somebody comes to tell me 'to come along'. Evidently I am not a very important prisoner, for until evening not one Yank bothers about Knechtsteden and its inhabitants.

7 March 1945

At 0715 hours I grab my haversack and stroll casually out of the cloister. I thank the Dutch labourer for the food and refuge in 'the time of crisis'.

Two hundred metres in front of the cloister is an inn. The Stars and Stripes flutter over the building. In front of it there is a light tank and a guard. As I walk up to this Yank, I leave behind me the stigma of having been associated with those Nazi criminals. Yes, it has finally come true: I step into the freedom of captivity.

Chapter 4

Special Forces (3)

Kampfgruppe von der Heydte

Document 4/1[1]

Parachute Battle Group von der Heydte

Three PW from Battle Group von der Heydte, captured and interrogated by Ninth US Army, have provided an interesting account of the unit which made the parachute jump presaging the opening of the current German Offensive. Captured at 1500 hours on 17 December 1944, their story describes the remarkable manner in which men are being thrown into the present all-out enemy effort.

The PW were very security minded, apparently having been briefed very carefully on how to behave in case of capture. All of them carried instruction sheets in regard to possible interrogation but their statements, though confused as to minor details, give a clear general picture.

Parachute Battle Group von der Heydte is presumed to be of battalion strength with at least three parachute companies under command. These PW belonged to Parachute Company z.B.V. Le Coutre which is organized into three platoons of three sections each. The company's total strength was one officer and 90 other tanks. Each section was equipped with 1 LMG, rifles (98K), machine pistols 38, pistols and hand grenades.

All men (PW, dead and wounded) who have so far been encountered from the group that took part in the parachute attack of 17 Dec, formerly belonged to the Parachute Assault Battalion of the Parachute Army,

1. ISUM 172, 23 December 1944.

which had been forming at Lichtenvoorde (Holland) since the middle of November 1944. This process was interrupted when part of the men assigned to Parachute Assault Battalion were pulled out and assigned to Parachute *Kampfgruppe* von der Heydte at Aalten around 10 December.

These men moved to a rest area in Westphalia (exact location not known), until 16 December, when Parachute Company z.B.V. Le Coutre left on three trucks and went to the airport at Paderborn, ostensibly for a practice jump. On the way one truck broke down, and two of the three sections on it were put on the other trucks, while the third section remained on the broken-down vehicle which finally limped into the airport at 0400 hours 17 December. When the company reached their planes the men were informed that this was going to be a combat jump behind US lines. Except for the one section, the company jumped between midnight and 0300 hours 17 December, the last one landing at 0500. The men were told to jump between two fires which would be burning in the vicinity of a road junction at which they were to assemble and to receive instructions as to their mission. 2nd Lt Le Coutre was to give these instructions. The men that jumped during the earlier period report that more than two fires were burning, that they became so confused that only very small groups assembled, and that they never located the road junction, while the last section at 0500 hours saw two fires burning very dimly, and also was scattered, never locating the assembly point.

The planes used in the operation were JU-52, each of which carried one section of ten other ranks, with their weapons, and several boxes of ammo which were dropped by parachute. Neither the men nor the plane carried any explosives or any heavy weapons. Every man was equipped with a spade. Upon landing, and finding themselves scattered, the men hid until daybreak; then tried to locate each other. One POW stated that during the night he was challenged at an AA position by a US soldiers, who made no attempt to investigate when the PW did not answer the challenge. PW walked off and approached the AA position from another side, and succeeded in killing a Staff Sergeant. Of the 20 men dropped in the area two separate groups formed during the early morning hours, both of which were engaged by US troops. One, consisting of four men, was encountered at K853525, and lost one killed, three PW (two of whom are critically wounded). The second, a group of two men, was observed calmly setting up an LMG next to a US AA position. One was killed and the other taken prisoner.

Document 4/2[2]

More About Parachute Battle Group von der Heydte

Another report on Parachute Battle Group Von der Heydte gives further details to those contained in yesterday's Intelligence Summary on the organization and methods of this unit. The Company 'Le Coutre' referred to yesterday is not contained in the organization cited here, but the name may well have been an alternative one for one of the three companies listed below or may even denote a fourth company.

These PW who numbered 14, of which ten were trained parachutists, have been interrogated by First US Army. They stated that the three companies of the Battle Group were known as:

Company Wiegand Comd: *Oberfeldwebel* Geiss (Lt Wiegand was ill)
Company Peters Comd: *Oberfähnrich* Peters
Company Wagner Comd: *Leutnant* Wagner

All three companies have three platoons each: Company Peters is reported to have 160 men; the other two companies 120–150 men each. Companies Wiegand and Wagner are reported to have two LMGs per platoon; the rest of the personnel is armed with German and Italian MPs as well as with Mauser 98K rifles. In addition, each man is equipped with two hand grenades.

Company Peters has three LMGs per platoon; the rest of the personnel have K98 rifles and two hand grenades each. This company is also known to have a reserve platoon which is equipped with 2 x 8 cm mortars. The company also has a communications platoon with an unknown number of small radio sets (the other two companies probably have the same); the following ammunition was carried: each rifle 100 rounds, each MP 200–300 rounds, each MG 1500 rounds.

The ammunition and MGs were dropped in separate containers. Each man was equipped with a white camouflage jacket, and each man carried two days' rations. Gas masks were worn, and the men were also given 'Losantin' powder for anti-gas protection.[3]

2. ISUM 173, 20 December, from First U.S. Army.
3. Introduced in 1935, Losantin was a skin decontaminant in tablet form used a protection against mustard gas. It was mixed with water to form a paste that was applied to those areas of the body that might be susceptible to injury from this type of gas.

It was impossible to get a clear picture of the exact mission of the unit, but from all indications the unit was not dropped for sabotage purposes (the equipment would hardly warrant this supposition), but rather for tactical reasons – to sever our supply lines on the main Eupen-Malmedy highway and prevent our reinforcements from reaching the front in that sector. How much this mission should have coincided with the current German counter-attack could not be ascertained. The whole project was kept highly secret; the men on the ground and the section commanders were told only their immediate mission and were also to receive further instructions after landing. The mission of *Unteroffizier* Gall from company Wiegand was to secure the main highway near Heisterberg, approximately at K8118. All the road intersections were supposed to be occupied by parachutists. No alternate orders were issued in case the mission did not go off according to plan.

None of the PW had seen a map before their jump; they had an approximate idea that they were to be dropped 50 km behind the lines at a spot which was not occupied by our troops. Some of the PW had the naive idea of getting back to the German lines in case they were lost. PW heard only vague rumours that strong German infantry and tank forces were also to make an attack in the same direction.

It is known that shortly before 6th Parachute Regiment came down to this sector, Lieutenant-Colonel von der Heydte was detached from the regiment and sent to Aalten to organize a new unit. The new '*Kampfgruppe*' was formed on 9 December in Winterswyk and left immediately for Sennelager near Paderborn where it received further replacements, both jumpers and non-jumpers from Gardelegen and Salzwedel. They were not volunteers; they were drafted into the unit without knowing what the plans were. On 14 December the unit was sent to the area of Helpup approximately 17 km from Bielefeld. Here the unit received two days of infantry training and the men were told in brief that at some unknown date, they might be used as real parachute troops. Much to their surprise, the promised mission was scheduled for the morning of 16 December. The men were briefed on the terrain with the help of blackboards, but no names of towns were mentioned. They also received their parachutes and emergency rations for two days. Everything was set, but the trucks which were supposed to have taken them to the airport arrived too late and the mission had to be abandoned because daylight had set in in the meantime. The men were told to turn in their parachutes and it was understood that the mission was called off.

Lieutenant-Colonel von der Heydte gave a short talk to the men and was complaining about the inexcusable negligence on the part of the officer who was responsible for the delay of the trucks. He pointed out that the attack had to be postponed now, indefinitely, but he promised them that they would be used more than once yet. Then the men returned to their barracks. At night they were alarmed again, and this time the trucks arrived in time and the men were taken to an airport near Paderborn where they were separated into sections and led to their respective JU52s. Each plane carried one section. The planes left between 0300–0400 hours. Company Peters was loaded on 16–18 planes. It is unknown how much of the personnel and equipment landed at the pre-arranged places or how far they succeeded in reorganizing on the ground. One section from Company Wiegand is known to have been dropped at the wrong destination, and was captured intact.

Document 4/3[4]

Freiherr von der Heydte's Last Battle

The exploits of Lieutenant-Colonel von der Heydte and his notorious 6th Parachute Regiment have haunted many a vital sector on the Western front ever since the opening days of the invasion. Two months ago, von der Heydte himself was reported to have left his regiment and to be on his way to Germany from western Holland for the purpose of commanding a Battle School. Nothing further was heard from him until the opening stages of the current German offensive, in which a force of paratroops under his command were dropped with a view to cutting the North-South road through Eupen. As the dejected colonel, now a PW himself, stated to his interrogators, only 35 of the 106 aircraft which set out on the night of 15/16 December arrived at the correct dropping area. The failure of the operation he attributed mainly to this, and to the haste with which the plan was laid on.

The Battle Group had orders to hold on for two days at the end of which time they were to be relieved. The following account of von der Heydte's last

4. ISUM 176, 23 December 1944, from Second Army Intelligence Summary 202, 22 December 1944, and First U.S. Army Reports.

battle is the result of interrogation by First US Army of captured members of his paratroop force.

At 1600 hours, 19 December, remnants of the Battle Group von der Heydte (approximately 300 men strong) were still in position east of the main Eupen-Malmedy highway, and they were still waiting for the Panzer spearheads which were supposed to join up with them by 1700 hours on 17 December. The men were hungry (they had had no food in two days) and cold (only a few of the blankets which had been dropped to them by parachute had been found), but their spirits were still high; they had the utmost confidence in their spirited leader von der Heydte, and shared his mystic belief that somehow they would be salvaged.

The worst part about the situation was that the Battle Group was completely cut off and had no communication with the outside world. None of the radios which were dropped by parachute were found, and the men did not know what was going on. Ammunition was plentiful, but weapons were scarce; they had between them 14–15 MGs, 2 x 8 cm mortars, MPs, anti-tank rifles, bazookas, and hand grenades. Nevertheless, the Battle Group built an all-round defensive position in the woods and had orders to resist any attack. They did not care to take the initiative though. An attempt was made on the night of 17 December to supply the paratroopers with extra food, ammunition, and a 36-man heavy platoon, but obviously this mission did not have much success either (three JU 52s left from the open field near Sennelager, Paderborn at 1900 hours, 17 December and were supposed to discharge their cargo on a pre-arranged light signal). In the afternoon of 19 December, the hungry Battle Group sent out eight men with the mission to search for parachute food containers. They found some containers, but they contained ammunition and *Panzerfausts* from which the caps were unscrewed. During their further search two of the men were captured – the rest turned back, but there was still no food. It seems probable that the remnants of the Battle Group, if they have not done so already, will try to make their way back to the German lines. There was some talk about it on the morning of 19 December; they were talking about going back in an easterly direction.

The main reason for the failure of 'Exercise Heydte' was the strong wind and the poor atmospheric conditions at the time of the landing. The strong wind dispersed the individual jumpers' weapons and supplies to all corners. Assembling under these conditions was difficult. Many of the men lost their weapons during the jump, and quite a few appear to have injured themselves while landing on the ground. It can be reasonably assumed that in the wide areas of the snow-covered pine woods of Malmedy a number of parachutists with broken legs and collar bones are dying a slow death from starvation, freezing and exhaustion.

A number of the troopers were dropped at the wrong place (in Aschweiler, Kornelimünster, etc.) and a number of the JU 52s were shot down before they reached their objective. Our AA crews have given the troop transports a hot reception on their way, and many of the pilots discharged their cargo prematurely due to the disturbing influence of our Flak.

PW confirm previous reports that several (number unknown) SS officers and men jumped with the Battle Group von der Heyte and were supposed to act as forward observers for the advancing SS tank columns. Their fate could not be ascertained, but several parachute PW relate jokingly that they heard that these so-called 'tough boys' were scared to death before their first jump.

What happened to all of the approximately 900 men who jumped, will probably never be known. Some of them have undoubtedly succeeded in getting back to the German lines; some may have even joined up with the advancing Panzer spearheads – others were killed or captured. One thing is certain, though: the Battle Group von der Heydte has not accomplished its mission – whether it was to cut our supply lines or to intercept our retreating troops.

Document 4/4[5]

Personality: Lieutenant-Colonel von der Heydte

Wartime Intelligence Officer's Comments

The following is the interrogation report of Lieutenant-Colonel von der Heydte, commander of the parachute unit that was dropped in the Ardennes at the start of the current Rundstedt offensive. He was captured on 21 December at Monschau.

5. ISUM 179, 26 December 1944, from First U.S. Army G-2 Report.

(1) His Career

Lieutenant-Colonel von der Heydte joined the army in 1925 as a private. Two years later, after he attained the rank of sergeant, he was kicked by a horse and had to leave the service. Following this he entered the University of Vienna and in 1930, he received a $15,000 Carnegie Institute Endowment to study international law. He has come to 'like' the Americans for this and with his pockets full of money, he could even afford to date the daughter of the American Military Attache in Vienna. In 1935 he joined the army, received a commission and a rapid promotion and in 1938 he was a captain in the German General Staff. This life seemed too quiet for him and he joined the parachute arm soon afterwards. His first action in this was was as CO of a Battalion in the 3 Parachute Regiment in Russia. Then came the airborne invasion of Crete, and for this he received the '*Ritterkreuz*'. Following that, he was on the staff of the 'Ramcke-Brigade' in Africa and after some fancy running to the west, he found himself in Italy where he fought for a while against Badoglio troops. When Ramcke formed his 2nd Parachute Division in Kőln-Wahn, he became CO of 6 Parachute Regiment and was in action with this unit throughout the battle of France and Holland. On 30 September 1944 he received the '*Eichenlaub zum Ritterkreuz*'[6] from Hermann Goering in person and on 25 October 1944 he left the 6 Parachute Regiment to form the nucleus for his infamous jumping mission. PW, though he disclaims any party connections and claims to be a knightly soldier, is a dangerous character and his soft and allegedly intelligent talk was full of falsity and Nazi propaganda. He is extremely shrewd, speaks fluent English – and as could be expected, he offered only fragmentary information.

(2) The Operation

PW claims that approximately 1200 of his unit were dropped by two groups of 53 JU 52 planes each (from Transport Group 30, CO Major Baumann). He further claims that his unit had six Companies and was 1200 men strong. (All other PW gave identical information that the unit had only five Companies and that the maximum strength of the Battle Group was 800–900 men. It is very probable that Lieutenant-Colonel von der Heydte was lying deliberately in order to mislead us.)

6. Oak Leaves to the Knight's Cross.

PW states that he received his mission from Colonel General Student[7] on 10 December. Then he had a conference with General Peltz[8] (in charge of the Luftwaffe for the offensive) and discussed the details for the landing with him. General Peltz promised him the best available pilots for the operation. On 12 December he went to Sepp Dietrich's HQ (refused to disclose location) and there he found out that the code name for his mission was 'Stösser'. Sepp Dietrich[9] told him that he is planning to knock the Americans out of the war (he'll show them) and he also promised him that his unit will be relieved by 1700 17 December by one of his SS Panzer Divisions – whichever gets there first. One SS *Obersturmführer* and two men from the 12th SS jumped with Colonel von der Heydte and they were supposed to act as forward observers for the advancing tank column. Their radios were destroyed during the jump and consequently there were no communications. (PW claims that he suggested to Sepp Dietrich to have Artillery FO's jump with the troops and adds that he learned this trick from the Americans in Normandy.) PW evaded all questions on the mission of the offensive, but suggested that all SS Divisions from 1–12 were connected with it and that *Oberstgruppenführer* Sepp Dietrich is in charge. PW was very much surprised when he found out that Monschau was in our hands; he had no information about the progress of the offensive.

(3) *Personalities*

Sepp Dietrich: PW referred to him as a '*Wachtmeister*' [sergeant-major] who has no knowledge of military affairs and claims that he is not fit to lead an army. He is the only *Oberstgruppenführer* (Colonel General) in the SS and he possesses all possible German decorations. He describes his HQ as swarming with SS Generals and adds dryly that it is very easy to become a General in the SS. He believes that many of these Generals have been transferred from the '*Allgemeine SS*'.[10] PW states that he would

7. *Generaloberst* Kurt Student (1890–1978) was the creator of the German paratroop units and in late 1944 was commanding Army Group H in Holland.
8. *Generalmajor* Dietrich Peltz (1914–2001) was a highly-decorated bomber pilot who commanded the Luftwaffe during the Ardennes offensive and was responsible for Operation *Bodenplatte*, the mass attack on Allied airfields carried out on 1 January 1945.
9. *Oberstgruppenführer* Josef ('Sepp') Dietrich (1892–1966) commanded Sixth Panzer Army during the Ardennes offensive.
10. The *Allegemeine* or 'general' SS was the administrative element of the service as opposed to the *Waffen* or 'armed' SS and the concentration camp guards. It numbered nearly half a million full and part-time members by 1944 when it became subject to the draft. Many senior *Allegemeine SS* officers were appointed generals in the *Waffen SS*.

have preferred to serve under another commander than Sepp Dietrich, but orders are orders.

Rundstedt: PW states that he is an old, sick man who is C in C West in name only as the Army Group commanders are in charge of the operations. He suggests though that Himmler may have a strong hand in army matters.

Student: He is in command of Army Group 'H'. Lieutenant-General Schlemm[11] is in charge of Parachute Army HQ.

Hermann Goering: PW was decorated by him at the end of September at the Luftwaffe Ministry in Berlin. He states that the Marshal has lost some weight, and that he also took off some of his Rumanian, Bulgarian and Finnish decorations.[12] The Marshal made a statement that he once formed the most powerful Luftwaffe in the world out of nothing, and saw it disintegrate into nothing, and that he can and will rebuild the Luftwaffe out of nothing once more. PW believes that the main reason for the establishing of new Parachute Divisions from former Luftwaffe personnel is Goering's desire to have a buffer against the SS Divisions. PW claims that the new Parachute Divisions are just as big a joke as the now dissolved Luftwaffe Field Divisions.

Wilke[13] (5th Parachute Division): PW considers him a very poor General and likens him to General Heyking,[14] former CO of 6th Parachute Division who is in our captivity. He said that the Germans were winners when we captured Heyking.

(4) Asides

Possible new German parachute landings: PW believed that they are probable even though he admits that the Germans lack trained parachutists. However, he claims that one does not need any trained parachutsts to jump, any infantryman can do the job. He states that the Germans have sufficient planes, gliders and leaders for such an undertaking.

Length of War?: Until a stalemate is reached on the Western Front and the Allies come to realise that 'the only menace to the world is Bolshevism'. The Germans can win the war because they are smarter than we are.

11. *General der Fallschirmtruppe* Alfred Schlemm (1894–1986) commanded First Parachute Army in Holland.
12. These three nations had broken with Nazi Germany in the preceding six months.
13. *Generalleutnant* Gustav Wilke (1898–1977).
14. *Generalleutnant* Rüdiger von Heyking (1894–1956), former commander of 6th Parachute Division, was captured at Mons in 1944.

Destruction of German Industry: The industry has been decentralized: 'You can destroy cities, but it is impossible to destroy German industry'.

Final Comment: 'Should you hear over the radio that I received the '*Schwerter zum Ritterkreuz*',[15] please notify me'.

15. Swords to the Knight's Cross. Von der Heydte did not receive this decoration. After the war, he became a professor of International Law and a brigadier-general in the *Bundeswehr* reserve force. An adherent of conservative political ideology, he was involved in a number of scandals in the 1960s involving attempts to muzzle the press and the disappearance of party funds. Von der Heydte died in 1994 at the age of 87.

Chapter 5

Formation and Unit Organization and History

Document 5/1[1]

Organization: 1st SS Panzer Division

Further details of the revived 1st SS Panzer Division have been given by PW of 1 SS Panzer Regiment, 2nd SS Panzer Grenadier Regiment and 1st SS Panzer Recce Unit. (Information from PW concerning 1st SS Panzer Grenadier Regiment was published in First Canadian Army Intelligence Summary 174, 21 December 1944).

1st SS Panzer Regiment was luckier than the Panzer Grenadiers and was able to salvage 50% of its battle-experienced veterans from France. The remaining 50% were exclusively from the SS Panzer Replacement Regiment which is now located at Paderborn. The Replacement Regiment, which provides reinforcements for all SS Panzer Regiments, normally contains 1500–2000 men, to whom it is able to give an average of 20 weeks' training. In the new Panzer Regiment these two groups are intermingled so that both classes are generally represented in a tank.

After its reforming in the Hannover area, 1st SS Panzer Regiment left in late November for Duren, travelling by train as far as Liblar F34 and by road the rest of the way. On 14 December it moved to the Eiffel moving either by day in bad weather or at night. Organization of the regiment is given as follows:

I Battalion:	HQ Company: 2 Panthers and 100 men
	1–4 Companies each 17 Panthers and an average of 120 men

1. ISUM 176, 23 December 1944, from Second Army Intelligence Summary 202, 22 December 1944, adapted from First U.S. Army Interrogation Reports.

II Battalion:	HQ Company: two Panthers 5–8 Companies each 17 Mark IVs and 120 men
Engineer Company:	It appears that 1, 2, 6 and 7 Companies were combined to form one mixed battalion for the attack; 3, 4, 5 and 8 Companies had no tanks up to 1 December, and are believed to have remained in barracks at Ramten near Hannover because of the lack of equipment. In addition both battalions in the Panzer Regiment keep an 'overstrength' training company of 250 men back at Ramten from which they draw the replacements they need. It is possible that this is a misinterpretation of the leaving-behind of the crews for whom there are no tanks.

PW agree that there are no Tigers or Assault Guns in the Panzer Regiment; on the other hand one PW had seen 13 Assault Guns in the assembly area and there was general agreement that Tiger tanks were attached to the regiment for the attack. One PW said the Tigers came from an SS Corps Tank Battalion, and another gave the total working with them as 21 Tiger II, a possible figure in view of the fact that only half of the Panzer Regiment was present. An interesting point is that for the attack the tanks carried parachutists, which allows 4–5 men to ride on each tank.

2nd SS Panzer Grenadier Regiment, which had suffered more heavily than the Panzer Regiment in France, has but 10% of trained veterans. 60% are recruits from the *Hitlerjugend* with a maximum of three months' training behind them, 15% are retrained GAF personnel of varying ages, and 15% come from miscellaneous sources. The history of the reforming and movement to the battle area of 2nd SS Panzer Grenadier Regiment is the same as that of the Panzer Regiment.

2nd SS Panzer Grenadier Regiment is organized into three battalions, each of four companies; average company strength is 140–160 men. PW could give no information on regimental companies.

In III Battalion companies are organized as follows:

9, 10, 11 Companies	(each) three light platoons of 6 LMG 42 and 8 MPs one heavy platoon of 2 HMGs, 2 x 8 cm mortars, 4 x 20 mm Flak. In addition every man in the company carried a *Panzerfaust*, having been

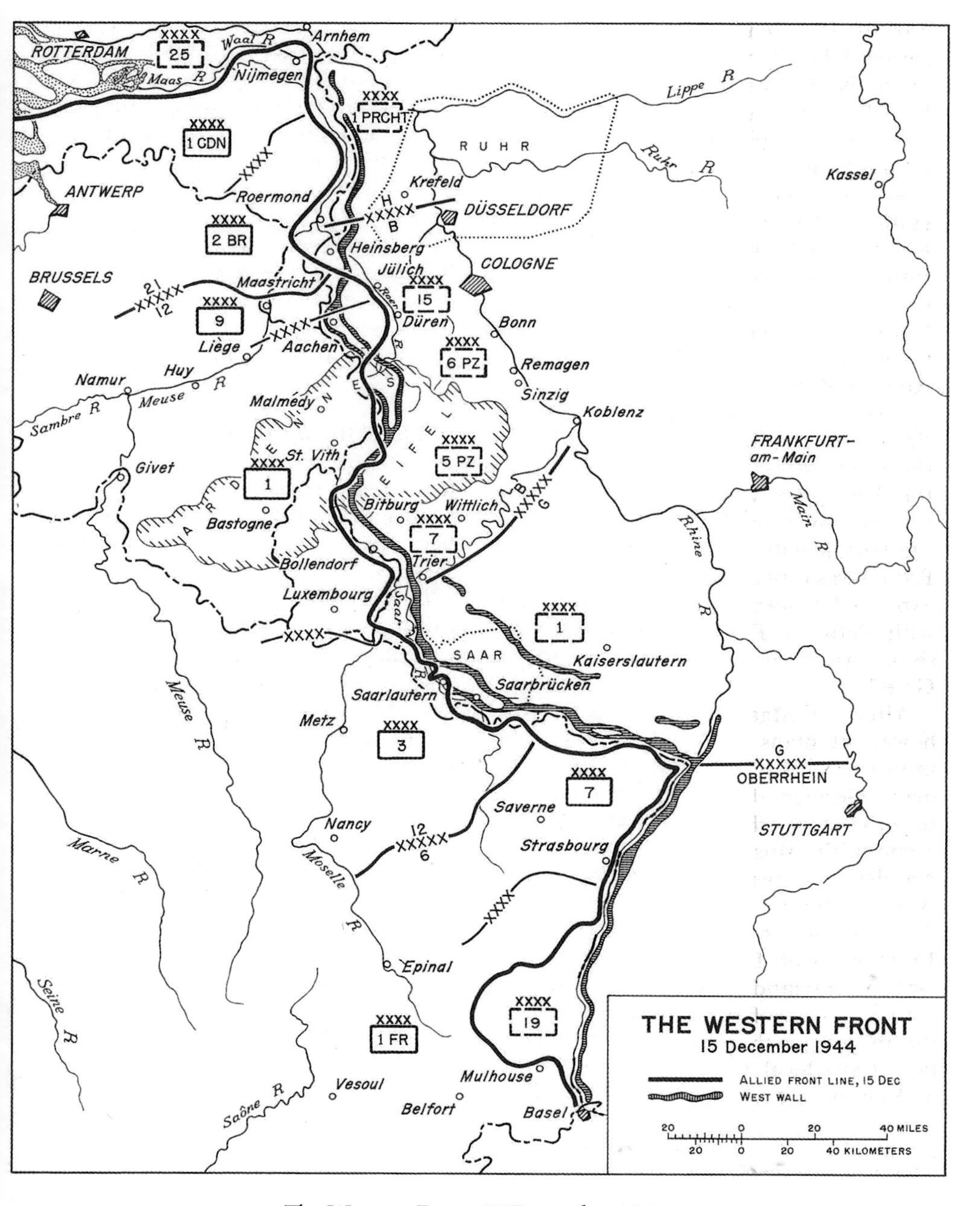

The Western Front, 15 December 1944.

Above: A Tiger II of the 501st SS Heavy Tank Battalion moving up to the front line immediately prior to the offensive to join *Kampfgruppe* Peiper. Most of these heavy armoured vehicles were lost, the greater part abandoned for lack of fuel.

Top left: Panther tanks on their way to the front. Wherever possible, the Wehrmacht used rail transport to move armoured vehicles, saving engine and track life.

Left: A Panther of Skorzeny's 150th Panzer Brigade disguised as an American armoured vehicle. The brigade had several dozen such vehicles.

Standartenführer Otto Skorzeny (1908–75), commanding 150th Panzer Brigade and the Third Reich's foremost commando leader.

American soldiers examining an abandoned *Sturmgeschütz* from Skorzeny's 150th Panzer Brigade. Note the attempt to disguise it as an American vehicle. The brigade had five such vehicles.

A wolf in sheep's clothing: a Panther disguised as an M10 tank destroyer. Note the Allied white star insignia and the use of plates to change the vehicle's outline.

Execution of three members of Skorzeny's commando, captured wearing U.S. uniforms and shot as spies. As many as eighteen of Skorzeny's men suffered a similar fate.

Malmedy 13 km
St. Vith 8

Left: Although often misidentified as Joachim Peiper, this cigar-smoking NCO in this shot is from 1st SS Panzer Reconnaissance Battalion. This is a staged shot taken on 17 December near Kaiserbarracke.

Below left: American infantrymen from the 119th Regiment surrender to grinning panzer grenadiers from *Kampfgruppe* Peiper in Stoumont. The roles would shortly be reversed.

Right: Standartenführer Joachim Peiper (1915–76), commander of *Kampfgruppe* Peiper. This photo was taken in April 1944.

Below: The Waffen SS of *Kampfgruppe* Peiper disgraced themselves by murdering helpless civilians and prisoners. These are some of the eighty-six Americans shot at Baugnez on 17 December 1944.

Left: Major Hal McCowan was taken prisoner by Peiper but later escaped. His account of his time in German captivity is an interesting document. This is a postwar photo.

Right: A Tiger II and passengers who are only too pleased to get a ride. This photo was taken on 18 December 1944.

Below right: A broken-down Tiger II of the 501st SS Heavy Tank Battalion being examined by American engineers.

Below: The same Tiger II as at above right with happy paratroopers on board is photographed advancing on 18 December.

Left: Oberstleutnant Friedrich, *Freiherr* von der Heydte (1907–94). A veteran paratroop commander with a distinguished record, von der Heydte commanded the luckless paratroop *Kampfgruppe* that attempted to drop behind American lines.

Right: A Panther tank advances while its crew sits outside the turret. Overcast weather during the first days of the German attack grounded Allied aircraft and the Wehrmacht took full advantage of it.

Below: German engineers constructed this bridge near Losheim. Vehicles of 1st SS Panzer Division cross while a 20mm flak gun stands guard.

The Poster Boy of the Ardennes. This photogenic machine-gunner from 1st SS Panzer Grenadier Regiment has been featured in numerous books on the Ardennes battle. Note the knife inserted into his coat.

A Tiger II tank passes a column of American prisoners in the first days of the offensive. The King Tiger was a feared and respected opponent for Allied tank crews.

German troops pass burning American vehicles. This is a staged scene from a German film made near Poteau on 18 December that was later captured by the U.S. Army.

Above: This carefully posed shot shows a Waffen SS NCO waving his men forward. He is armed with a *Sturmgewehr* 44, the first true assault rifle.

Above right: Another staged shot of men of 1st SS Panzer Grenadier Regiment taken at Poteau on 18 December.

Right: A disabled Tiger II tank after the battle ended. The Tiger II was a tough opponent but it could be knocked out. Most were lost by lack of fuel rather than Allied action.

A disabled Mk IV tank. This example is equipped with *Schurzen* or skirts as protection against hollow-charge weapons. By the last year of the war, the Mk IV was becoming obsolescent.

	promised two days' leave for every US tank destroyed.
12 Company:	mortar platoon of 4 x 12 cm mortars; gun platoon of 7 x 7.5 cm Kwk (mounted on ? SPW); AA platoon of unknown number of 20 mm guns

1st SS Panzer Recce Unit contains a mixture of veterans and various new recruits in about the same proportion as the Panzer Grenadiers; the story of its reforming and move to the battle area also resembles this. Unfortunately PW statements on its organization are too vague to be of much use, but it is noteworthy that the reconnaissance unit, like the battalions in the Panzer Regiment, contains a training company of 100 men which was left behind at Minden when the battalion departed on 1 December for Norvenich F24.

Personalities of the Division are given as follows:

GOC 1st SS Pz Division	*Oberführer* Wilhelm Mohnke[2]
Comd 1st SS Pz Regiment	*Obersturmführer* Joachim Peiper
I/1st SS Pz Regiment	*Sturmführer* Werner Potschke[3]
II/1st SS Pz Regiment	*Hauptsturmführer* Gerhard Nuske
Comd 2nd SS Pz Gr. Regt	*Sturmführer* Rudolf Sandig[4]
I/2nd SS Pz Gr Regt	*Hauptsturmführer* Becker[5]
III/2nd SS Pz Gr Regt	*Sturmbahnführer* Josef Diefenthal[6]
CO 2nd SS Panzer Recce Unit	*Sturmbahnführer* Gustav Knittel[7]

Mohnke, who started the campaign as Commander 26 SS Panzer Grenadier Regiment, took command of 1st SS Panzer Division in October; he was last reported as a *Sturmführer* but his promotion is not surprising. He was awarded the Ritterkreuz on 17 July. All the remaining Commanders, except Nuske and Diefenthal, held the same positions before the reforming of the division; Diefenthal was known as commander of a battalion battle group from the division, which remained behind in October in the Eiffel sector.

2. *Oberführer* Wilhelm Mohnke (1911–2001) commanded the 1st SS Panzer Division during the Ardennes offensive. Although he was accused of ordering the murder of British and Canadian prisoners of war, he was never brought to justice.
3. *Sturmführer* Werner Potschke (1914–45).
4. *Sturmführer* Rudolf Sandig (1911–94).
5. This officer cannot be identified from the information given.
6. *Sturmbahnführer* Josef Diefenthal (1915–2001).
7. *Sturmbahnführer* Gustav Knittel (1914–76).

Document 5/2[8]

1st SS Panzer Division: Mission and Atrocities

PW from 1st SS Panzer Regiment, 1st SS Panzer Grenadier Regiment, 1st SS Panzer Artillery Regiment and 501st SS Heavy Panzer Battalion have given the following information about this division.

It is the interrogator's opinion that even the poorly trained elements (and there were many such in the unit) were hand picked for downright fanaticism and absolute loyalty to their ideals. They fought to the bitter end – and are still insolent.

The mission of 1st SS Panzer Grenadier Regiment was to tie up with *Einheit* Peiper (the tank component of 1st SS) and then to push forward to Liège. It did not succeed. *Einheit* Peiper (or rather what remained of it) was cornered in La Gleize. It had remained there expecting ammunition and petrol which never arrived. Each tank had carried 700 litres of petrol when the attack began, enough to carry it 200–250 km. The unit had gone as far forward as it could on its own and then had to stop. When the supplies did not come through, the tanks were destroyed and the men surrendered.

Hundreds of vehicles and tanks were left standing along the roads in this operation, the victims of motor trouble, air attack and poor driving (given by PW in order of importance). These motor difficulties, so far as *Leibstandarte Adolf Hitler*[9] in particular was concerned, seemed to be on an unprecedented scale.

The Panzer 'Regiment' was only a mixed battalion – 1, 2, 6, 7 Companies and 9 (Engineer) Company with 3 Company of the Division Engineer Battalion attached. Tanks of the heavy SS Panzer Battalion 501 (3 companies with *Königstiger* tanks) were also on hand. Although the normal complement of 3 Company of Battalion 501 was 14–15 Tigers, the actual number it had was 6. These were all destroyed. Numbers of tanks in 1 and 2 Companies of the unit are unknown. The men of 3 Company were told that they were not up to strength because it was impossible to manufacture and deliver enough tanks in the face of our bombing activities.

At least 10 of the 18 guns of I Battalion of 1st SS Artillery Regiment (presence of only 2 battalions confirmed – any others very doubtful) have been knocked out.

8. ISUM 182, 29 December 1944, from First U.S. Army.
9. The formal title of the 1st SS Panzer Division.

Both 1st SS Panzer Grenadier Regiment and 2nd SS Panzer Grenadier Regiment have suffered heavily. The losses of the latter are believed to be in excess of 50%.

Estimated 1st SS Panzer Grenadier Regiment present strengths are:

6 Company	40 men
7 Company	20 men
9 Company	40 men
11 Company	50 men

PW also told the following story:

On 18 December 1944, the Engineer Platoon of HQ Company of 1st SS Recce Battalion, while on reconnaissance in the Stavelot area prior to attack, were ordered by their platoon leader (*Untersturmführer* Dröge[10]) to do away with all civilians who came in sight. Dröge is in our hands, either seriously wounded or dead. An identical order was given by the platoon leader of the bicycle platoon, *Untersturmführer* Kollotschny.[11] Further, one PW heard the company commander, *Untersturmführer* Foltz,[12] deliver the same instructions from a motor vehicle. The men carried out their orders well, even exceeding them in their zeal to do their German duty. In the village of Parfondruy (K705005) 20 civilians of all ages and sexes were slaughtered. Some were shot on the street. Others were assembled in a barn and butchered there. After the blood bath, a match was put to the barn and the contents consumed. It is believed that PW hoped in this way to hide what they had done.

Samples of the confessions obtained follow:

> 'The civilians were picked up on the streets and brought into a barn. Then they were shot.'
>
> 'I myself, SS Private Rosenke, shot two civilians. They were a man and a woman, about 45 years old.'
>
> 'These 20 civilians were then shot and the barn was set on fire. All members of the platoon participated in the action.'
>
> 'When both Belgians noticed that they were to be shot, they tried to escape. Therefore I, and several of my friends, shot and killed the fleeing Belgians.'
>
> 'We had the mission to reconnoitre Stavelot. Before we could march into

10. Possibly *Untersturmführer* Heinrich Dröge (1922–44), who fought with the 1st SS Panzer Division and was killed during the Ardennes offensive.
11. Possibly *Untersturmführer* Gunther Kollotschny, b. 1924.
12. This officer cannot be identified from the information given.

the village, we had to advance left of it to find out how strong and where the American artillery was. We had to pass through a village. Before we got into it, *Leutnant* Dröge gave the order to shoot everybody there. I was at the end of the platoon. I know many civilians were herded into the barn and then shot. As I followed the platoon to the scene of the incident, I received the order from the *Leutnant* to burn the barn down with the help of a PFC, a parachutist.'

Document 5/3[13]

9th SS Panzer Division 'Hohenstaufen'

295 Prisoners of War of 9th SS Division *Hohenstaufen* were selected for a survey similar to that on 62nd Volksgrenadier Division. Care was exercised to select a representative cross-section of PW; however, it should be borne in mind that no PW from Tank and Artillery regiments passed through Army Cage during period. According to interrogation reports, these units contain better calibre soldiers than the *Volksdeutsche*-studded Panzer Grenadiers which supplied the bulk of personnel surveyed.

From this survey it would appear that the latest edition of SS Division *Hohenstaufen* appears far below the standards previously established by the Division, and is certainly in no way reminiscent of the *Hohenstaufen* of Normandy days. With well over half the men civilians or RAD youngsters on D-Day and a sizeable portion of the rest 'Fortress Germany' commandos, it is no surprise that even the handful of excellent veteran SS NCO's failed to produce a topnotch fighting unit.

Of the four groups surveyed, those inducted in 1943 make by far the best impression from the military angle. All but two Prisoners of War in this category have been with the SS since induction; 35% admitted they volunteered for this political army. They decidedly outrank all others in experience, 66% having seen action prior to the invasion. This contrasts sharply with the group inducted earlier in 1943, 58% of whose members received their baptism of fire in Rundstedt's Do-or-Die offensive. The 1943 recruits also appear to have received a more thorough training in almost

13. ISUM 201, 17 January 1945, from First U.S. Army.

all infantry weapons. The group also boasts a good fighting age – 53% have not yet reached their 23rd birthday, while the oldest are only in their early thirties. These superior military qualities are reflected in comparatively high morale which leaves 58% in this class confident of German victory.

Only 37% of PW came from Germany proper, an additional 8% from Austria, Sudetenland, and Alsace-Lorraine. Almost two out of three of the remainder are Ukrainians, the rest a motley crew from the Balkans, Poland, and the Baltic States. One lone Italian represented the former Axis junior partner. The number of *Volksdeutsche* rises drastically from a mere 13% in the pre-1943 group to 81% of those inducted after 1 August 1944. With few exceptions, these foreigners appeared exceedingly unintelligent – even if their inability to speak German moderately well is taken into consideration.

Approximately half of PW under 26 years of age were members of the Hitler Youth with the other half largely accounted for by foreigners or farm boys whose essential occupation after school hours was considered a satisfactory excuse by the HY authorities. Some others undoubtedly feared unpleasant consequences – despite assurances to the contrary – and failed to admit their membership. This factor has probably also impaired the accuracy of the figures on Nazi Party membership, nevertheless 12% reported themselves as having participated in one of the Nazi organizations, a marked increase over the 1% Party men in the 62nd Volksgrenadier Division.

One out of six PW interrogated claimed to have volunteered for the SS, while another 7% were willing to offer their services to the Wehrmacht. As expected, the percentage of draftees increased sharply in 1944. The *Volksdeutsche*, especially, appeared none too happy about their arm of service. At the conclusion of one interrogation, three Hungarians pleaded, 'Can't you please see to it that we won't have to associate any more with those SS men'.

Median age of 9th SS Division *Hohenstaufen* is 24. There is a wide age distribution ranging from 16–44. Heaviest concentration is in age classes 18–20 and 31–40. The influx of older men from the recent draft group has raised the Division's over-35 percentage to 22%. In this connection it is interesting to note that only 13% of the 62nd Volksgrenadier Division PW surveyed were 36 or older with no one having reached his 40th birthday.

If the *Hohenstaufen*'s current crop of PW is typical of all SS troops, it would dispel the notion that the SS receives superior weapons training. As a matter of fact, there is an incredible lack of infantry training apparent in the rookies of late 1944 vintage. 18% of this group had never fired a rifle before commitment. Most of these seem to be *Volksdeutsche* from

7 Mountain Infantry Training and Replacement Battalion in Italy, who explained their training at the rifle range was called off on account of rain. Most of these 'foreigners' had no training whatever with other weapons. But even the relative veterans cannot boast a thorough small arms education. Most of them have at least a cursory acquaintance with the LMG and hand grenade; nearly all the Flak transferees in the pre-1943 class feigned complete ignorance of the LMG. Surprisingly few have had instruction in the personal AT weapons, the bazooka and *Panzerfaust*, explaining that only special groups in each training outfit were selected to receive lessons; instruction in the bayonet often appears to have been limited to an hour as part of the manual of arms.

With the medical combing-out boards trying to outdo each other in salvaging battered Nazis from the hospitals and recruiting other replacements from former discard piles, medical classifications are beginning to lose significance. 7% of PW listed as 4F or near-4F seven months ago, have since been reclassified as combat material. Interrogators, upon seeing a 'bkv' (limited combat service) of 62nd Volksgrenadier Division equipped with a glass eye, were astonished; but were even more amazed when one of Hitler's Elite, who is now classified 'kv' (full combat service), arrived similarly handicapped.

The great majority of the German element in the group questioned still registered belief in German victory, although the preponderance of *Volksdeutsche* tipped the scale to the 'war-is-lost' side. One in five claimed to be positive that the Nazis would succeed somehow.

Outside of the replacement units, the GAF contributed most of the Division personnel. These comb-outs are anything but enthusiastic about their transfer to the SS. It also appears that the best soldiers were concentrated in the heavy companies.

The *Hohenstaufen* looks as if it is once more badly in need of a re-formation. If a reorganization takes place, it may be expected that the new personnel will closely resemble the men of the current issue. Perhaps an even greater percentage of *Volksdeutsche* and GAF discards will be in this hodge-podge of a military 'one-pot dish' [stew] – with a few experienced NCOs providing an insufficient seasoning.

Document 5/4[14]

12th SS Panzer Division

Some history of the arrival of the 26th SS Panzer Grenadier Regiment, 12th SS Panzer Division, was obtained from prisoners who passed through the Division cage. The regiment was originally stationed along with the rest of the division near Cologne, where its chief mission, as a part of the Sixth Panzer Army, was to sit like a raven overlooking the plans of the Allied operation staffs. On 12 December, General Sepp Dietrich, commanding the Sixth Panzer Army, appeared and told the men they were to embark on the crucial blow; the regiment mounted its organic armoured personnel carriers and moved to the area of the breakthrough by the route of Alrath (2274) – Romerskirchen – Königsdorf – Altenrath – Etternich – Morenhoven – Altenahr – Honigen – Adenau (4298) – Honerath – Krahwinkel (0393) – Bullingen. There the III Battalion of the Regiment, of which the prisoners were members, rested, fed up on American rations (it was the first hot meal since leaving the Cologne area), and gassed up on American gas. Many of the men were issued American field jackets, heavy winter underwear and American cigarettes.

The trip down took six days, and the battalion arrived in Bullingen on 16 December. There was no serious difficulty with gasoline supply on the way south, although at several points the convoy had to pull up and wait for supplies to arrive from the rear. The supplies, however, always did arrive within a reasonable time; the PW were sure that the gasoline always came from the rear and not from the front.

During one of these waits between Adenau and Honerath one prisoner got off the carrier and roamed around the neighbourhood. During his roamings he came upon the sites of three V-1 launching platforms, all in full operation. These he pointed out at 422941, 444949 and 457962. The area is in the Nürburg Ring, a former cross-country automobile race course.

The PW reported that the roads down were jammed with vehicles, but that a fairly efficient traffic control system had been set up. Several times they were stopped to allow high priority convoys through. One of these convoys was an approximate battalion of men dressed in American field jackets and fatigues, riding in American 6x6s and jeeps. The PW's battalion commander explained that these were special troops who would operate

14. ISUM 179, 26 December 1944, from First U.S. Infantry Division G-2 Report.

behind the American lines; they could be identified by bandages on their heads and a yellow rectangular patch on the left shoulder. This encounter took place on the other side of Bullingen.

On the night of 22 December the battalion was alerted and rode up to the Schoppen area to assemble for an attack. At Schoppen they left their vehicles and marched towards Butgenbach, the objective of the attack. Halfway along the road they stopped to join up with a force of 25 tanks – 15 from the tank regiment of the 12th SS Division and 10 Wehrmacht tanks. The Wehrmacht tanks were late, owing to gasoline difficulties. As many men as possible were mounted on the tanks, the rest walked alongside, and the attack took off at 0300. The first accident occurred when the force ran into a lone Sherman cruising the area; one German tank was knocked out and the whole column was ignominiously machine-gunned. Later a second tank was lost to artillery fire. Still later, the battalion ran into the 26th US Infantry.

The PW said that the I and II Battalions of the 26th SS Panzer Grenadier Regiment followed the III Battalion out of Bullingen to Schoppen and were to exploit any breakthrough. The mission of the II Battalion, in fact, was to occupy Butgenbach after it had been taken.

The PW were told in an original briefing that the 12th SS and the 1st SS were to make the initial attack. The 9th SS Division was to exploit the breakthrough of the 12th SS and the 2nd SS was to follow the 1st SS. The only indication that this plan had been followed was the fact that the PW saw one anti-aircraft battalion of 9th SS in Schoppen, a town that seems to be as busy as a rabbit-warren with SS troops.

Other information: the tank regiment of 12th SS is believed by the PW to be with the 9th SS Division to the rear (i.e. to the south). Of 125 men in the 10th Company, III Battalion, 20 were veterans of the fighting in Normandy. One of the PW was 16 years old. Division commander of 12th SS is General Kraas;[15] of the 26th Panzer Grenadier Regiment Colonel Krause;[16] of the 11th Company *Leutnant* Latter.

15. *Obersturmbannführer* Hugo Kraas (1911–80).
16. *Sturmbannführer* Bernard Krause (1910–45).

Document 5/5[17]

501st SS Heavy Panzer Battalion

A Rumanian PW, of HQ Company 501st SS Heavy Panzer Battalion, captured in La Gleize, gave the following organization of the unit:

501st SS Tank Battalion consists of:

an HQ Company, three Tank Companies and a 4 Company

Tank Company: (135 men) has three platoons each having four Tiger II tanks; two Tiger II tanks belonging to Company HQ make a total of 14 tanks per company and 42 in the Battalion

4 Company: according to PW this Company has not been completely formed yet, and remained behind in the Bielefeld area. It consists of:

one AA platoon with 4 x 2.0 cm *Flakvierlings*
one Reconnaissance Platoon (42 men) having six SPWs (armoured halftracks)
one Engineer Platoon (32 men); composition unknown to PW

HQ Company: (150 men) HQ Platoon, Signal Platoon, and an Ordnance Section with four trucks

PW had been with the unit since February 1944, at which time it was in Mons, Belgium undergoing training. About the beginning of May the Battalion moved to France and at that time PW was sent away for two months on a special mission. He returned to his unit on 16 July in the Caen sector. This commitment ended with the decimation of the Battalion. The remnants were withdrawn to Germany and reformation began in early September in Bielefeld. According to PW, replacements came from Latvia and consisted one third of older men. Tanks were brought to the unit in early November and PW believes they came from Magdeburg. About 5 December the unit moved from Bielefeld to a wooded area near Euskirchen at F3126 and moved again five days later to the Stavelot sector. Here the unit was committed on 17 December.

In May PW and several of his comrades were sent from France to Thorn, East Prussia. There they picked up three halftrack motorcycles with instructions to drive these across Germany, Belgium and France back

17. ISUM 183, 30 January 1945, from First U.S. Army.

to their unit. The installation at Thorn is known as the *Heereszeugamt*. PW could not describe it because he never actually went to the place, the motorcycles were delivered to him at a railway station.

PW was told by friends in his unit that fuel was to be flown in and dropped by parachute once their attack in the Stavelot sector got under way.

Document 5/6[18]

Führer Escort Brigade

A knowledgeable and co-operative officer PW from Führer Escort Brigade gives the following information:

The troops in the Führer Escort Brigade consisted of picked elite men of the average of 21 years. The majority had received decorations for close-quarter fighting in the east and the west. The commanders were usually holders of the Knight's Cross.

The uniforms worn in this formation varied. The members of the panzer regiment wore the normal black uniform of the panzer troops. The 3rd Company of the Panzer Grenadier Battalion which was an SS Company, wore SS uniform with an Adolf Hitler armband. The Panzer Grenadier Battalions wore ordinary army infantry uniforms or the panzer grenadier cut uniform (double-breasted, field grey tunic). Everybody, with the exception of troops belonging to the Hermann Goering Division or to the *Leibstandarte*, wore '*Grossdeutschland*' as an armband.

The Tank Regiment had a tank battalion which was detached from the division *Grossdeutschland* and originally was equipped with Mark IV tanks. PW believes it went into action with Panther tanks. It consisted of four companies. In addition, Battalion HQ had a platoon of AA tanks equipped with 4 x 2 cm AA on Mark IV chassis. PW does not know the exact number of tanks in the battalion. The Assault Gun Battalion (formerly 200 Assault Gun Battalion) constituted the remainder of the Tank Regiment.

About a quarter to one third of all units in the Brigade were attached to the Field Replacement Battalion, which was intended to supply battle reinforcements direct to the units. I and II Panzer Grenadier Battalions had

18. ISUM 203, 19 January 1945, from SHAEF.

about 260 men in their infantry companies, but 90 of these were behind with the Field Replacement Battalion. III Panzer Grenadier Battalion went into action with about 140 men in its individual companies and left about 70 men per company behind with the Field Replacement Battalion. Similarly about a third of the tank and assault guns in the Tank Regiment were left with the Field Replacement Battalion. Two guns per artillery troop were likewise disposed of. As well as from the Field Replacement Battalion, reinforcements for the Führer Escort Brigade were obtained from the *Grossdeutschland* depot at Cottbus, near Frankfurt on the Oder.

PW attended a conference at the Reichs Chancellery about 10 December. It was restricted to Army, Corps, Divisional and Brigade (not Regimental) Commanders, and certain officers from the Führer Escort Brigade. Hitler spoke and stated that the Ardennes offensive was to reach the Meuse in two days and Antwerp in three weeks. This would enable Germany to achieve the following three objectives:

(1) the encirclement of 48 Allied Divisions or a general Allied withdrawal
(2) to gain time, viz. at least four weeks, for the consolidation of German war industry, particularly the sunthetic oil industry
(3) by accentuating political difficulties on the Continent and by propaganda, to detach one of the Allies from the war

PW mentions the following Führer guard troops were not committed to action:

929 Grenadier Battalion – remaining at Rastenburg
Führer Air Signals Battalion – remaining at Rastenburg with a company at Berchtesgaden
Führer Signals Battalion
One SS Company affiliated to *Leibstandarte Adolf Hitler*
Seven further troops of the AA Battalion (including railway AA)

The whereabouts of the last two in this list is unknown to PW.

Document 5/7[19]

506th Heavy Tank Battalion

As hitherto the principal proprietor of Tiger IIs on the Western Front, 506th Heavy Tank Battalion, deserves special attention. The details given by a number of knowledgeable PW recently are fairly informative.

It seems clear that the battalion has, contrary to earlier indications, suffered considerable losses. The original three companies were committed in Holland with a total of 45 tanks; one was lost there, and another eight later in the Düren area. While resting in the Noithausen area, welcome reinforcements arrived in the form of Tank Company 'Hummel'. This unit had been raised in September 1944 from 500 Tank Replacement and Training Battalion at Paderborn, and made an unfortunate debut north of Nijmegen, where the training Tiger Is with which it had been supplied, developed so many faults that few reached the battle area.

Oberleutnant Hummel, however, was still the possessor of eleven Tigers when his unit became 6 Company, 506 Heavy Tank Battalion in Noithausen in December 1944. At about the same time, six new Tiger IIs arrived from Paderborn, so the battalion entered the Ardennes battle with the formidable total of fifty-three tanks.

After the retreat, however, only twenty-nine remained. Six were known to have fallen to US artillery and tanks, and the remainder are supposed to have been destroyed by their own crews. Nine, indeed, are stated to have run out of fuel near Dasburg P8562, and it is unlikely that they would have been allowed to remain intact.

Subsequent history is a sad story of shortages of fuel and visits to workshops. The battalion was ordered at the end of January to move to the Julich-Düren area, but the plan was cancelled. From 8 February, the unit supported 2nd Panzer Division in the Rommersheim (L0777) – Fleringen (L1179) area with a number of runners that rose from four to fifteen as fitters worked frantically to remedy defects. Although fighting dug-in in a purely defensive role, one tank was lost to artillery fire on 10 February; the total remaining – twenty-eight – is confirmed by PW as being the strength of the battalion at the time of their capture on 15 February.

19. ISUM 250, 7 March 1945, from SHAEF Intelligence Notes, 3 March 1945.

Document 5/8[20]

Sorting Out the Paratroops

Amongst the parachute formations in the west, the Order of Battle problem has been consistently complicated by the inconsistent numbering of regiments within divisions, and worse still, the tendency to form *ad hoc* battle groups with an operational role before they are absorbed into normal divisional formations. Since early in September 1944 when the High Command desperately flung hastily-assembled units on to the Maas to stop the Allied advance, there has been constant reference to various personalities with the most frequently heard names being men like Erdmann, Menzel, Grasmehl, Hardegg, Müller, Hermann, Hubner, Jungwirt, Gramse, Crahs, Hütz, Lecoutre, Wiegand and Adler. These men have largely been associated with the labour pains involved in the formation of 7th and 8th Parachute Divisions, as well as the ambitious programme of the Parachute AOK[21] for the organization of 9th, 10th, 11th and 12th Parachute Divisions. The drive in the east as well as the current western offensive so dampened this ambitious programme that to date only 7th and 8th Parachute Divisions have emerged after 2nd, 3rd, 5th and 6th Parachute Divisions have been reinforced and reformed.

The bulk of paratroops in the west have variously made their way into the present parachute troop divisions through the remnants of the GAF Field Divisions, conversion of air crews and ground crews of the Luftwaffe to an infantry role, and finally the parachutists who were originally designed to carry out parachute jumps. Personnel of the GAF, training for either a ground or an air role, carried out their training in *Flieger Ausbildungsregimente.*[22] Of these, a number seem to have been converted wholesale to provide manpower for the new paratroop divisions. 51st *Flieger Ausbildungsregiment* at Tilburg, 53rd *Flieger Ausbildungsregiment* at Groningen and 93rd *Flieger Ausbildungsregiment* at Winterswijk seem to have provided the bulk of personnel first met when the Allies invaded Holland. It is probable that their proximity to the actual fighting determined their conversion, and while 51st *Flieger Ausbildungsregiment* may no longer exist, both 53rd and 93rd still seem to provide personnel for the *Fallschirmjäger AOK.*

20. ISUM 244, 1 March 1945.
21. *Armee Oberkommando* or headquarters, here a reference to First Parachute Army.
22. Training regiments.

On the other hand the regiments used for training paratroops proper did not seem to be numbered, but rather carried the name of their regimental commander. Thus there was *Fallschirmjäger Ersatz und Ausbildungsregiment* Hardegg being formed at Bitsch, France late in August 1944, and *Fallschirmjäger Ersatz und Ausbildungsregiment* Grasmehl, stationed at Warn, near Cologne. These units carried on their training as complete regiments, and when needed for an operational role they were merely upgraded and given a number and made part of a parachute division. This policy of training complete regiments independent of divisions, and then combining the regiments into a parachute division, may explain the reason for the piecemeal manner in which parachute divisions made their way to the front. The regiments seemed to come independently to take up a part of the line, and when two or three regiments had arrived they were provided with an official divisional number.

Document 5/9[23]

History of 23rd Parachute Regiment: Interrogation of *Freiherr* von Frankenburg

(1) Personal History

Fähnrich (Cadet) Richard Alexander *Freiherr* von Frankenburg is a deserter from 23 Parachute Regiment who came into our lines on 25 December 1944 at E759665. Twenty-two years old, intelligent, a willing talker, he is of noble birth and his mother, born von Brauchitsch, is a distant relative of the Field Marshal. A thorough investigation has convinced his interrogators that his story is reliable. After completing his studies as an engineer he volunteered for the GAF in August 1942. After the normal period of training he was sent to Russia with 1/Luftwaffe Regiment 1 in October 1943 and by 15 January 1944 he was an officer cadet at *Luftwaffekriegsschule* 13 at Halle, where he stayed until 20 October 1944. From there he took a Parachute Officers' course at Quedlinburg where he qualified as a platoon commander and was sent on 2 November to Parachute Regiment 'C' being organized in Magdeburg. About the middle of November the regiment

23. ISUM 181, 28 December 1944.

was converted to 23 Parachute Regiment, and he states that a friend of his was sent from the same Parachute Officers' School to Regiment 'B' in Brandenburg.

(2) Formation of 23 Parachute Regiment

23 Parachute Regiment began formation early in November at the *Flak Kaserne* [Anti-aircraft barracks] in Magdeburg. This barracks dates from about 1926 and is of a standard design. It can accommodate about 2000 men. In November the following units were stationed there:

2 and 3 Battalions 23rd Parachute Regiment	1000	(1st Battalion quartered in town)
Leicht Flak Ersatz Abteilung 7[24]	400	
HQ Einsatz Gruppe Magdeburg	200	
Luftschutz Abteilung[25]	300	

The barracks were then uncomfortably full. The procedure in forming 23rd Parachute Regiment was for the Regimental staff to arrive first, followed by the battalion staff. Drafts then began to arrive at a fairly even rate, reported to Regimental HQ where a nominal roll was made out and the men allotted to battalions. This procedure was then repeated at battalions and the men allotted to companies. No nominal roll was received before the arrival of the drafts. The latter were evenly distributed in the regiment so that all companies grew at about the same rate.

Personnel consisted of 10% experienced paratroops, several fresh from convalescence after wounds in Italy, 50% from disbanded GAF Field Divisions, and 40% from a wide variety of GAF sources. Of this total 20% were volunteers for parachute divisions, and less than 10% had actually been trained to jump.

The drafts arrived badly clothed at Magdeburg and the period there was partly spent in equipping and arming them, arms arriving last.

Training consisted of approximately seven hours per day tactical training, and two hours weapon training. The former never involved more than a company-scale exercise and cooperation between arms seems noticeably lacking.

(3) Movements of 23rd Parachute Regiment

23rd Parachute Regiment left Magdeburg on 6 December 1944. PW did not return there from a course until 6 December and joined the Regimental

24. Light Anti-Aircraft Training Battalion 7.
25. Air Raid Protection Battalion.

Rear Party, which by 14 December was some 400 strong, 150 being personnel returning from leave or hospital and the remainder, drafts to bring the Regiment up to strength, which had arrived too late. The Rear Party entrained at Magdeburg-Friedrichstadt station, taking two hours to load. Besides wagons for personnel, there was a wagon for ammunition and arms (only small arms), and flats for 30 MC [motorcycles] and 12 TCVs [trucks]. The latter were loaded from a permanent ramp.

The train left Magdeburg at 2000 hours on 14 December and travelled via Oldenburg, Groningen (arrived 15 December 1730 hours) Zwolle (16 December 0500 hours) Apeldoorn to Amersfoort (16 December 1000 hours). This part of the journey was completed with no stops of more than one hour, by day and night, and special arrangements seem to have been made to get the train along quickly. PW described this as a 'supervised' journey (*mit Fahrtüberwachung*) but knew of no good reason for the hurry. The train remained near Amersfoort on 16 December until 2000 hours, and then moved on to Utrecht, arriving at 2130 hours. Here they found the rest of the Regiment quartered in houses widely scattered over the town.

On 19 December PW states that the whole Regiment moved off by march route at 2200 hours, and marching until dawn, reached Renswoude E5098. Here troops spent the day resting, some in bivouacs, others in houses, the owners being awakened to receive their unannounced guests.

Troops were not allowed out of doors, except to fetch food. Next night they marched to Schaarsbergen E7283 where the day was spent in the same way. On the night 21–22 December they should have marched to Zevenaar E8571 but stopped at Duiven E8273. They took over the positions from 16th Parachute Regiment about 0130 hours on 23 December 1944.

(4) Organization of 23rd Parachute Regiment

The Regiment had three battalions which PW thought had the same organization. As far as PW knew, 13, 14 and 15 Companies exist in theory only. 2 Battalion contained four companies. 5, 6 and 7 Companies each had three platoons of three sections. WE strength of the sections was 1 NCO and 8 OR, but one section of PWs platoon had 1 NCO and 11 OR. Each section had one MG 42, the largest having two, which PW thought exceptional. Section Commanders had MPS [submachine guns], the rest of the section [Mauser] Carbines 98, two discharger cups per section and hand grenades. Each company had, in addition, an anti-tank section of 4–6 men each with two *Panzerfausts.* 8 Company contained two MMG platoons (8 MG), one platoon of 4 x 8 cm Mortars and, according to WE, only a light infantry gun platoon.

Transport was very scarce. In fact PW's company had six or seven horse-drawn carts where the WE allowed one car, one MC and 3 lorries. At Battalion 6, 7 cars and the same number of MC were available at Magdeburg but were not used owing to the shortage of petrol.

PW knew of no formation signs.

(5) 2nd Parachute Division

PW thinks he belongs to 2nd Parachute Division or to 6th Parachute Division for the following reasons: he has only heard of five parachute divisions and knows that 2nd Parachute Division was destroyed. Therefore, a new Parachute Division must be either a reformed 2nd Parachute Division or 6th Parachute Division. He had never heard of 7th Parachute Division. With regard to the equations between Parachute Regiments with numbers and with letters, he says that, knowing that in the case of his own unit Parachute Regiment 'C' is Parachute Regiment 23, it logically follows that Regiment 'B' is 22 and 'A' is 21. He admits, however, that this numbering of Regiments does not logically fit in with the existence of only six Parachute Divisions, each of three regiments. He knows nothing of 85th Division and did not know to what Division 16th Parachute Regiment belonged. Nor had he heard of 17th or 18th Parachute Regiments.

(6) Circumstances of Desertion

Freiherr von Falkenburg has the same attitude to Nazi Germany that has been noticed in other aristocratic PW, namely a rather lofty disdain, and an intellectual contempt for the Nazis. His views appear to be those of an intellectual undergraduate with a taste for politics. Having been three times questioned by the Gestapo as a result of publishing a small periodical for private circulation (maximum 50 copies), the last time in October, he had for some time been thinking of deserting but had lacked the opportunity hitherto. After arriving at the front a patrol of four men from his Battalion had all been lost owing to German mines of whose presence they were unaware, as 16th Parachute Regiment, on moving out, had handed over no mine plans. When his company commander ordered him out on patrol with two others, PW used this fact to convince the company commander that the task would be performed more economically if he went alone. He thus created what would appear to be a legitimate set of circumstances under which to desert. The story of his troubles with the Gestapo was not known in the Regiment and thus he would not be suspected of desertion – at any rate for some time. When it was suggested that a patrol had subsequently been sent out to look for his body, PW replied that the fact suggested that the idea of desertion had not occurred to Higher Authority. When asked how a member of an aristocratic and traditionally military family could, under any circumstances, be guilty of desertion, he replied that since the attempt on Hitler's life on 20 July, his family circumstances provided a reason for desertion from Hitler's army.

(7) Attack by 88 Corps

PW claimed that he had seen a handwritten order by the Regimental Commander requesting proposals by Battalion Commanders for feint attacks on Halderen in support of an operation by 88th Corps, suggestions to be submitted by 2000 hours on 23 December 1944. Asked how he should see such an order at 7 Company HQ, PW explained that he had not seen the order arrive, and did not know what had happened to it subsequently. Possibly it had been brought from the Regiment by an LO and left at 7 Company for onward transmission to Battalion. When the Company Commander saw him reading it, he indicated that the order was no concern of PW and put it away.

Document 5/10[26]

The Present State of 3rd Parachute Division

A large number of PW from 3rd Parachute Division recently interrogated at First US Army Cage have given a vivid account of the continued disintegration of this once-formidable formation. Holding the right shoulder of the salient in the Ardennes since the start of the Rundstedt offensive, the cold weather and the steadily attacking Americans have done their combined best to cool the ardour of these formerly fanatical Nazis.

Rumour has it that 3rd Parachute Division is to be withdrawn from combat if and when the Artillery Regiment is forced to retreat beyond Wereth P9395. The division is then to reassemble in Karl-Hüls, Westphalia and subsequently to refit in the area of Dresden, with Div HQ in Dresden. PW believe that when this relief occurs 2nd Parachute Division will take their place. The notorious Lieutenant-General Schimpf[27] of Normandy fame

26. ISUM 213, 29 January 1945.
27. See Document 13/5 below.

has come back to command the division, and Major-General Wadehn,[28] their temporary OC, has gone to take over the newly-formed 8th Parachute Division. With the advent of Schimpf a number of conflicting reports have begun to circulate among the men. According to one source he has requested the immediate relief of the division; according to another he has reasserted that the division would stay in combat until its remnants can all eat from one field kitchen.

The fighting strength of the division is astonishingly low, and it is believed that 8th Parachute Regiment has already been pulled out. PW report that 5 and 9th Parachute Regiments have received reinforcements but had each not more than 300 men on 24 January 1945. The division continues to get reinforcements from a Field Replacement Regiment, Parachute AOK, in Winterswijk A37 in Holland and from Salzwedel. The last shipment from the latter place, arriving on the Front on 20 January 1945, numbered approximately 500 men from various branches of the GAF.

All PW agree that the morale of the troops has never been as low as it is now. PW of 5th Parachute Regiment (Commander: Lieutenant Becker) recount spitefully that according to a new regimental order any paratrooper contracting frozen limbs is punished with three days' solitary confinement and forfeits all furlough claims for a period of one year. A statement to this effect is entered in the soldier's paybook.

One PW, on his way to the battalion aid station to be treated for frozen feet, was halted by the Regimental Commander, subjected to a tongue-lashing, and chased back to the front lines. PW state that they will have to stay in the line until their feet are frozen blue. In addition, troops suffer from stomach cramps, dysentery, undernourishment and exhaustion. Several PW state they had nothing to eat for four days.

During the period 15–24 January personnel of 2 Company 5 Parachute Regiment received hot meals only four times. Three of these meals, however, had grown stale before reaching the front lines and could not be consumed. The 'daily' ration, which arrives every two or three days, consists of one third of a loaf of bread, 50 grams of margarine and 80 grams of canned sausages. No liquid was served during the last week. Upon the request of the battalion doctor, the Commander of 1 Battalion 5th Parachute Regiment recently reported to the Regimental Commander that the state of health of the troops was critical ('*gesundheitszustandbedenklich*'), but was told in reply that these considerations were deemed irrelevant ('*scheissegal*') and that everybody was to stay in combat regardless of his degree of exhaustion.

28. *Generalmajor* Walter Wadehn (1896–1949).

As a consequence, the men have become either totally indifferent or resentful. Some have already broken down and are being dragged along by their comrades; others are deserting to our lines. In fact the number of desertions from this once so proud division is growing astonishingly large.

Document 5/11[29]

Radio Intercept Regiment West

PW interrogated by Third US Army have given some fairly detailed information on the workings of the German radio intercept service as applied to their own unit. In spite of odd statements to the contrary, most PW who have served in such units claim that a large body of information is obtained from this source.

(i) Organization and Function

The regiment is attached and directly responsible to the *Reichsluftfahrtministerium*,[30] Berlin, and a daily consolidated report is sent to Berlin by this organization. The regiment itself disseminates pertinent information directly to field Headquarters, divisions and independent units in the field. With its fourteen companies this regiment covers radio intelligence information at the Western Front.

I Battalion: 1, 2, 3, 4, 5 and 7 Companies have the task of jamming Allied military transmissions.

II Battalion: 6, 11, 12 and 13 Companies are engaged in intercepting Allied messages and they also do the same work as III Battalion.

III Battalion: 8, 9, 10 and 14 Companies do the following work: 8 Company specialises in ultra short-wave sets, monitoring the inter-plane messages of Allied Air Forces; they usually work on a 750–900 metre band. 9 Company has approximately 40 short-wave receivers. Four of these sets are used by interpreters searching the wave length for transmissions. These cover 2000–6000 Kilohertz (Kilocycle). There are two receivers permanently on 2580 and 2780 kilocycles (since D-Day), used by the Allied Forces for air recce (according to PW). 34 sets work on code and morse reception. In

29. ISUM 308, 1 May 1945, from First U.S. Army.
30. Ministry of Aviation, responsible for technical development in the Luftwaffe.

addition, the company has an '*Auswertestelle*' – an interpretation-evaluation section of 40–50 men; an '*Entzifferstelle*' (deciphering-decoding section) of 40–50 men; a '*Teilauswertestelle*' (an evaluation of direction finding results section) of 30–40 men. 10 Company has the same function as 9 Company. 14 Company does the work of '*Auswertung*' (evaluation).

Chapter 6

Letters To and From the Front

Document 6/1[1]

'We MARCH!': A German Soldier to His Sister, *c.* 14 December 1944

I write during one of the great hours before we attack . . . full of expectation for what the next days will bring. Everyone who has been here the last two days and nights (especially nights), who has witnessed hour after hour the assembly of our crack divisions, who has heard the constant rattling of Panzers, knows that something is up . . . we attack and throw the enemy from our homeland. That is a holy task!

[On the envelope]: 'Ruth! Ruth! Ruth! We MARCH!'

Document 6/2[2]

Christmas in the Ardennes

Wartime Intelligence Officer's Comments

The following item extracted from captured documents found in the Ardennes shows what some of the front-line troops engaged in the Rundstedt offensive were thinking on Christmas Day.

1. 1st U.S. Division G-2 After Action Report, December 1944, quoted in MacDonald, *A Time for Trumpets*, 90.
2. ISUM 203, 19 January 1945.

A German soldier writes to his wife in Troppau on 25 December

We have been on our way through Belgium from 16 until 24 December without a break. No rest, nor sleep at all. On 24 we thought we'd get a day's rest, but our joy was brief. My Christmas presents consisted after twelve days, of washing, shaving and five hours' sleep, but we are on our way again. The main thing is that the Americans are on the run . . . Nevertheless, the Americans conducted themselves very decently towards the population, who can only say good things about them . . . I estimate that 80% of my company are either dead or wounded . . . We cleared an enemy supply dump. Everybody took things he wanted most. I took only chocolate. I have all my pockets and my musette bag full of it. I eat chocolate all the time, in order to sweeten somewhat this wretched life . . . Don't worry about me. The worst is behind me. Now this is just a hunt. The Americans hardly got to fire a round, and the American PW say they are war-weary, and don't want to hear anything more about the war. Things might move very quickly in the west.

Document 6/3[3]

Ardennes Letter

Wartime Intelligence Officer's Comments

A letter from a Battalion commander in the 9th SS Panzer Division to the notorious Skorzeny, the man responsible for the rescue of Mussolini and for Operation Greiff, gives insight into the reaction of good Nazis to the abortive offensive:

7. 1. 44
(obviously should be 45)
before Bastogne

Dear Comrade Skorzeny!

I take the opportunity of a rest period to give you a brief report of the situation. For the past three days I have been Battalion Commander

3. ISUM 219, 4 February 1945.

of the 1 Battalion Panzer Grenadier Regiment 20 of the '*Hohenstaufen*'; unhappily under the unfavourable circumstances of the moment. We lie before Bastogne with the order to defend the southern flank of the breakthrough spearhead coming from the Eifel. Because of poor conditions – inadequate training of the men and very deficient supply, especially clothing – I am having heavy casualties. In particular, through artillery and – as soon as the weather clears up – through *Jabos*. Yesterday I received a replacement of 200 men, unfortunately practically all elderly men from the Ukraine, some of whom do not understand German. Yes, if I had only a small number of NCOs here of the type you sent me at Heinrichsburg!

So there is a shortage of everything, but here it is the kind of man that counts. I have learned these days what it means, for instance, to have to attack without one's heavy weapons – anti-tank guns and mortars cannot be brought up because of lack of vehicles – or to have to lie on the frozen ground as a target for the enemy and fighter bombers. But – and one can call this lucky – it is not going any better with the Americans. They have some companies of 10 or 15 rifles so that they don't stand firm up-front. Thus, my opinion is that if we had one division here, trained and equipped with the 'elan' our forces had in 1939 or 1940 and the motor vehicles we now lack, we would have chased our opponents into the water long ago. Well, we will and must succeed one day.

My best regards to you and also to my comrades of VIS and those at Orienburg. Heil Hitler!

Yours,
Karl Appel
SS *Hauptsturmführer* and Battalion Commander

Document 6/4[4]

Letters from Home

To Feldwebel Heinrich Blum FPN L62027 D
From his wife in Wiesbaden.

Dear Heffes,

After having written you a letter this morning, I will write you this quick note. Heffes, we are in such a tumult here you would never believe it. We hover here in constant danger of our lives. We had another attack yesterday and half the town is demolished. We sat in the air raid shelter here at the hospital; the chaplain gave us all the last blessing, in case we were hit; you can imagine the agitation. My temperature was 40 degrees when I came out of the shelter.

Heffes, it is in fact flying bombs which are being dropped on us now. You hear them coming clearly every half hour, and then they explode with a roar. Heffes, I can tell you that my nerves are at the end of their tether. We did not sleep for three hours and lay here in the hospital actually with our clothes on in bed. No one wants to stay in Wiesbaden any longer. It is catastrophic, you wouldn't believe what it looks like. My poor children, my poor heart aches. We sat in the shelter again this morning from eight until one o'clock. And this evening we shall certainly be bombarded again, as they always send flying bombs over here at night. I will close now in the hope that we are still alive when the letter reaches you.

To Corporal August Haxter, PFN 35039 B
From his family at Dortmund-Schüren

Dear August,

On the last day of the old year, as well as on New Year's Day, the English and Americans had plans for us. On these two days they intended to make a good ending to one year, as well as a good beginning to the next, for we had continuous alerts throughout. New (enemy aircraft) formations were repeatedly reported. During the evening of New Year's Day, the Homrichs were visiting us, and about 1900 hours when a heavily laden aircraft passed overhead, Mrs. Homrich made the remark, 'there goes another one with asthma'. Since no comment had been made on the radio, we paid no more attention to it, because only single enemy aircraft

4. ISUM 222, 7 February 1945.

were being reported outside our district. However, two minutes later, the warning 'Enemy aircraft approaching' was sounded, and immediately afterwards, 'Enemy aircraft overhead'. We at once hurried to the shelter and just as we reached it, the first bomb landed, and as we reached our place inside, the second one fell after which we heard no more, the doors having been shut. I presume now, however, that the English must have miscalculated, because the target to be attacked was said to have been the centre of Dortmund.

The Christmas-tree flares hovered over Halde, and there were two more back towards Aplerbeck. In addition, red and green light shells were used to mark the target. There was no shortage of phosphorus bombs either, but it really was not the usual terror attack, since the main attack was being carried out at Wuppertal, which makes me think that the attack was really intended for Dortmund proper. Unfortunately, as has often happened before, the alert was too late, and as a result of this negligence a number of lives were sacrificed. Every shelter in Dortmund has its dead, and Hörde had one shelter, at whose entrance, I regret to say, 29 dead and over 100 injured were found. The immediate cause of their deaths was not bombs. They were actually trampled to death at the steps of the entrance as panic-stricken people rushed into the shelter. One can only shake one's head at the prevalence of such conditions. On New Year's Day no warning alert was given, only the 'Aircraft overhead'.

Document 6/5[5]

Three Whispers from the Reich

Wartime Intelligence Officer's Comments

The effects of the bombing offensive, of the manpower shortage and of the increasing lack of heating facilities are well illustrated in the three letters printed below, all expressing the same dreary resignation which still is not despair.

5. ISUM 248, 5 March 1945.

Netzschkau
8 January 1945

My dear Bubchen,

The Tommies seem to like it here pretty well or they wouldn't be quite so liberal with their eggs (bombs) for the people of Plauen. Since Monday, only the Prudelver train has been running. I have to walk again unless I want to wait for hours and delay the work. Dresden has had its share too; I hear that all three rail yards have been hit and as a result there are no communications from above or below. We have not had any milk for fourteen days as it comes from the dairy in Plauen. The Mönchauer stretch is passable only to Rogensburg, and the Leipzig-Magdeburg line has had bad delays. There were no trains at all this morning, no sign of one until one o'clock in the afternoon. We are in the midst of it all, and the railway yards are full of travellers who cannot get any farther. Those who don't have to travel far are the lucky ones these days. Ten horses couldn't get me away from home; my six kilometres to Netzschkau are quite enough for me.

To: L Cpl Paul Kemper, FPN 32470A
From: Else Kemper *Dornberg, 3 February 1945*

Dear Paul,

From your letter I see that you are still getting along alright, and I can still say the same about us, too. It's a whole year since you have been here now, we'll hardly know each other, but the war will and must finally come to an end. Karl, who put in thirteen months in the AA service, was released (he's still a big strong chap) and he remustered for the heavy artillery. He will apparently be called up again in the course of the month. Yesterday he went to Oberbrechen. I too have good prospects of becoming a soldier once again, but even that or anything else that may come cannot shake us. Let us pray that Our Lord God have mercy on us, especially in our dying hour. What can happen to us after all? We pray daily in Holy Mass for you and for all our members, that all may go well with you. Generally speaking, everything is satisfactory.

To: L Cpl Josel Keusser FPN L62227a
From: Thea Keusser *Scharmede, 7 February 1945*

Dear Josef,

In Scharmede Mia Appelbaum and Mia Vossebürger are to go into uniform, imagine that! I think there are several others who will have to go, but I don't know who they are. It has really gone too far. I hope this war will be over soon. We have no heat now as we are completely out of coal. No one can stand that for very long, I can tell you. I get here at 6.30 in the morning as my train starts at 6.20. I am usually chilled to the bone by the time the others get here at 8 o'clock.

Chapter 7

Diaries

Document 7/1[1]

An Infantry Officer's Diary of the Ardennes

Wartime Intelligence Officer's Comments

The following diary of Leutnant Martin Opitz of 1 Company 295th Regiment of 18th Volksgrenadier Division and translated by 30th US Infantry Division is an interesting study of an officer's reaction to the battle of the Ardennes. Leutnant Opitz is 24 years of age and from July 1944 to November 1944, attended the Officers' Candidate School at Thorn.

At first we see the enthusiastic new lieutenant eager for battle and with the light of victory in his eyes. Four weeks in the Eifel and the burning flame of Teutonic arrogance has been almost extinguished. On 17 December 'there is a general feeling of elation, everybody is cheerful' and on 12 January 'everything looks hopeless'. So died the vaunted ambitions of the Wehrmacht's last offensive.

22 November 1944

Graduated as a lieutenant.

1. ISUM 207, 23 January 1945.

13 December

Twenty officers will leave for the front. They will be platoon leaders in a Volksgrenadier division under Army Group B. We shall travel via Remagen (Rhineland). I have very much enjoyed working with the Hitler Youth Organization and silently hoped that this would become my permanent assignment. Besides, I also hoped to spend Christmas at home. Yet, what is all that if I can go to the front again after having been in the rear areas for more than six months!

15 December

The train was scheduled to arrive at Giessen at 0700, however, we reached Wetzlar at 1330. We had to take a local to Koblenz. There is a two-hour delay in the departure. During an air alert we left the station. Almost five hours are required to travel the fifty miles to Koblenz . . . We stay in the shelter until 0400. People in this shelter live here from raid to raid, that is, they stay here day and night. I am unable to recognise the city of Koblenz now. All our beautiful old German cities are devastated, what a loss!

16 December

The train to Remagen is overcrowded. At 0730 we arrive. We get orders to go back to Koblenz to the Officers Replacement Pool, Army Group B. The sight of Koblenz is terrifying. Ruins on both sides of the Rhine. By truck we finally arrive at Bendorf where we get billets in private homes. The afternoon is sunny; Anglo-American bombers travel east, undisturbed by the fire of a Flak battery . . .

17 December

Today is a sunny Sunday. The Anglo-American flyers arrive early. Alert signal, Alarm, All clear, another alarm, so it goes all day long. The first officers leave for the front. We hear that Army Group B is advancing since 0300 this morning. There is a general feeling of elation, everybody is cheerful . . . The official communique is still cautious . . .

18 December

0630, the flyers are attacking already. Transferred to 18 Volksgrenadier Division at Mautenscheid, Eifel. I leave at 1230 during an air raid. 1700 at Army. Our Army Group is advancing west.

19 December

The roads are crowded with advancing columns. Via Prüm we slowly reach Schönberg. Traffic is extremely heavy. Prisoners, and more prisoners. All

Americans. Buzz bombs fly towards the west. I talk to German civilians and ask them how the Americans behaved during the occupation. They were all favourably impressed. Our attack coincided with an American relief and a regrouping of their forces.

20 December

Clear sky – *Jabo* weather, yet none turn up. All the advancing units are picking up American vehicles, to become motorized. It is like a giantic flood forward which gives proof of German power and German organization. Who would have expected a German attack like this one, right before Christmas? Everybody is enthusiastic, especially the *Landsers.*

21 December

The attack on St Vith begins at 1515 after an assault by the engineers. A new division – 62nd *Volksgrenadier* – passes through. During the whole day no enemy airplane. Official communique: Winter battle in Belgium – 7000 PW in the Snow Eifel (that is with us), 20,000 altogether.

22 December

We move to St Vith and are billeted with a German family. The women sleep in a cellar and we have a room upstairs.

24 December

Christmas Sunday. We stay at the house all day, in the cellar. At noon a bomb lands immediately in front of our house. The cellar holds out but the house is in ruins. The bombing goes on all day. In the evening most of the people pack their things and leave – and that on Christmas Eve. This night we sleep in the cellar. Two bombs land close by, but nothing happens.

25 December

We move to Hinderhausen. We prefer to walk instead of using a car on the main highway. The American *Jabos* keep on attacking everything which moves on the roads. Lucky for us that we got out of St Vith. We walk across the fields from hedgerow to hedgerow, the *Jabos* are driving us from the roads. Even so we have to hit the dirt time and again. One time a bomb lands 30 feet from us. Fortunately the terrain is muddy so that only dirt flies around, but there are no fragments. We stop at a farmhouse between Rodt and Hinderhausen.

This is a brilliant day. The sky is clear, the sun is shining. Only the *Jabos* hanging in the air like a swarm of wasps. High up formations of bombers pass without any interference from us, direction east. Which German city will suffer today? Thousands of bombers go by.

At 1600 American bombers destroy St Vith completely. Within a few minutes they unload their bombs which level whatever has been left of that town. Many don't see the end of this Christmas day.

Yet my luck lasts: Yesterday the bomb landing on the house with me in the cellar, today bomb landing 30 feet away, then the fact that I did not stay in St Vith . .

26 December

St Vith is still burning. At about noon 15–20 German fighters turn up. For a while everything is quiet. Later in the afternoon like yesterday, formations of American bombers come from the southeast and again St Vith is the target. The bomb carpets come close to our village. I have never seen anything like that in all my life. The whole countryside is covered by one big cloud of smoke and fire.

In the evening I walk back to St Vith. The devastation is hardly believable. All streets are burning. Where once houses were one can see nothing but big craters. Only very few people are here trying to rescue some of their belongings. Cattle are howling, ammunition exploding, tires burst; there is a strong smell of burnt rubber. Delayed action bombs still go off and we have to seek cover frequently.

27 December

Over St Vith and Neuendorf there is a thick cloud of smoke. Again the *Jabos* are over us like wasps. From 1000 to 1730 I direct traffic. The *Jabos* keep on attacking. Flak gets a few of the planes, among them two of our fighters. It gets colder and colder. There is heavy fighting in Bastogne. Echternach? Malmedy? Who is there? Artillery fire is coming closer.

28 December

Cloudy day. No *Jabos*. What a relief!

29 December

Clear day, but only a few *Jabos*. In the afternoon big formations of American bombers fly towards the east again.

New Year's Eve

Thanks to providence the Führer has been with us and has given us strength to endure and to fight for victory. My prayer on the threshold of the New Year: With the Führer's and our strength, to end this war victoriously. A *Volksgrenadier* Division marches by (694th Regiment, 340th Division).

2 January 1945

Transferred to 66 Corps.

3 January

On foot to Hinderhausen, by truck to St Piel and Blanche-Fontaine. Corps has moved. From there to Petit Langlier. I report and they send me back to my old place.

4 January

It snows all night. We go skiing. We are lucky and find some wine in the cellar of a deserted house. When I get back there are orders waiting for me to go to Blanche-Fontaine again and to report to the Ops Staff of Corps Felber.

5 January

Corps decides to send me back again.

7 January

I am definitely leaving now. Heavy artillery hits our village by day and night.

8 January

Artillery fire during the whole day. In the evening it gets quiet. The night is quiet. It is snowing.

9 January

The HQ of an Engineer Battalion moves into the house. 50 bottles of wine from Ligneuville help to put us in a good mood. At 1600 artillery starts coming in. It does not bother us, but the engineers move out. The Americans break through from Stavelot in the direction Wanne–Grand Halleux–Vielsalm.

10 January

Bombers in the morning. Why don't we use ski troops and sleds? We would be definitely superior to the Americans who are fully motorized. I leave for Logbierme to take over 1st Company, 295th Regiment.

11 January

I have oriented myself. 7 Company, 295 Regiment comes to relieve us. Two American patrols were captured. The Americans behaved impossibly (He refers to the carelessness of patrols from an attached infantry regiment in crossing open fields under German observation). We go back to Coulee. Artillery keeps coming in during the night march.

12 January

HQ Company moves in. Everything looks hopeless. Towards evening we start marching to Krombach.

Wartime Intelligence Officer's Comments

Leutnant Opitz was wounded and captured on 16 January 1945.

Document 7/2[2]

Diary of a Disgruntled Panzergrenadier

Wartime Intelligence Officer's Comments

The following extracts from the diary of Obergefreiter Singer I/2nd Panzer Grenadier Regiment of 2nd Panzer Division were translated at the Second Army PW Cage. Here we see the cynical realism of the 'old sweat' as he takes part in the big Rundstedt offensive. To news of big German advances his only comment is the caustic 'So What?', and twelve days after the offensive begins he decides that six years of being 'pushed around' is indeed a 'bellyful'.

27 November 1944

Told we were being posted to 2nd Panzer Division. By train from Mahrisch-Weisskirchen via Prag–Nurnberg–Bonn–Koblenz–Wittlich. Plenty of excitement on the journey, including a bombing attack on Koblenz.

2. ISUM 197, 13 January 1945.

11 December 1944

Detrained at Wittlich, by truck to Eisenschmitt. Two days in huts at Himmelrodt (?) trying to get our clothes dry. Heard two V-1s going over towards the enemy (we hope).

14 December 1944

Parade at 1400 hours – told we were moving off. We've never cursed so much in our lives before – we are to march 25 kms, still with wet boots. We started at 1710 hours, the first few kilometres weren't too bad, but after a time my boots began to take their revenge on me. Went through several villages; don't remember any of them.

15 December 1944

0215 hours arrived at Elens (?). Into billets; at least it's warm. Boots off and asleep until 1000 hours, then they call the roll to see who is missing. At 1130 hours we get some cold food because the field cooker has got lost on the way. At 1620 hours we're off again – direction? Forward. We march and march – soon my old wound is hurting again, so Schneider and I and a few others stop a truck and get a lift to Waxweiler and from there to Irrhausen.

16 December 1944

All the way we had a job to get along because of all the transport on the roads. Before we got to Irrhausen we heard the American artillery firing at the ground ahead of us. Got to Irrhausen at 0300 hours. Our kit had got lost through an accident to the truck that was carrying it, so all we could do was lie on our bellies and freeze. At 0430 hours the rest of the Company turned up, and we got put into billets. We were in a deserted farmhouse, and it wasn't long before we had some baked potatoes. All the time there's a stream of troops moving up the road. As far as we can make out we have put in a really big attack, and the enemy has already been pushed back 10 kilometres or more. So what? Either this is the last push we can make and it will soon be peace, or we shall soon have had it. Let's hope there's peace soon anyway.

At 1900 hours we're thinking of going to bed, when a 15 cm shell lands outside, so we clear off quick to the local squire's house which is a bit better protected. After about an hour the others come crawling in too, for the other house has had a direct hit. Anyway we can get a bit of sleep . . .

17 December 1944

Still in Irrhausen. In the evening we saw a dozen [American] PW on their way back to the collecting point. Later we moved on to Clervaux – it took three days to capture this place. When we got there the castle (?) was still burning.

23 December 1944

Moved in SPW (half-track troop-carrying vehicle) to Bande, where we spent Christmas Eve. We may not be lonely, but we're certainly far from home – perhaps we shall never get home again.

25 December 1944

We move again to Hargimont. Here we are split up; I go to s.2, 1 Battalion, 1 Company. We move again, but only 1 kilometre, then the SPW packs up. So once again we get a chance to sleep one more night, but with artillery music.

28 December 1944

Another two days gone by, and the SPW is nearly ready, then we shall have to chase after the Company again. The Devil only knows where it is. If only the war would end – I've had a bellyful – six years I've been pushed around now.

31 December 1944

Our SPW is ready at last – we go off after the Company. It is in action at Rochefort. We got to the town at 1600 hours, but had such a greeting from the artillery that we dived into the nearest cellar. The company was forward and we couldn't get to it before dark. As we arrived the Americans broke into the town, and we were sent to help hold them off. The artillery certainly does a good job for the American Boy (sic). All we could do was get into cover. A sleepless night . . .

1 January 1945

Defensive positions at Dupont (?), then to Han-sur-Lesse, and another sleepless night . . .

2 January 1945

Back to Lesterney as a standing patrol, living in a pile of hay. A third sleepless night, and so cold that our greatcoats are quite useless. We are treated like so many cattle . . .

3 January 1945

When the patrols are relieved they forget all about us, so if the enemy comes we're in the bag. At least we shall have finished with all this bloody nonsense . . .

4 January 1945

Captured at 1100 hours. Five tanks against us two – what could we do? – after five days in the open or in holes in the ground . . .

Document 7/3[3]

Christmas in the Ardennes

Wartime Intelligence Officer's Comments

The following items extracted from captured diary illustrates what one front-line German soldier was thinking on Christmas Day.

Entries in a German OR's diary dated 25 December 1944 state:

> Slept last night in a barn. At 1100 the enemy attacked . . . with planes and tanks. It can hardly be worse in hell. At 1700 we move out again. Our driver burned to death in his car. The Lord saved me. We are in a village which is encircled by the enemy. Hundreds of people have had to lose their lives today. I can hardly understand how it was possible for us to escape from the barrage . . .

In his last entry on 26 December the soldier wrote:

> We are still encircled. A larger tank unit is said to be on its way to relieve us. Will this be possible? I don't care any more. If not, I go into captivity . . . at 1130 the fighting is coming closer . . . Shall we be relieved? . . . This is my saddest Christmas.'

3. ISUM 203, 19 January 1945.

Document 7/4[4]

A Sniper's Diary

Wartime Intelligence Officer's Comments

The following is the translation of an extract from the diary of a member of 7 Company, 982nd Volksgrenadier Regiment of 272nd Volksgrenadier Division. The PW was a sharpshooter, and this extract comprises his 'score' at the end of December and the beginning of January.

'My Score as a Sharpshooter'

1st Score:

29 December 1944 in sector of 1st Platoon, 7th Company, 982nd *Volksgrenadier* Regiment, above the road bend and at a distance of 400 metres: Of three enemy soldiers standing talking to one another in a group, I aimed and fired at the one in the middle who doubled up and fell to the ground.

Witness: Observer Corporal ____

2nd Score:

1 January 1945 in sector of 6 Company, 986th Volksgrenadier Regiment, on the wood road near bunker. At 0900, right after a relief of sentries, one soldier stood still. I fired, and the soldier fell and was immediately carried away by two others who appeared from the left.

Witness: Observer Corporal ____

3rd Score:

1 January 1945 in the same sector and on the same wood road. Three men came to the right of the dugout. To all appearances, they were discussing where my first shot had come from and pointing in various directions. I got the middle one in my sights and he fell over on to his side. The other two immediately jumped into the dugout. Time: 0920.

Witness: Observer Corporal ____

4. ISUM 198, 14 January 1945, from XIX U.S. Corps.

4th Score:

Same sector and place. A soldier who was standing, visible down to his web belt, in a connecting trench immediately in front of the dugout, was brought into my sights and fell. My observer was, at the time, watching another enemy soldier chopping wood and accordingly did not see the man fall. He did, however, see the wood chopper go to the fallen man's aid. Time: 1515.

Witness: Observer Corporal ____

5th Score:

Same sector and place. The sentry in the foxhole obscured by trees, grew careless and left the foxhole, appearing out by the trees. As I had the place zeroed in, all I had to do was squeeze the trigger and he fell to the left into the ditch. Time: 1625.

Witness: Observer Corporal ____

Wartime Intelligence Officer's Comments

The PW, when interrogated, said that he found the US soldiers 'easy marks' and that they exposed themselves carelessly. The reason for keeping this careful score was that after ten successful shots, properly witnessed, a sharp-shooter received a seven-day furlough.

Document 7/5[5]

From Victory to Defeat: Diary of an Artillery Officer

Wartime Intelligence Officer's Comments

Another diary of a German officer in the Ardennes presents again the study of an enthusiastic expectation of Teutonic victory at the start of the Rundstedt offensive, which had died to a grim realization of defeat in only five short weeks. The writer, Leutnant Behmen of 1818th Artillery Regiment of 18th Volksgrenadier Division, curiously enough comes from the same division

5. ISUM 214, 30 January 1945.

as did Leutnant Opitz whose diary appeared in First Canadian Army Intelligence Summary Number 207 dated 23 January 1945. In both accounts the flame of promised victory on 16 December is snuffed out by the combined efforts of Allied dive bombers, artillery and attacking infantry.

16 December 1944

First day of attack. The sky was lit up along the whole front. A terrific barrage is laid on the whole time. By noon reports of the first successes come in. The population of Puppeln is very enthusiastic. At 2 o'clock the infantry is in motion. Casualties are not light. It was there that the Americans were echeloned in depth.

17 December

Our fighter planes still control the air in the morning and afternoon.

18 December

The infantry is before St Vith. The men hear the wildest rumours of successes, but the official notices are very laconic about the attack.

19 December

Endless columns of prisoners pass; at first, about a hundred, half of them negroes, later another thousand. Our car gets stuck on the road. I get out and walk. *Generalfeldmarschall* Model himself directs traffic. (He's a little, undistinguished looking man with a monocle). Now the thing is going. The roads are littered with destroyed American vehicles, cars and tanks. Another column of prisoners passes. I count over a thousand men. In Ameler there is a column of 1,500 men with about 50 officers, and a Lieutenant-Colonel who had asked to surrender.

20 December

According to statements of the civilians, the American soldiers did not conduct themselves badly at all. Mostly they slept apart from the civilians, and since they had enough to eat, they were able to give some to the civilians. Only the 'White Army' (revenge) was at its worst. Many persons were taken away from their homes. Civilians too tell us that the Americans were completely surprised when our attack started. The American soldiers have shown little spirit for fighting. Most of them often said, 'what do we want here? At home we can have everything much better'. That was the spirit of the common soldier. If the officers thought that way??? . . . A rumour was set going that Eisenhower was taken prisoner. It will probably prove to be only a rumour.

21 December

Roads still clogged, but traffic continues. Vehicles are almost exclusively captured American equipment. It was a tremendous haul. In the morning an American artillery battery gave itself up. This night St Vith has fallen.

22 December

After St Vith is taken, traffic flows continuously. If enemy planes had appeared, it would have been a terrible disaster. An infantry division, and infantry regiment HQ are set up in town. Also our artillery battalion HQ. We went to tank up at a large gasoline and food supply depot which the Americans had near a monastery, but all the stuff was already gone, except for half a can of gasoline.

23 December

We sight strong bomber formations flying toward Germany. Saw two of them shot down.

24 December

Dive bombers attack and hit a house in front of me. Two metres more and it would have been me. We take our car and race toward St Vith. Here, dive bombers attack again and strafe all the roads. By four o'clock, we counted 12 shot down by AA. During the night more bombs fall. At 0430 a terrific crash awakens me. Windows break, and the little house seems to be falling apart.

25 December

We are ordered to proceed to Hinderhausen. Over us circle enemy planes. All along the road, there are tremendous bomb craters but it seems that very little was hit. Shortly before reaching Hinderhausen, we see a dive bomber start for us. We are able to stop the truck in time to get off the road as the bullets start flying about us. Nothing is to be seen of our air force; where is it? The heavy bombers fly toward the Reich, quiet and undisturbed. The AA is getting heavier but it doesn't seem to bother them. Only two bombers are knocked down. The pilots 'hit the silk' but the dogs are lucky, and the wind drives them toward the West. They actually regain enemy territory. If they had landed in our lines we'd slay them; in the evening, we see the first in St Vith. I could cry from rage, and tear the prisoners apart.

26 December

During the afternoon, we undergo the second large-scale attack on St Vith. Large bomber formations pass, and then the bombs drop; 100 tons, and heavier. The house shakes, and the windows break; the terrorized family seeks refuge in the cellar. Babies cry, but the bombers keep on coming. It looks as though they were dropping phosphorus. There's nothing left of St Vith. Hours later, heavy smoke clouds are still rising.

29 December

The division is now ordered to secure the northern flank in the direction Malmedy-Perrieres.

1 January 1945

We had hardly moved into our new quarters when the artillery started shelling us. We had expected it. I sent all men to the cellars.

10–13 January

Our position is under continuous artillery fire. On the 12th at eight o'clock, the Americans laid down a heavy concentration of fire. Then the enemy infantry attacked. On our left, Otaimont is in enemy hands. He is now attacking Hedomont, driving southeast and breaking through. We have lost contact with our forward observer. Battalion gives the command to withdraw to our alternate position. During the evening, we move three guns into a new position at Recht.

14 January

Almost every house in the village has been hit. The barrage lasts all morning. Radio communication to Battalion is excellent (for the first time in my two and a half years of Army experience). In the afternoon the enemy attacks again. I alert all gun crews, but I will not fire for fear of giving away our positions. I call Battalion for a concentration of fire. The fire falls behind the enemy, and is not too effective. In the evening, we strengthen our position with MG and outposts.

16 January

Four weeks ago our attack started. How quickly everything has changed! Here, again, we receive continuous fire from the enemy. During the day Recht is under heavy fire. Around noon, an order comes through to withdraw, one gun at a time, and to assemble at new positions. Dive bombers are active again. Because of this, the guns are forced to withdraw slowly. I wonder if we'll ever see the field kitchen again. We have only one two-wheeled cart left for transport, and no horse. I hope the horse will show up some day.

17 January

Nine AM. It is fairly quiet. The front line is new in front of Ochsen Barracks to the right of Dellburg. This is where the First Battery is employed as front-line infantry. I hope that the weather remains cloudy, so that it's more difficult for the fighter-bombers. I hear that *Leutnant* Dahel, CO of the 8th Battery, is missing, and that the CO of the 1st Battery was killed. Officer casualties are heavy.

18 January

The night was very lively. We received continuous artillery fire on our positions. We expected an attack through the large gap which exists in our MLR, but nothing happened.

20 January

I am ordered to organize anti-tank defence at St Vith. For the first time since Christmas I'm in St Vith again. The town is in ruins, but we will defend the ruins. I am sending the Signal Platoon back to Andler. We expect the attack on St Vith. Only small forces are available for the defence. The pessimists in the unit speak of a little Stalingrad (*KleinStalingrad*).

21 January

There are no new messages. The battle noises come closer to town. We can already see the infantry on some of the heights. I am organizing everything for a last defence. Rumour has it that the Tommies (?) have surrounded the town. Some even believe it. At high commands, they believe that we will be forced to yield. These rear-echelon men!!! I am neither optimistic nor pessimistic, and I don't give up hope. When the kitchen goes back I will send all personnel not immediately needed back with it. During the day it is unnaturally quiet. Will the enemy surround the town? I'm sending back all of my personal belongings. One never knows. I wonder what Heide is doing? The news from the Eastern Front is very serious. There must be a decisive change very soon; what we need is submarines and airplanes. Only those things can still help us.

22 January

Nothing new during the night. At eight o'clock, the enemy recommences his saturation fire from the direction of Nieder Emel. Exactly one year ago, on 22 January 1944, I was in this same fix. At that time, as a non-com, I was involved in the retreat north of Galhelina; now, as a battery commander of a battery used as anti-tank security. The front lines are just as hazy now as they were then. Exactly one month ago, we took St Vith . . .

Document 7/6[6]

Diary of a Stoic Panzergrenadier

Wartime Intelligence Officer's Comments

The following are extracts from the stoical, but naively charming, diary of Karl Blank of 6 Company, 104th Panzer Grenadier Regiment [of 15th Panzergrenadier Division], in his peregrinations to and from the Eifel and up to the Reichswald area. They enhance the impression already gained, that 15th Panzer Grenadier Division can have had little time to refit between the two battles, or indeed do anything except move rather aimlessly from place to place, keeping sanitary all the while.

The carefree abandon with which the author records his impressions of the battles of the Ardennes and Reichswald is, to say the least, refreshing. The process of extraction [translation?] *is not responsible for the staccato style, which is the diarist's own.*

6 January 1945

From Advanced Transit Camp to Schlossheck, 7 kilometres southwest of Prühm. Spent night in Town Hall cellar. Air raid warning.

9 January

To St Vith with ambulance, thence by lorry to Oberblessingen. Night at a signalman's cabin.

10 January

On the road for Ufflingen and Boxhorn. Lorry ditched with trailer at Boxhorn. Drove all night to

11 January

Neroth near Gerolstein. Very cold. Feet like ice. 16 hours on lorry. Good billet. People friendly. Night at Neroth with the Sonnen family.

6. ISUM 240, 28 February 1945.

12 January

Transferred to II Battalion 104th Regiment. Another night at Frau Sonnen's.

13 January

Left for Gees on foot, thence lorry to Blewingen. II Battalion moved to Steiningen, frequently got stuck on the way.

14 January

Sent to 6 Company at Utzerath (L48). Two hours' march with full kit. Company Commander Second Lieutenant Zölsch.

17 January

Stiff neck and back. Did some skiing.

18 January

Got angina. Painted my throat with iodine. Cleaned my gums.

22 January

No skis. Marched to Steiningen via Darscheid.

23 January

Supposed to move but couldn't. No petrol.

24 January

Battalion marched back to Gochs. Got myself tattooed.

27 January

Left Utzerath for Leidenborn at 2400 hours.

28 January

Hot and cold rations issued from battalion kitchen. Left for Lunebach (L07).

29 January

Icy cold all night. Organized a room and stove. Got undressed.

30 January

Organized a new stove. Personnel allotted to platoons and sections. One loaf of bread for ten men.

31 January

Pea soup again. Not a bite of bread.

1 February

Dry vegetables. Still no bread, only butter and tobacco.

2 February

Left Lunebach for Nüten (L21) near Münstereifel (L31). At 1030 hours arrived at glider depot and spent two hours looking for a bed to sleep in.

3 February

Washed and shaved. Air activity. Fetched petrol at night from Mechernich (F22).

4 February

Petrol issue. Moved to Haardt (? Haardt A09).

5 February

Left Haardt for Bockhold (A01) near Strälen (E91) via Süchteln (F09). Looked for billet.

6 February

Cleaned my rifle. Spent night in a bed.

7 February

Deloused. Read a novel.

8 February

New reinforcements. Now in 2nd Platoon.

11 February

Assembly area in wood. Fired *Panzerfaust* and *Ofenrohr*. Left for Goch-Cleve area.

12 February

Concentration area in the Hochwald. Some casualties.

13 February

New positions near Goch behind the Reichswald. Patrol activity. Ziebner wounded. Artillery fire to our left. First sleep for four days.

14 February

Quiet day. New Company Commander. Roast duck. Miscellaneous mail from home.

Chapter 8

Tactics and Methods

Document 8/1[1]

German Soldier, Use Your Eyes!

Wartime Intelligence Officer's Comments

Attached is a reproduction in translation of an enemy training pamphlet, entitled 'German Soldier, Use Your Eyes!'. This document, complete with rhymed explanation of the cleverly sketched illustrations, is one of the better examples of German instructional methods. Translation is by First Canadian Army Documents Section.

Use your eyes! Mark this well! Good
'Intelligence' may save your blood.
It furthers our Commanders' ends
If they know what the foe intends.

A prisoner brought in by you
Means one patrol you needn't do.
And if we first know who is where
It's no great problem to infer
Enemy strengths and armaments,
by methods of 'Intelligence'.

1. ISUM 253, 10 March 1945.

Watch carefully a captured man
He'll discard papers, if he can,
Tickets, signs or even letters
Are enemy Intelligence matters.

It's true a dead man tells no tale,
But be observant. Do not fail
To take away his shoulder titles,
Documents and such like trifles
And search his pack for there's a hope
That you may find an envelope.

And if some time you have the luck
To come across a knocked-out truck,
A quick sketch roughly to resemble
The enemy Divisional emblem
Will bring you thanks from 'Higher-ups'.

Especially efficient men
Note types of captured tanks, and when
They can, they look inside the box
For radio and signals Docs.

To be of any use at all
It's most important you recall
To send us back with 'when and where'
What you've discovered then and there.
The sooner we receive the news
The greater it will be of use.

So use your eyes, and all you send
(The small things too), will fit and blend
Into a picture we can use
Against the Bolsheviks and Jews
We must use all that comes to hand
To defend our Fatherland.

Document 8/2[2]

Tricky American Methods of Fighting

Wartime Intelligence Officer's Comments

A captured order from 3rd Parachute Division dated 13 January 1945 mentions the following items:

(1) An officer from 277 *Volksgrenadier* Division encountered a group of American soldiers in German uniform on 1 January 1945. They called out in German, 'Halt, don't shoot, we are German soldiers.' The Americans then opened fire at close range, killing the officer.

(2) German soldiers returned from American PW camps and related the following: They are given cards to fill out, calling for name, date of birth, address and unit. The cards were supposedly to be used to notify next of kin as to whereabouts of the German PW. Actually they were used to obtain military information from the PW. According to the Geneva Convention a PW is required to give only name, rank, date of birth and home address. To answer any other question is treasonable. It has been determined beyond the shadow of a doubt that the enemy uses the information thus obtained not to notify next of kin, but for the purposes of propaganda by leaflets and radio.

Document 8/3[3]

Awards for Breaking Out of Encirclement

Wartime Intelligence Officer's Comments

The following translation of a document captured on 22 January on the American front stresses the importance the German High Command places on the fight put up by their own troops once they have been cut off.

2. ISUM 215, 31 January 1945, from XVIII U.S. Airborne Corps.
3. ISUM 215, 31 January 1945, from XVIII U.S. Airborne Corps.

HQ II Parachute Corps Corps HQ, 2 January 1945
Chief of Staff

The enclosed order of Supreme Headquarters of the Army of 8 December 1944 in conformity with the Führer's decree regarding awarding of decoration to members of the Army who have fought their way out of encirclement, is hereby brought to your attention.

It has been repeatedly affirmed in orders to this HQ that strict rule be applied in the awarding of decorations under this order, and that the proposals for awards be forwarded to this HQ for review. The conferring of close-combat bars on the basis of the aforementioned orders, is to be the personal responsibility of divisional commanders as to review. The award of close-combat bars is contingent on the soldier's having taken part in a specified minimum number of close-combat engagements. If this contingency does not exist, the award is illegal and the decoration is to be recalled. Should a soldier be in a position to prove, on the day of the award, that he had in the meantime acquired additional close-combat credits, such credits are to be included for the purpose of determining his eligibility. The final, valid total is to be entered into his service record.

Valid on: 25 January 1945 Draft copy signed
Meindl[4]

Document 8/4[5]

Another Ten Commandments

Wartime Intelligence Officer's Comments

Among the documents salvaged from the wreck of the recent enemy attacks at Zetten E8172 was the following list of instructions for sentries and patrols. While it contributes little enough to our knowledge of the enemy's sentry methods, it is interesting as a sample of the kind of instruction he finds it necessary to distribute among front-line troops.

4. *General der Fallschirmtruppe* Eugen Meindl (1892–1951), the corps commander.
5. ISUM 208, 24 January 1945.

Ten Commandments for Sentries and Patrols

1. I am a sentry: my alertness prevents bloodshed.
2. My duty is to be suspicious.
3. My duty is to halt all strangers.
4. I do not give information without first seeing the man's paybook.
5. My duty is to ask every stranger who he is, where he comes from, where he is going to, and why.
6. As a sentry I carry my weapon under my arm without fail.
7. At night I halt everyone and have each one show me his identification, even those who know the password. While I am inspecting the papers, my fellow sentry stands a few yards away to keep me covered.
8. My rifle is a weapon to shoot with. I fire on everyone who tries to run away, who fails to perform or acts in opposition to my orders.
9. As OP sentry I must see without being seen by the enemy (camouflage in soldierly manner).
10. As OP sentry I report to my superiors without interrupting my observation of the enemy position. Eyes remain fixed on the enemy. When lying down I report lying down, even to a General.

Document 8/5[6]

The Germans Prepare for the Winter

Wartime Intelligence Officer's Comments

The Germans, confronted with the prospect of fighting a winter campaign on both fronts, are desperately trying to make ends meet. Climatic conditions naturally will make it necessary to shift priority on winter equipment to the Eastern front, and this has up to date been carried out, much to the detriment of the freezing Heinies on the Western front. Belief amongst troops interrogated is that clothing and other essential winter equipment will arrive here for distribution on or about 1 December. Advance issue, however, has

6. ISUM 146, 23 November 1944, from First U.S. Army G-2 Periodic Report 21 November 1944.

taken place in some units. This, together with T/Es issued, gives a rather representative picture of what kind of paraphernalia the German Army will carry this winter.

PW interrogated included most of the units now in contact with First US Army. An effort was made to question primarily men who were informed about QM-issue (supply sergeants, HQ men employed in the QM offices).

Questions asked were:

(a) What winter equipment has been or is to be issued in your unit?
(b) Do you know of any new or unusual items of clothing and equipment ready for issue?
(c) What additional food distribution is planned for the winter?

Clothing issued to date

Items issued in this paragraph have by no means been issued to all troops in all units. It may be expected, however, that as soon as the German '*Nachschub*' begins to bring up the winter supplies, the following will be standard equipment:

1 Pullover (*Schlupfjacke*), light grey, cotton substitute
1 pair of gloves, dark grey, cotton substitute with half sleeves
1 (additional) blanket – brings total to 2
1 set of long winter underwear, heavy-knit, short fibre cotton, grey colour. Drawers have a 10 cm wide felt waist band
1 hood (*Kopfschutz*), green-grey, wool, with neck protection
Winter overcoat: cloth coat, with imitation rayon lining (quilted), with head cover attached
Rubber boots: those were issued so far to outposts, patrols, officers and engineers
Wristlets: 4 inches long, fitting around wrist as protection
Cotton stockings: heavy knit, no toes or heels, held in place by a strip of tape approx 1 inch around instep – full length (up to crotch)
'*Brustwärmer*': described as a tricot strip to wind around chest. Referred to as a 'brassiere for men'.

Special Equipment issued to date

Many items so far have only been issued to special troops such as engineers, assault troops and guard companies (who have long hours and stationary posts).

Vest: form of US Navy life-jacket, initiation knit, woven rayon long sleeve jacket with imitation rayon, caracule lining, colour steel grey, panama weave.

Rubber overshoes: made of thin rubber, same shape as German boots, half-knee length; with a strip to tighten. Sole is made of somewhat hard rubber.

Camouflage suit: colour white inside, camouflaged pattern outside (like German shelterhalf). Reversible. Wool padding inside, impregnated and water-repellant. Inner lining consists of poplin coloured lining, loosely woven. Has pockets inside as well as outside. Jacket designed for double buttoning with 2-inch overlapping flap. Strap runs around the waist making for snug wear. (This article was issued to all troops in Russia in 1943).

Special German Winter Equipment

Most of the following equipment has been specially designed for cold and dry winter weather and was used by the Germans during the winter campaigns of 1942 and 1943 on the Eastern and Southeastern Fronts. Some of the items shown may, however, also be used in cold and damp weather and are almost certain to make an early appearance on the Western Front.

Rubber pants and jackets: No further details are available. PW from the 12th Infantry Division stated that this clothing has already been delivered to their company supply room, but for some reason, perhaps the planned withdrawal of the Division, was transported to rear echelons again on 15 November.

Cloak with hood, made out of oil cloth: This is a one-piece garment, reaching down to the ankles. Some few have already been shipped to this front.

Cloth coat with heavy padding, white: Coat looks like a quilt and is almost as thick. It was issued in Russia to static troops.

Sheep-skin Jacket: Worn as a vest, it has no sleeves and no collar. Lining yellowish serge. This jacket is likely to be introduced to troops on the Western Front, if supply is adequate.

Camouflage coat, canvas: Coat has hood attached, is reversible with one side white and one side grey. It has been issued so far only to ski troops. Not to be confused with padded camouflage suit.

Gloves: In Russia it was found that the best protection against cold is secured by wearing 3 pairs, as follows:

Silk gloves

Woollen gloves

Woollen mittens, with leather back

The mittens have sleeves reaching up to the elbows and can be tied by means of attached tape. Another piece of tape, about a yard long, ties the mittens together so that they can be slung over the shoulders. This combination of gloves may soon be found in the west.

Knee warmers, knitted wool: Same as wristlet, about 8" long, they can be slipped around knees for additional protection.

Shoes:

(a) Leather with felt padding and inner sole. These may be issued in place of regular shoes
(b) Felt and horse hair boots. Half-knee length. Because of the material used this boot is not well suited for the Western front. When soaking wet it begins to fall apart. Since it is not a very substantial piece of clothing it has been ruled that a pair of
(c) Rubber overshoes must be worn over it. These can be tightened around the legs by means of attached string.

Fatigue uniform, 2-piece green herringbone: This piece of equipment is very similar to our own fatigue uniform and is now frequently worn over the regular uniform to give additional protection against the cold.

NOTE: Many additional items, such as ear muffs, fur coats, etc. were issued to German troops fighting during the Russian winters. These things presented a motley appearance, having been collected from the civilian population through the '*Winterhilfe*'.[7]

Improvisations

As mentioned in the introduction, the Germans have to utilize any and every means at their disposal to keep their soldiers at least fairly warm. The following expediencies have been adopted:

(a) Soldiers were told to go into evacuated houses and 'find' some warming garments. Everything was looted including silk under-garments which some PW were sporting.
(b) PW used paper and cardboard to pad their clothes.
(c) Wrappings and improvised leggings around feet and legs have proved to be a successful preventative against frostbite.

7. The *Winterhilfe* ('Winter Help') was a pre-war charitable organization that collected food and clothing for the needy. During the war it collected warm garments for the troops at the front, particularly the Russian Front.

(d) Soldiers are issued with tubes of frost-prevention cream which they rub on exposed body parts.
(e) Germans were able to deplete the Italian Army depots before their withdrawal from Italy. Thus, special issue of Italian overcoats, shoes and jackets was made possible.
(f) Bed sheets are wrapped around uniforms, filling the double function of warming 'garment' and camouflage in snow.
(g) An extra button is sewn on to the sleeve of the blouse in order to be able to button the sleeve all the way.

Other Preparations for Winter

The Germans are drawing upon their experience gained in the last few years. Thus they will use the following 'tricks' to adapt themselves to the change of temperature as well as terrain.

(a) For snowy terrain they will be issued with a piece of white cloth to fit over their steel helmets. This will make for excellent camouflage.
(b) If the mittens mentioned above are issued, the infantry will most likely receive an attachment for the gun trigger. Some units have already received this gadget which enables them to fire with their mittens on.
(c) Vehicles probably will be painted a grey-white camouflage colour with irregular grey stripes.
(d) German troops have been told to take the bolt off their [Mauser] K98 when not actually using it and to put it in their pockets. This will keep the hammer in working order in spite of severe cold.
(e) A different oil will be used on weapons during the winter. It will be a solution of ⅔ of oil and ⅓ of petrol. This mixture necessitates the changing of oil every day, because this lubricant causes rust.
(f) Approximately the same solution will be used as winter lubricant for vehicles.
(g) In order to prevent the effects of the glare produced by the snow, a green filter is attached to the sighting apparatus of artillery and mortar pieces. PW states that accuracy of sighting in winter is greatly improved by this device.
(h) In the summer, MG ammunition and MG ammunition belts are oiled. In the winter, however, the Germans exclusively use shells made of black iron. These are waxed, not oiled. The MG 42 is said to be particularly sensitive in this respect and will give a lot of trouble if the belt is oiled or oiled brass bullets are used. It appears as if the MG 34 is less choosy.

(i) German snipers and bazooka men have been instructed to aim somewhat higher, as range is believed to be less in winter weather.

Sidelights on Survey

(a) Strange as it may seem, the opportunities to salvage clothes appear to be excellent in the German Army. This is accounted for by the fact that worn-out items are rarely destroyed, but are constantly mended and repaired, or the material is re-used. This enables the German QMG to be very lenient in its salvage regulations for frontline troops. Clothing stock is kept all the way down to company. A soldier who has a worn-out piece of equipment gets permission from his CO to go to the supply chamber (which is open every day) and draw new equipment in exchange for the damaged item. Thus salvage is handled without red tape and very promptly.

(b) Winter clothing, like any other item of equipment, is issued as late as compatible with the well-being of the troops. Perhaps this is done to cut down wear and tear. Added to this is the fact that the German High Command considers troops in bunkers 'as not being exposed to winter climate'.

(c) Significant is the remark of Captain Zeitz, CO of 1 Coy, 48 Regiment. When approached by PW Theodor Schlosser, who worked in the supply tent of the company, and asked to request certain articles of winter clothing, this officer is reported to have said, 'What is the hurry? If the boys feel too snug and warm, they lose their fighting spirit. These men fight best when they are cold and shivering.' Consequently, members of this company came into this Cage looking like walking ice blocks.

Document 8/6[8]

What the Americans Fear Most

66 Corps HQ, 14 December 44
G-3 – Nr. 2212/44 Secret

Numerous testimonies of prisoners contend that the American soldier fears most the German tanks in their present tactics, next to the well-directed artillery fire. It is noted that the German panzers attack in flocks of 3–4 and are fighting their goals with concentrated fire. The exact aiming is especially expressed by prisoners. According to prisoner's opinion, the German tank force fights far better in the Aachen sector than in Normandy.

This fact is to be made known immediately to all Panzer troops and assault gun brigades.

Further statements of prisoners showed that houses, adopted for strongpoints, can be successfully attacked by bazookas. Attacked in this way American strongpoint crews surrendered in most instances immediately, deprived of observation due to dust clouds caused by explosions, and affected by the destructive effect of the shelling.

Successful use of bazookas in fighting for strongpoints is to be made known immediately to all units equipped with bazookas.

For the 'Generalkommando'
C of S 62nd Volksgrenadier Division
Signed Siebert

8. ISUM 172, 19 December 1944.

Document 8/7[9]

German Tactics in Attack

Wartime Intelligence Officer's Comments

The following are translated extracts from a directive on tactics issued by the commander of Fifth Panzer Army on 30 November:

During an attack no weapon must remain idle. In cases where vehicles or prime movers drawing weapons or ammunition break down, weapons and ammunition will be reloaded into other vehicles immediately. Orders for this may be given by any officer or NCO acting as an officer.

When going over from the attack to the defence, even if only temporarily, all supporting weapons should be concentrated around the commander of the unit that is to be supported so that he can control the fire plan. Only thus can effective defence be assured.

Commanders up to and including divisional commanders should be where they can obtain the best overall view of the battlefield and where they can intervene personally at a moment's notice. They must not only lead their men, but they must also direct the extensive and varied fire of supporting weapons. We still attack too much with our legs, and not enough with our weapons.

When you make contact with the enemy, push ahead immediately, that is, quickly and brutally with every ounce of energy. Do not hit on the hands and between the eyes. Form definite strongpoints, not so much by concentrations of troops, but by determined concentration of all available weapons. In attacking, infantry and armoured units still do not spread out sufficiently. Advance where the terrain is most suitable. Under these conditions, intervals between platoons, companies, etc., are not disadvantageous. On the contrary, they are desirable, because they force the enemy to scatter his fire. The tank company also must spread out. The range of the cannon facilitates this. If we spread out, it is frequently possible to force parts of the enemy unit to fall back, especially when we catch them before they have completed their defence preparations.

Watch for every opportunity to execute encircling manoeuvres, bypass enemy strongpoints and large towns. Attacking units which meet only little

9. ISUM 185, 1 January 1945, from 12 Army Group.

or no enemy resistance must advance speedily towards their target, and only afterwards will they execute a flanking movement against the enemy they bypassed. They will destroy him by attacking his flanks and his rear.

Anti-tank guns must be destroyed. If tanks or assault guns cannot do the job, they must be cut off by a pincer movement with the support of tanks and assault guns, and aided by our light and heavy weapons and artillery. This will, in most cases, force them to withdraw. Spread out in order to scatter the enemy fire.

Document 8/8[10]

Battalion Defence in the Ardennes

Wartime Intelligence Officer's Comments

The following translated document of I Battalion 183rd Grenadier Regiment of 62nd Volksgrenadier Division indicates some of the methods enemy infantry are adopting to hold the ground so dearly gained in the Ardennes.

I Battalion, 183 Grenadier Regiment — Battalion HQ
62nd Volksgrenadier Division — 31 December 1944

1. The main battle zone must be held against any and all enemy attacks.
2. It must be expected that enemy artillery preparations will disrupt our lines of communication. This will force lower unit commanders to make many independent decisions. In making these decisions, the following motto should be followed: 'Fight to the last bullet' regardless of the situation to the right or that on the left.
3. The enemy infantry must be stopped in our main battle zone, and if possible before reaching it.
4. During enemy artillery fire all troops will remain in their foxholes. Only one responsible man is to be placed in a position from which he can observe the battlefield. Our weapons will not be placed in their firing positions until it is clearly established that the enemy infantry is attacking. Fire will only be opened at effective ranges (LMGs not over

10. ISUM 196, 12 January 1945, from First U.S. Army.

400 metres, and MPs not over 200 metres). Care must be exercised in the expenditure of ammunition, since we cannot obtain additional supplies during the actual battle.

5. Hostile infantry must never be allowed to constitute a serious threat to us.
6. It has been found that high casualties are not suffered unless troops abandon their foxholes and retreat. Therefore, all men must remain in their positions until the enemy attack is repulsed.
7. The strongpoint at Trois Ponts must be developed so elaborately that a weak attack by enemy infantry will not be able to overrun it.
8. The 4th Company will develop a fire plan which will enable it to continue its defensive fires even after a disruption of communications.
9. Enemy tanks which cannot be destroyed in close combat and break through, constitute no threat. They will be destroyed further to the rear.
10. Medium mortar and light infantry howitzer emplacements will be developed into strongpoints and will, if necessary, defend themselves independently.
11. We are defending our own homeland and I therefore demand the utmost effort by everyone without consideration.

Signed: Illegible
Captain and Battalion Commander

Document 8/9[11]

Loading and Movement of Heavy Tanks

Wartime Intelligence Officer's Comments

The following account obtained through interrogation of an observant PW captured by the Second Army provides a number of interesting details on current procedure in a movement involving loading and unloading of tanks:

His unit, 1 Company, 2nd SS Panzer Regiment, received marching orders

11. ISUM 199, 14 January 1945, SHAEF Communications Summary, 8 January 1945.

without previous warning on the evening of 9 December, and moved off to Paderborn station with their twelve Panthers an hour later. The tanks maintained a 200-yard interval not only on the road, but also on reaching the station, moving up as required.

The company commander doubled as Loading Officer and the loading was carried out on a combined end and side-loading ramp. A rake of twelve heavy flats was positioned for the operation. The first tank drove up the end-loading ramp and travelled over the flats to a point near the centre of the rake, where it stopped. The following tanks in the queue drove up behind it, each occupying one flat, until the rear half was completely loaded. At the same time, side-loading was taking place on the flats in the front half of the rake. The tanks drove onto the flats obliquely and then twisted on their tracks. Wooden wedges were placed under the tank tracks but no chains or ropes were used to secure the tanks in place. The loading occupied approximately one hour and a half.

After this the train and the wagon is placed between the locomotive and the first flat, and others between all the other flats. The remarshalling consumed about an hour, the total loading process therefore requiring between 2½ and 3 hours.

The box wagons remained completely empty. The tank crews had to leave their kits with the company transport which followed later. Crews were ordered to stay inside their tanks throughout the entire journey, a precaution, the PW assumed, to avoid losses from strafing aircraft. The only exception was for the tank commander who was allowed to look out of the turret and, if necessary, to use the dismantled hull LMG as an AA weapon. There was no flak wagon in the train. PW claimed that the rail journey lasted 28 hours. The tanks travelled with full petrol tanks. He could give no details of the route followed, but believed the Rhine was crossed near Düsseldorf. The time given by PW was presumably some 72 hours after departure, and the remainder of the time was probably spent on sidings during daylight hours.

Detraining took place on an open line during the night of 12–13 December between Cologne and Berheim at a spot identified by the PW as the 'Roselaarheide area'. Two ramps of bolted girders decked with baulks of timber, had been provided at this spot, apparently by the regimental engineer company. They were 7 metres long, 4 metres deep and on the wagon-side the same height as the floor of the flat, and were so placed that two tanks, with the empty box wagon between them, could be unloaded simultaneously. The tanks twisted on their tracks, proceeded down the ramps, and headed straight for a nearby wood for cover. Unloading began at the head of the train. As soon as the first two tanks were off, the locomotive moved on to bring the next pair into position at the ramps. The whole unloading lasted less than an hour and a half, then the tank column moved off by road to Julich, maintaining a 100-metre interval.

The PW also described an emergency method of unloading in the absence of ramps which he had witnessed in Russia. The locomotive was uncoupled and moved a short distance forward with the first empty box wagon. The tank on the first flat then drove slowly forward. As it got to the edge of the flat its weight caused the wagon to tip up and the tank drove off onto the line and moved away. The locomotive then backed up, was coupled, and withdrew the emptied flat and next box wagon so that the next tank could repeat the process. If the flat falls back as the tank leaves it in such a way as to become derailed, it could easily, PW claims, be put back again by use of a jack which is attached to the wagon.

Document 8/10[12]

Security Measures for the Ardennes Offensive

Wartime Intelligence Officer's Comments

Interrogation at First US Army Cage of NCOs and OR of units participating in the German attack of 16 December 1944 in the Ardennes brought out the following points in regard to security measures taken by the enemy prior to attack.

(1) Signal security. Prior to an attack, all code names, call signs and code keys are changed. From jumping off point to a depth of 3 kilometres all telephone lines have to be strung double. This precaution makes it extremely difficult to tap a wire. The use of authenticators between telephone stations is stringently enforced. Only a small number of picked signal men are allowed to use telephones, in order to cut calls to a minimum and in order to ensure that only a few men have knowledge

12. ISUM 207, 23 January 1945.

of new call signs, coordinate codes, etc. The use of walkie-talkies is forbidden. Whenever possible messengers are used for communication, accompanied by a liaison officer if a message is very important.

(2) Violation of black out regulations before an attack will result in severe disciplinary action. All troop movements, usually of no greater than company strength, take place at night. Both men and vehicles stay under cover during daytime. If time permits, the heavy equipment such as tanks and artillery pieces are brought to the marshalling area piecemeal, in order not to arouse the suspicion of Allied night reconnaissance.

(3) Troops are usually given security lectures. They are warned not to talk about military things, not even to neighbouring units. Some unit commanders are known to have collected Soldbuchs before attacks, others told troops in case of capture to destroy them or tear out page 4 and 17 respectively.

(4) Road signs with unit codenames are used as sparingly as possible. Unit insignias and vehicle markings, however, are not removed. The disadvantages of removing the latter proved to outweigh the advantage obtained by a greater degree of security. It was found, for instance, that troop and vehicular traffic was slowed down in the absence of identifying markings, and that it was hard to apprehend stragglers and deserters.

(5) Orientation of officers as to mission is given at the last possible moment. Even then, they are given exact information only about the sector and unit with which they are directly concerned

(6) H-hour is usually set between 0200 and 0400 in order to achieve a greater element of surprise.

Summarizing the enemy's security preparations, it may be said that he is not employing any new or unusual means to ensure greater secrecy. His main strength in this respect lies in his rigid reinforcement of the above-mentioned security programme.

Document 8/11[13]

A German Tank Man Talks About German Tanks

Wartime Intelligence Officer's Comments

The following report is compiled from the further questioning of PW from 3 Panzer Regiment of 2nd Panzer Division. Previously, the same prisoner provided interrogators with an account of his regiment's destruction in the Ardennes offensive. In this report, he reveals some interesting facts about a new model Panther tank now in use by the Germans.

The tank is known as the 'Gustav' Panther and its Maybach motor produces 730 horse power – 130 horse power advantage over its predecessor, the 'Friedrich' Panther. The 'Gustav' however, must be refitted with a new motor every 1000 kilometres. But despite this drawback, the tank still has more durability than the 'Friedrich'. However, the 'Gustav' trails the mileage capacity of the Mark IV Maybach engine, which requires replacement only after 1500 kilometres. But the Mark IV Maybach has only 320 horse power and is considered much inferior to the new motor. PW declared that installing a new motor is a very simple and speedy operation that can be performed right in the battleline. A crane-mounted wrecker drives up, the armour-plate bolts over the engine are loosened, and the crane uncovers the engine. The engine bolts are removed, the crane removes the engine and lifts in a new one, total time consumed is six hours.

This engine, as all Maybach motors, has a high compression ratio of 8:1. That means eight units of gas mixture sucked into the cylinder are compressed into one unit prior to combustion.

The five gasoline tanks of the 'Gustav' Panther hold 730–750 litres, sufficient to keep the tank rolling 70–80 kilometres in cross-country movement and 100–130 kilometres on surfaced roads. Of interest in this connection was the PW's remarks on the experience of German tank men with captured American gasoline. When they filled up with red gas their motors operated very smoothly, knocking ceased and carbonisation of the spark plugs was greatly reduced. When changing gears, German gasoline will cause thunderous back-fires and sheets of flame shooting out of the exhaust. The American gas eliminated this. PW's vehicle tanked twice

13. ISUM 208, 24 January 1945, from Third U.S. Army.

on American gas, once in Bourcy P6364 and again in Noville P5864. PW declared that their gasoline supply, from various sources, was good during the initial stages of the counter-offensive. But when the skies cleared and the swarms of Allied fighter-bombers descended, the gasoline supply evaporated.

The PW described the Panther as an oil eater. It requires an initial fill of 28 litres in the gear box, and each day thereafter another 3–4 litres must be added. Theoretically, oil must be changed at the 100, 250, 500 and 1000 kilometre marks, but the PW said this was never done because of lack of oil.

As explained by the PW the steering mechanism of the 'Gustav' appears to have been made independent of the main power drive, by means of the '*Uberlagerungsantrieb*' (Heterodyne drive of epicyclic gear?). Through this mechanism, which apparently is constructed on the order of a differential transmission, the tank may turn in its tracks, one track works backwards while the other continues forward so that the tank comes to rest in its original tracks after the completed turn.

Also, the 66-cm wide steel tracks give the tank an exceptional amount of flotation. PW boasted that the terrain test for the 'Gustav' consists of sending out a man in deep mud. If he does not sink into the muck, the Panther also will not bog down. When new, the track consists of 68 steel links, but after 200–300 kilometres some of the links are removed to compensate for stretching. The life span of the track is about that of the motor. On slick roads steel spikes are added to the tracks to prevent side-slippage.

According to the PW the Panther can easily make 30–35 kilometres per hour in cross-country driving on firm ground. On roads the speedometer can be pushed up to 55 kilometres per hour. The Panther manages moderately rough terrain as smoothly as a boat, a deceptive feature, the PW declared, which has caused many drivers to ram the 75mm gun into embankments.

As explained by the PW, the primary mission of the German tank is to provide the heavy mobile punch. That is the reason why the Germans have gone to such great lengths to increase the calibre and muzzle velocity of their tank guns. The better the gun, the better the tank, according to German thinking. Machine guns play a secondary role, and are comparatively little used. Further, the Germans have built their recent tanks on the theory that the enemy will at all times be superior in mechanization and mobile weapons of war. Therefore, a hard-hitting, steel crushing tank is necessary to clear the way so that the Panzer Grenadier (armoured infantry) can move up with his automatic weapons. Conforming to this tactical doctrine, the Panther has a super-long 75mm gun. The PW declared they were trained to engage a Sherman tank at a range of 2000 to 2200 metres without hesitation. The preferable range of 800–900 metres will improve accuracy, but not add much to the punch. The gun has an optical sight which bears three gradations, one for high explosive shells, one for armour piercing shells, and the third for the co-axially mounted machine gun. Each gradation has its own range subdivision. According to the PW the gun is seldom, or never, used as indirect artillery.

Each Panther has an ultra-short wave receiver and transmitter. They are the 'Caesar' and 'Bertha' models, but PW did not know to which set either of the names apply.

In the line of gadgets, the PW said the 'Gustav' sports an automatic fire extinguisher which will flash a 'fire in the motor' signal on the driver's dash board and simultaneously flood the engine with chemical foam whenever the motor temperature registers 120 degrees (Centigrade). Also, an 'Aggregate' apparatus can be operated from the dash board which will refill the battery with acid whenever it runs low. There is also a 'Fuchsgerät'; a coiled pipe to which a blow torch may be applied. In extreme cold this will flood the cooling system of the motor with hot water.

Concerning tactics, the PW had limited knowledge. He was taught that in the approach march the tanks moved in column, covered by 8-wheel armoured reconnaissance cars ahead. These vehicles, the PW stated, are part of the reconnaissance platoon that each Panzer battalion has. If contact is made with hostile armour, the platoons fan out and attack, echeloned in depth. However, in the battle around Novile 5864, 25 December, these tactics were not followed. Captain Hingst, CO of I Battalion (the PW belonged to II Battalion), ordered all tanks to attack in a shallow skirmish line. The American commander apparently quickly sized up the situation and in 45 minutes his Shermans blasted six Panthers to oblivion. The Germans withdrew, Hingst was replaced by a Captain Scheer, CO of II Battalion, and what was left of the two battalions was combined in a KG Scheer. He then chose to by-pass the American pocket of resistance.

One interesting disclosure by the PW was the confirmation of the existence of a German order that, in case a hopeless situation develops, where a unit is threatened with capture of annihilation, all officers and senior NCOs are to withdraw and report to the next higher command. PW declared this measure was adopted to reduce the heavy battle losses in unit leaders.

Another interesting revelation was confirmation of a sharp schism between Wehrmacht and SS. 2nd Panzer Division is a Wehrmacht unit. The PW stated that in pep talks to the troops during the offensive, the men were egged on by playing upon the feeling between the Wehrmacht and the SS. Among the things they were told was that Sepp Dietrich, SS generalissimo, had entered Brussels, a galling claim in view of the fact that 2nd Panzer Division was still floundering around Noville. The PW declared that even the officers believed the falsehood. However, some of the Normandy veterans had strong doubts and privately expressed them.

A US tank officer, present at the interrogation of PW, summarised the information obtained from him as follows:

(1) The Germans have equipped the Panther tank track with special ice calks.[14] Tanks do not slip on icy hills.
(2) At the first round of enemy fire, any calibre, German tank crews button up. This slows down speed of tank, especially cross-country.
(3) The raw 'Gustav' Panther tank has a gadget, which from PW's description, appears to be an epicyclic gear arrangement which, in effect, acts as an auxiliary differential for the steering gear. PW thinks this is one of the most wonderful inventions of the war; but it yields results comparable to our own final drive in that both tracks revolve on a turn, however slow the rate for the inside track.
(4) German tank crews cover air vents in tank engine compartment in cold weather, thus forcing warm air inside the tank. This keeps the inside of the tank comfortable.
(5) Germans prefer to open fire on Sherman tanks at 2200 to 2000 metres. The closest PW tank opened fire was 800 to 900 metres.
(6) Platoons in his unit started out with five tanks. Favourite tactical formation: Inverted V; platoon leader in front.
(7) On level ground turret can be rotated by hand. Otherwise, turret binds.
(8) Power take-off for turret traverse is under centre of turret floor, through floor at this point, then by linkage to gun cradle where it connects with an air compression unit attached to gun recoil system, thence to turret ring at front centre. Linkage is wholly mechanical. PW says power take-off joins propeller shaft at a special gear box. Engine speed determines traversing speed.
(9) PW says muzzle brake takes 70 per cent of gun recoil.

14. Special tracks with projections that grip the ice.

(10) PW thinks Panther tank is better than Royal Tiger.
(11) PW says two 18-ton half-tracks with a V mast are used for evacuating Panther tanks.
(12) PW says Mark IV is no good. Armour is too thin.

Document 8/12[15]

Tactical Employment of a Werfer Regiment

Wartime Intelligence Officer's Comments

The following document presents some criticisms of and comments on the tactical employment of 54 Werfer (Rocket Projector) Regiment in the Ardennes.

Criticism of the Present Commitment

54th Werfer Regiment *Regiment HQ, 7 January 1945*
Regimental Commander

(1) March Discipline
Columns are inadequately supervised as to intervals and pace because the leaders are rarely found with their columns. During halts, the driver should maintain intervals and personally keep them from being occupied. Don't park vehicles too close together. Damaged radiators, and in the case of attack by ground or air, considerable loss of men and materials, are the consequences.

(2) Operation of Prime Movers by Inexperienced Drivers
It should be the practice of every driver to make as little use as possible of the brakes and especially of the hand brakes. Every time the brakes are used, it means loss of power, that is, additional consumption of gasoline. The good truck driver does not drive as if he were driving a tank. Curves are to be taken in the manner of a cyclist, making no use of hand brakes. I have seen drivers allow their motors to run for hours during traffic congestion without proper admonition by either the *Werfer* Officer or

15. ISUM 214, 30 January 1945, from First U.S. Army G-2 Report, 28 January 1945.

Battery Commander in charge. The discipline of men on trucks resembles that of a band of gypsies. The discipline of men on a march reflects upon that of the entire troop.

(3) Installation of Firing Positions

Every time positions are changed it is noticed that those batteries which required longest time to go into position, required the least time to get out of position. On the other hand, it is always the same unit which functions promptly and reliably. Survey must be conducted quickly and accurately, as must be the placing of *Werfers* into position and their preparation for firing. This is the first pre-requisite: speedy preparation for firing. The time required for going into position is the battery's weakest point. Immediate readiness for firing is the battery's primary protection. For that purpose, two men are required for each Werfer. The others will, in the meantime, be digging fox-holes.

(4) Installation of Communication Lines

When the battery takes position, the radio must automatically be set for reception from battalion, and remain tuned in until telephone communications are established. Battalion HQs have to make contact with batteries and regiments in like manner. Circumstances might require a change of positions, hence the above precautions of maintaining everywhere uninterrupted communications with higher units. Laxity and negligence prove costly. Everyone, especially the guides, should be of assistance to the wire teams of regiments and battalions. Thoughtful planning pays dividends in time and accomplishments. It is taking us entirely too long to establish nets of communications. Under all circumstances the installation and putting to use of all communications must be accomplished within two hours at the most. Lateral communications between battalions and between batteries is hereby ordered once and for all.

Communication will be from Right to Left. Installers of lines are also responsible for their maintenance. Trouble-shooting, however, will be conducted from both ends. The battalion and battery commanders must continually check compliance with these orders. Insufficient personnel man communications. Operators must know the names of all commanders, COs, and assistants. The discipline of these operators is unsatisfactory – it almost resembles that of civilians. Transmission of orders is long-winded. I repeatedly miss military precision. The accurate and immediate compliance with these orders is made impossible by the unmilitary practice of adding personal conversation to the transmission of orders. The Service takes precedence over friendship. I hereby forbid the familiar form of address 'Du' between officers when transmitting orders. In case of breakdown of telephone communications, the switchboard is to notify the radio station so that the radio can bridge the gap in the transmission. It is essential that telephone communication exists between the exchange and radio station to enable immediate radio connection. In this respect also, proper supervision by officers in charge, that is signal officers, is lacking. I request commanders to keep an eye on these matters and to punish negligence.

(5) Reports of Positions

Reports of positions come in too slowly. I have to express my compliments to the I Battalion for its expeditious handling and transmission of reports on positions and orders for firing. Also the self-propelled battery worked satisfactorily. The other battalions are in need of great improvement in order to measure up to the I Battalion.

It is repeatedly evidenced that targets are not marked on map or firing plans. Assignment of targets is hereby considerably delayed. The preparations for getting ready to fire take much too long. Men should go to the *Werfer* at once upon receipt of mission, meanwhile the forward observer figures out the commands to take aim and gives them to the battery which then sets its sights. Every opportunity for observed firing should be exploited. The switch from primary to secondary targets must be indicated on the pre-arranged range card. The weather messages are to be received continuously.

(6) It is the duty of every officer personally to observe the target area. Officers in buildings or pillboxes who delegate the fire position to sergeants are no officers. The greatest responsibility of officers is to be everywhere themselves and to check up on the compliance with carrying out orders. I demand greater efforts from battery commanders. Shooting by battalion does not make them superfluous, on the contrary, the success of the commitment depends upon them.

(7) The performance of the forward observers and the liaison officers is not satisfactory. Officers who send only one message per day disqualify themselves. Everything that happens in the observation area is to be reported. The regiment will decide whether it is important. The regiment evaluates. The attitude of Lt Lerch does not befit an officer. It is the duty of every battalion to keep eyes and ears on the enemy. Disruption of radio communications does not release anybody from the responsibility of getting messages through. A messenger is to be on hand at all times. Every message is

important and no observation should remain unused. The *Werfer* units were justly proud that they offered the best communications to the divisions. It must be our ambition to reach this goal again and to maintain it. I fear that the forward observers do not install their radio stations nor supervise them properly. I demand of all to give their utmost and to achieve the greatest possible good. A great deal depends on these communications. A great deal for battery, battalion, and the outcome of this war.

(8) The sixth year of war should harden us and find us the more experienced. Under no circumstances must we deviate from our goal. The enemy is to be attacked with every means. Every possible harm is to be inflicted upon him.

The fulfillment of duty will bring victory!

(signed) Braunwarth

Document 8/13[16]

Reduction of Casualties in 116th Panzer Division

Wartime Intelligence Officer's Comments

The following are extracts from a document captured recently from 60 Panzer Grenadier Regiment. The document is a directive from the GOC 116th Panzer Division on methods of reducing casualties to a minimum. The document is dated November 1944, but the lessons must be presumed to be doubly applicable in view of the two subsequent major batterings inflicted on this division.

Minimising of Casualties

Introduction

In this sixth year of war, when the demand for manpower is becoming an ever more pressing problem for the home and battle fronts, it is more than ever the duty of every commander to use all means to avoid unnecessary casualties.

To this end I am issuing the following instructions:

16. ISUM 233, 18 February 1945.

Tactical Principles for Commanders

(1) Frontal attacks, and frontal deployment of all weapons must be the exception. As a general rule, flanking manoeuvres should be practised in all situations and by all arms.
(2) The MLR should generally be sited on the reverse slope (adequate field of fire, anti-tank protection). On the forward slope, only battle outposts or advanced positions, if terrain and tactical situation is suitable.
(3) Frequent changes in lay-out of posts and heavy weapons.
(4) Liberal use of dummy positions.
(5) Boys and insufficiently trained and experienced reinforcement troops (e.g. GAF troops) must be split up among experienced personnel.
(6) Construction of weapon pits, OP etc., must be undertaken without delay and in adequate depth. (SWEAT SAVES BLOOD).

Miscellaneous

(1) A number of officers and officials tend to adopt an attitude of indifference. This needs checking sharply.
(2) Officers to show no false bravado. They will wear their steel helmets wherever their men do, and take the same precautions as they require of their troops when under enemy fire.
(3) Dress of officers on the battlefield (concealment of map cases, sporting of elegant riding-breeches, etc.).
(4) Infantrymen must not hug the tanks for protection. Tanks attract the fire of all arms.
(5) VD must be combatted. (In future I will have anyone who does not observe the regulations on this subject charged with self-mutilation).
(6) Every means must be used to avoid losses of material (loss of one's weapon is shameful, and the feeling of personal obligation to stand by it must be re-awakened).
(7) Importance of the NSFO.[17] (Repeated instruction necessary on the consequences that can ensue from becoming a PW).

Signed
Von Waldenburg[18]

17. NSFO or *Nationalsozialistischer Führungsoffizier* was charged with the political indoctrination of the troops, the dissemination of propaganda and the maintenance of morale. NSFO officers appeared in the last year of the war and they were not generally very popular.
18. *Generalmajor* Siegfried von Waldenburg, commanding 116th Panzer Division.

Document 8/14[19]

Feldmarschall Model on War

Wartime Intelligence Officer's Comments

The following is a translation of a document, signed by Field Marshal Model, discussing British and American attack procedure and suggesting the proper counter measures. A copy was received on 22 February by 27 Volksgrenadier Regiment of 12 Volksgrenadier Division.

High Command of Army Group B HQ, 14 February 1945
G-3, No. 1762/45 Secret.

Trapping the Beast – Tactics

Enemy Attack Procedure

The main characteristics of British/American attack procedures are:

action in accordance with a pre-determined plan
short-term objectives
feeling-out of the front by reconnaissance
reducing of individual strongpoints by the use of individual pincer attacks

Strengths: Commitment of material, use of main effort. Armoured forces everywhere. Short-term objectives that promise success. Unsuccessful frontal attacks are broken off and forces quickly regrouped.

Weaknesses: Infantry does not shove forward vigorously. It only follows the armoured forces and occupies the terrain. Rather long 'stops' after taking the goal of an attack. Very sensitive on the flanks.

Every infantry division is teamed with a Combat Command of an armoured division.

Formation in the attack is narrow and deep.

Every attack is prepared for by a concentration of artillery fire and strongest possible air support. Then, after feeling out the front, infantry units infiltrate into the soft points.

19. ISUM 245, 2 March 1945, from VII U.S. Corps.

To exploit a success, an armoured combat command is pressed ahead to attack with limited objectives. Usually the infantry remains where it is after the said combat command moves forward, moving up only after attaining its short-term objective in order to dig in before the armoured point, to act as security for the supply of the armoured command and to allow the artillery to change position. On the following day, the armoured command moves forward again past the stationary troops. This overlapping commitment is repeated schematically with continual reinforcements from the rear. When a breakthrough or penetration succeeds, the attack elements do not move very far forward, but turn inwards, in order to neutralize the enemy strongpoints by pincer attack. This procedure is used for the smallest local attacks as well as in large scale offensives.

Localities and strongpoints are bypassed by the attack elements, and are only mopped up by the infantry which closes in after thoroughgoing artillery preparation.

In order to forestall counterattacks, suspected assembly areas are immediately taken under concentrated artillery fire, if possible with observation by artillery planes, and the forward attack elements boxed in by artillery (‘*durch Feuerglocken abgeschirmt*’)

Early commitment of infantry automatic weapons for psychological effect.

Before the beginning of the enemy attack, it is desirable to harass the enemy by all conceivable means, to inflict the highest possible losses on him through projectors, artillery and night bombers, and thus to weaken him. He must be kept in the dark about our strength until the last moment, in order to increase his feeling of uncertainty.

The forward line is to be thinly posted before an impending attack. Heavy weapons are to be drawn back to the rear of the MLR. The strong points holding the front line must so channelize the enemy attack that the enemy runs into his own supporting fire. By laying all kinds of obstacles and traps in the rear areas of the MLR, considerable losses can be inflicted upon the enemy. Effectiveness is increased by laying S-mines.

For the battle on the MLR, ingeniousness, trickiness, adaptability, mobility, deception and camouflage are the prerequisites for later attacking and destroying the enemy. But above all, the independent action of individual assault patrols and anti-tank patrols, fighting in the strong-points, is of decisive significance.

As long as the MLR is well protected with every conceivable kind of engineer obstacle, it will always be difficult for the enemy to quickly develop his penetration into a breakthrough.

In this way time for planned countermeasures is won. It should be a principle that every pincer should be met by another pincer with the goal of destroying the enemy attack point. In order to make our traps and ditches effective, it should be a principle that they be covered by our own weapons.

Counterblows by local reserves (counter-pincers) in the depth of the MLR are so to be prepared and organized that they can be supported very economically, i.e. by explotation of all disposable forces, through the fire of mortars, anti-tank, and assault guns of all kinds, taking advantage of surprise. It is always necessary to recognize the enemy's main effort immediately, in resistance in our own flanks, and thus create the prerequisites for a counter-pincer.

Anti-tank weapons and MGs must be in ambush positions, so that they can open fire particularly effectively when the enemy has been lured through the obstacles and his attack has been channelized.

Counterblows (counter-pincers) on the enemy's flanks should cut him off decisively like a beast in a trap. They promise the greatest success if carried out at a time when the enemy is beginning to clean up trenches or is temporarily immobilized by small-arms fire and obstacles.

Individual guns of the artillery, tanks, and assault gun brigade of the division, kept constantly mobile as wandering guns, can be of decisive importance in the direct support of these counterblows.

If the counterblows do not succeed, and the enemy wins further ground on the MLR, the development of the situation must be recognized at once and counter-measures with a view to further development must be taken. Losses must be continually inflicted on the enemy by means of concentrated storming fire from the troops in the strongpoints, directed by the commanders of the strongpoints. The goal is to shatter the enemy attack more and more by these strongpoints, and to divert it from its direction. Only in this way can the enemy attack be gradually forced to slow down and to halt. And in this way the most essential prerequisites of limited counterattacks (counter-pincers, trap) are created!

There must be assault reserves in the artillery security zone, strengthened by assault guns and TDs,[20] as divisional reserves; these go into action, under the concentrated fire of all artillery, as soon as the enemy attack approaches the artillery security zone, in order to destroy the enemy before the artillery

20. Tank destroyers.

security zone through our own counter-pincer in collaboration with the strongpoints that are still fighting in the MLR. We also recommend partial smoke-screens in order to facilitate the approach, or the blinding of enemy units on the battlefield itself.

In the case of still stronger enemy breakthroughs, it is the duty of the leadership of corps and armies to commit quickly-brought-up motorized assault units and thus achieve the necessary counter-pincer or trap without loss of time; this must be brought into play with greatest impetus and with the goal of total annihilation of the beast.

Model
Feldmarschall

Document 8/15[21]

Testing of Allied and Enemy Tanks

Wartime Intelligence Officer's Comments

The interrogation by First US Army of a prisoner from 33 Panzer Regiment has provided some interesting data on the relative performance of Allied and enemy tanks. PW was an instructor from September to December at the Schiessschule der Panzertruppen in Putlos near Kiel, where the latest tank tactics were taught, and had previously had eight years' experience as a tankman. In spite of this, he was transferred to the infantry – just another indication that the Germans are running short of tanks.

The school in Putlos was used as the main proving ground for tanks and experiments were conducted there from September to December 1944 with the following results:

21. ISUM 250, 7 March 1945.

Tanks Compared: Panther, *Königstiger*, Sherman and Russian T 34

(1) Mobility

The Panther is regarded as the fastest tank on straight roads. The Sherman is the fastest in cross-country driving and also the most mobile of all tanks tested.

(2) Performance of Guns

The *Königstiger* can destroy any of the other named tanks at a distance of 3000–3500 metres (with a hit on the sides); the maximum range of the Panther is 2500–3000 metres; the maximum range of the T 34 (old model) and the Sherman is considered to be 2000–2500 metres.

(3) Stability

Experiments have been conducted with the Sherman and the Panther firing while on the move from a distance of 1500 metres.

Results:
Sherman – 9 hits out of 10 with the gun
Panther – 1 hit out of 10 with the gun
Sherman – 236 hits out of 250 with the MG
Panther – 120 hits out of 250 with the MG

(4) General Comparison

In spite of some advantages, the Sherman is considered inferior to the Panther, Tiger or T 34. German tank crews feel confident that they can more than match our Shermans even when outnumbered 2:1. They have a healthy respect for some of our anti-tank guns, however.

(5) Main Weaknesses of the Panther

The engine is too weak. The first engines developed 650 HP; later 700 HP Maybach engines were introduced and a 750 HP engine is now being installed in Panthers. Most breakdowns occur with the engines and sprocket wheels. There are not sufficient spare parts available for these and because of this many Panthers had to be destroyed by their own troops.

Document 8/16[22]

Gentle Order

Wartime Intelligence Officer's Comments

The following battalion Order of I/122nd Volksgrenadier Regiment of 176th Infantry Division gives a vivid insight into the character of some of the gentle souls now in command of German front line units. It also illustrates some of the problems being found amongst newly-organised formations of this type.

1 Battalion 1220 Volksgrenadier Regiment — Battalion HQ
22 December 1944

Battalion Order No. 17

Construction of Positions

It is ridiculous nonsense and contrary to all experience to post sentries in covered (roofed) positions. The man sees nothing, hears nothing and dozes.

Velvet, plush pillows, featherbeds don't belong to a position. This stuff is to disappear by midday Saturday and will be handed in for textile salvage.

Billets

I have inspected several billets today. There seemed hardly any cleanliness or order to be noticed. Arms, barrack stores, cooking utensils, steel helmets and respirators are to be laid out properly in their respective lines, exactly as they were in the days of 'Old Fritz' (Frederick the Great). If this pigsty does not show a marked improvement by Saturday, section and platoon commanders will be put under arrest. With effect from 23 December every billet will start to build its own latrines. Conditions in the latrines are simply outrageous.

Dress

The wearing of any type of scarf is forbidden, it is most unsoldierly. Every man in possession of a carbine will have two ammunition pouches and the carbine with him at all times. Sentries (except listening post and scouts) will wear steel helmets with net. Moustaches are to be kept short. Every man has opportunities to show his manliness in other ways. Trousers will be pushed

22. ISUM 211, 27 January 1945 (Source: 7 Armoured Divison).

well down into the boots, and they are not to be worn as knickerbockers. The leather equipment, belt, ammunition pouches and shoes are to be blackened. Boots will be dubbined, but the part above the ankle is to be polished. The rifle will be carried on the right shoulder, barrel pointing upwards. If I should see again a 'Sunday Sportsman' walking about with his rifle pointing downwards, he will be under arrest for seven days.

Fresh dirt only graces a soldier, but old filth shows the lazy.

If I see again anyone with a 'lion mane' or other fancy coiffure, I will cut his hair personally.

Drivers of horse wagons will drive wearing their rifles. The best rifle is no good if it is hidden away in the cart.

Salvage Collection

I found today a perfect flying jacket on the rubbish heap, about two metres from the billet entrance. This is quite impossible. Even if in this sixth year of the war we had everything in plenty, it would still be an amazing wastage, but it also shows utter disregard for the gigantic efforts made at home in equipping us. If by Saturday this situation has not radically improved, severest disciplinary action will be taken. Everybody must make it his own business to collect whatever waste materials he can get hold of; textiles, leather, empty cartridges, cardboard, bottles in whatever shape.

Chapter 9

Interrogation of Prisoners of War

Document 9/1[1]

Interrogation of Americans

These men were captured on both the Third and Seventh Army fronts by numerous enemy organizations. All were interrogated by the enemy, upon capture, at forward command posts, regimental command posts and division headquarters, as well as at the collecting point in Strasbourg. All enemy interrogators asked substantially the same questions laid down by higher headquarters.

The following standard questions were asked by all interrogators in the order shown:

(1) Name, rank, serial number
(2) Unit (down to company). Names of unit commanders.
(3) Why do you not wear gas masks?
When was the last time you had gas training?
Do you have gas with you? If so, where is it stored?
(4) How much artillery is attached to your division?
(5) When did you leave the States and from what port?
(6) Where did you land in France?
(7) How did you get to the line – by truck or rail?

1. ISUM 182, 29 December 1944, Seventh U.S. Army Intelligence Bulletin.

(8) Do you have a gasoline pipeline from the south?
If so, where is it?
(9) At Strasbourg, all men were interrogated by a man in civilian clothes in addition to Army interrogation. His questions were designed to find out what a man had done in civilian life so that he could be properly employed in a prisoner of war camp. Probably looking for skilled labour for war plants.
(10) What do you think of the Jews?
(11) Why are you fighting Germany?

Methods of interrogation in the order that they caused men to talk, were:

(1) Confronting the man with his own order of battle. A man would be asked his division and refuse to answer, whereupon the interrogator would say 'Don't waste my time, you are from Company C, 101st Infantry, 26 Division. You left the States on 25 September from New York, and arrived at Marseille on 2 October.' If this was not enough to shock the man he would continue.
(2) After taking dogtags and paybooks away from men they threatened to treat them as spies because they had no identification as soldiers unless they revealed their units and showed a knowledge of military things.
(3) Threats not to feed the prisoner.
(4) Making a prisoner stand in a corner in the cold.
(5) Putting him in the rain with no protection for a few hours.
(6) Interrogating the NCOs first and then telling the privates that the NCOs had told everything.
(7) Being kind and solicitous of the men's welfare.
(8) Threats to hand him over to the Gestapo.
(9) Threats to segregate Jewish prisoners.

Document 9/2[2]

German Methods of Handling Allied Prisoners, Dead and Casualties

Wartime Intelligence Officer's Comments

German methods of handling Allied dead, PW and captured documents are set out below in considerable detail in an undated and unsigned directive. In almost every detail, it will be noticed, enemy procedure resembles that followed by the Allies.

This document must not fall into enemy hands. This document may not be reproduced in part or in full.

Instructions for handling PW and captured papers and articles

(1) The Searching of PW
The thoroughness employed in searching PW depends upon the battle situation. In the case of heavy intakes, PW, once disarmed, will be taken to Battalion or Regimental HQ where they will be searched. When there are only a few PW, the search will be carried out at company level.

While en route to headquarters from the front line, PW must be closely watched and prevented from destroying or otherwise disposing of any papers. PW attempting to return to their dugouts to get blankets or leave the column will be stopped at the point of a weapon. It is frequent practice of PW to try to get out of sight to dispose of important orders, etc.

All articles, with the exception of Paybook and identity discs, will be removed from PW. Their personal effects will be returned to them by the Interrogating Officer. Articles taken from the PW must be kept separate and, if possible, bundled up and given to the escort for delivery to the Division Interrogating Officer.

The identity of wounded PW and if possible their units, must be established before evacuation to a Field Dressing Station, and the information telephoned to the Division Interrogating Officer immediately. Paybook, identity discs and other unimportant personal property including family photos, will be left with the wounded. All other articles such as maps, notebooks, pocket diaries, private letters and other papers,

2. ISUM 253, 10 March 1945.

camera, film, compass and files will be taken away and, together with unit flashes ripped from the upper sleeve, [sent] to the Divisional Interrogating Officer.

Enemy dead will be relieved of unit badges and other personal effects, paybooks and identity discs, will be sent to the Division Interrogating Officer immediately. After examination, these articles will be sent back to the next of kin through the International Red Cross and are to be handled with special care. Troops are forbidden to retain any such articles.

(2) Segregation of PW

Segregation of officers, NCOs and men will be done depending on the battle situation, at Battalion or equivalent HQs. Where a shortage of guards or transportation prevents immediate segregation, no discussion among the PW will be permitted.

(3) Interrogation of PW

Interrogations of, or conversation with PW by the troops are strictly forbidden. No concessions will be made prior to delivery at Division HQ. Interrogation will be done by the Divisional Interrogating Officer on arrival, or by the Interrogation teams sent down to troop level.

Forward interrogation will be authorized by the division, depending on the capabilities of the trained interpreter with the troop. The Division will make sure that interrogation reports dealing with any one sector are telephoned as soon as possible to the sub-unit concerned.

(4) Captured Documents and Articles

It is of prime importance that captured orders, maps and sketches be made use of and passed on as soon as possible. The troops must be made to understand, by repeated lectures, that every piece of paper may be of value to us. Enemy HQs, barracks and other occupied buildings must be searched for documents. Troops must be instructed not to dispose carelessly of papers when searching captured vehicles.

The forward unit will make no use of captured documents. However, brief reference to captured maps and papers may be made as directed by division. Recognized enemy intentions will be sent to Divisional HQ either by telephone or wireless.

Captured material must be sent to intelligence at division immediately by special DR [Dispatch Rider].

Captured equipment, ammunition or weapons, particularly concerning chemical warfare, must be left untouched and reported to Intelligence at Division and only forwarded on the instructions of Divisional HQ. In the case of a larger amount of booty being captured, the 'Special Section' will be summoned from Divisional HQ.

The following tags are to be placed on captured documents and personal effects:

Identification of Sender
Time of capture
Place of capture

Document 9/3[3]

German Interrogation Methods at Regimental Level

Wartime Intelligence Officer's Comments

The following document sets out a list of tactical questions which are to be asked by the interrogators of 246 Volksgrenadier Division in order to provide information of immediate interest at regimental level.

Grenadier Regiment 869 Regiment HQ, 18 January 1945

Subject: PW Interrogation
To: Int, 246 Volksgrenadier Division

The Regiment requests that the following information which is of direct value to the Regiment, be obtained from PW during interrogation.

(1) Since when in this position? (relief)
(2) Is the position under heavy German fire? (Infantry, Artillery fire).
(3) What were you told about location of enemy positions or what did you observe of the German positions?
(4) Strength and armament of PW's section and platoon.
(5) Where is HQ of section leader and platoon leader located? How far away is it and which route do you use to get there? Can you also reach the HQ during daytime without enemy observation?

3. ISUM 222, February 1945.

(6) At what time do the ammunition and kitchen trucks come up and where do they park?
(7) How well have the positions been constructed?
(8) Where is the neighbouring section located at night? How far is that from PW's position?
(9) What are the enemy's flare Standing Operational Instructions?
(10) How do you call for Mortar and Artillery barrage?
(11) What is the combat mission of your section, your platoon?
(12) Where are mines or road blocks located in vicinity of PW's position? Are they anti-personnel or anti-tank mines?

Signature Illegible

Chapter 10

Propaganda

Document 10/1[1]

What Germany is Saying: German Radio Propaganda 13–19 December 1944

(i) Military

After the delayed announcement on 18 December 1944 of the large-scale German counter-attack on the Western Front, German propagandists began to develop two lines of comment. The first consisted of claims that the German attack had taken the enemy completely by surprise and that considerable progress had been made before Allied commanders had realised the full scale of the offensive. The second propaganda line, intended for home consumption, asserted that the present attack was the answer to those who asked 'Where is the Führer? What exactly has become of the Luftwaffe? What is happening to our industries in the Saar and Ruhr areas?' The Führer, it was claimed, was safe and well, and had spent days and nights during the past few weeks in working out plans for the present offensive in the minutest detail.

Recent German comment on the fighting in the Saar area was to the effect that the war of movement which General Patton desired had been turned into positional warfare, thanks to the quality of the German defence.

1. ISUM 173, 20 December 1944, from Second British Army Intelligence Summary, 19 December 1944.

Concerning the Upper Rhine it was claimed that new fortifications had been brought into being there and that this part of the front line had been re-armed, both morally and materially.

In reviewing the whole of the Western Front the Germans repeatedly stated that the American Armies had sustained heavy losses. One commentator declared that the British had been unable to profit as they had hoped from American successes, and had been obliged to take over sectors formerly held by American troops.

(ii) Political

The German wireless tended to confine itself, in broadcasts to Germany, to giving news of events in Greece without comment. Details were also regularly given of alleged tension or disturbances in Italy, Rumania, Estonia, Finland and French North Africa. A typical allegation was: 'wherever the North Americans set foot starvation follows in their wake'.

After celebrating the anniversary of the Triple Alliance between Germany, Italy and Japan as a reminder of what von Ribbentrop described as 'the strongest military alliance in history', German propagandists turned their attention to the recent treaty between France and Soviet Russia. This treaty was represented as a snub to British diplomacy and a sign of complete French subservience to the Kremlin.

Recent declarations by the American Secretary of State, Mr. Stettinius, were interpreted by the Germans as giving American approval to Bolshevist politics in Europe, since he had raised no objection to the Soviet solution of the Polish problem and the Soviet treaty with France.

Allied plans for the post-war settlement of Europe were characterised as premature in view of the stubbornness of German resistance. One commentator declared that proposals for robbing Germany of East Prussia and Danzig would make her fight to the bitter end.

Document 10/2[2]

German Propaganda for Christmas 1944

Wartime Intelligence Officer's Comments

In addition to serenading the troops with Christmas carols, Goebbels sent over a volley of seasonal greetings in the form of three brand new propaganda pamphlets. Ranging from the subtle to the blunt, two of the pieces adopt the Christmas theme to make their points, while the third rather clumsily delves into the current Canadian conscription issue.

Hello There!

A rather pretty card announcing its presence with the above words, is by far the most sly and pointed. Printed in sky-blue and red, and splashed with a decorative evergreen design and colourful silver stars, the message it sends is simple, timely and one of the better bits of Goebbelesque.

> WE THOUGHT YOU WOULD BE HOME FOR CHRISTMAS
> Well boys – take it easy – you've been promised so many things –
> It's not your first and certainly not your last disappointment –
> Cheer up – console yourself with Jerry
> He wishes you a very Merry Christmas and the best of luck in the New Year

Hark . . . the Herald Angels Sing!

This one is not nearly as good. The Noel tidings are offset by a sinister, rather macabre painting on one side. A golden-haired, blue-eyed, ethereal child tearfully clutching a sprig of mistletoe is dominated by the shadowed figure of a dying Allied soldier, oozing symbolic blood from nose and lips. The caption cheerfully reads, 'Daddy, I'm so afraid.'

The message on the reverse side, surrounded by Woolworth-like imitations of angels, candles and hearts, has this to say:

> HARK . . . THE HERALD ANGELS SING!
> Well, soldier, here you are in 'No-Man's-Land' just before Christmas, far away from home and your loved ones. Your sweetheart or wife, your little girl, or perhaps even your little boy, don't you feel them worrying about

2. ISUM 179, 26 December 1944.

you, praying for you? Yes, old boy, praying and hoping you'll come home again soon. Will you come back, are you sure you will see those dear ones again?

This is Christmas-time, Yuletide ... the Yule-log, the mistletoe, the Christmas tree, whatever it is, it's home and all that you think fine to celebrate the day of our Saviour.

Man, have you thought about it, what if you don't come back ... what of those dear ones?

Well, soldier, 'PEACE ON EARTH GOOD WILL TOWARDS MEN' ... for where there's a will there's a way ... only 300 yards ahead and ... MERRY CHRISTMAS!

Canadian Soldiers!

Wartime Intelligence Officer's Comments

Entering into the already overcrowded Canadian political arena, Goebbels here employs the conscription problem to achieve his ends.[3] *The well-worn propaganda device of sowing mistrust amongst Allies is employed in the third pamphlet, but the bad spelling and Teutonic sentence structure does nothing but cloud both the issue and the design of the message. The Goebbels boys evidently haven't made up their minds whether we think conscription is a good or a bad idea.*

In the battle for the Scheldt estuary you have suffered such heavy losses that your War Minister, Mr. Ralston – who has resigned since then – had to ask for no less than 16,000 men as reinforcements. There was a big scandal behind the closed doors of your Government. Perhaps you know already that the opposition reproached the Government to let you bleed to death, because the British only to a small degree kept their promise to send British

3. During the Second World War Canadian men could be drafted into the army but only volunteers went overseas. Many conscripted men refused to volunteer and remained in Canada, being universally despised as 'Zombies'. The governing Liberal Party under Prime Minister Mackenzie King was reluctant to order the 'Zombies' overseas but in late 1944, as Canadian casualty rates rose in Northwest Europe, a political crisis broke out when some of Mackenzie King's ministers, including the Minister of Defence, resigned or threatened to resign unless the 'Zombies' were ordered overseas. Finally, in late 1944 this took place and although many deserted, approximately 15,000 'Zombies' saw active service in Europe.

divisions to relieve you. Ralston hasn't done anything against it, he didn't even protest! He is gone, and so is your Air Minister, Mr. Power – but the system remains the same as before. Now your Government will send to Europe those Canadian soldiers who are still at home – they will do it in spite of all demonstrations in the garrisons and, if need be, by force. They too shall die for the British. Obviously it is only right that the noble British race be saved at your expense.

The Allied Supreme Headquarters won't leave you in peace much longer. New offensives are planned, new and heavy sacrifices are to come, and new weapons of the Germans are ready everywhere.

What's all this for?

Are you to bleed here for Canada or are you to die for the British?

Wouldn't you prefer to wait until all is over? It's just a few steps which separate you from safety – take them!

Document 10/3[4]

What Germany is Saying: German Radio Propaganda for Week ending 14 January 1945

Military

In German news broadcasts and wireless propaganda during the past week, emphasis has been shifted successively from the battle in the Ardennes to the German offensive in northern Alsace and to the Russian offensive in southern Poland.

The Ardennes fighting was described as the 'winter battle' from the outset until 10 January, when the Wehrmacht communique referred to it as 'the defensive battle'. The change in the official interpretation of von Rundstedt's offensive was also reflected by the appearance in the news of references to the 'unimaginable severity' on the part of 'brave divisions'.

From 9 January onwards German listeners were encouraged to transfer their hopes of offensive successes from the Ardennes to Alsace. Commentators claimed that a concentric attack against Strasbourg was taking

4. ISUM 199, 15 January 1945.

shape. The American Seventh Army, they said, had been placed in a very precarious position and would be able to continue operations only after a wholesale regrouping.

The western front was relegated to second place on the evening of 13 January, when the news announcers declared that the opening of the long-awaited Russian winter offensive had been the biggest event of the previous twenty-four hours. German broadcasters claimed that the Wehrmacht had not been taken by surprise by the Russian onslaught and that many Russian tanks had been knocked out or destroyed. No precise claims were made by the Germans, however, and by insisting on the large scale of the new offensive and the probability of its spreading to other sectors of the eastern front they appeared to be preparing their people for news of setbacks.

Propagandists continued to make much of the 'miracle' of continued German resistance, but the call for effort and sacrifice remained as insistent as ever. The need for adequate training of the *Volkssturm* was stressed in a broadcast which described the help given by the film industry in providing training films which concentrated on the essential rudiments of soldiering and on points of practical value in the front line.

Political

William Joyce[5] was at some pains to convince British listeners that Germany had not been forced to adopt a 'last-ditch strategy'. The general picture presented to the outside world by the German wireless was, indeed, of a Germany who held out to a stricken Europe, from the wealth of her experience and wisdom, the only possible hope of salvation. Persistent emphasis was laid on the 'chaos' behind the Allied front lines in liberated countries. On the strength of this the Allies were denounced, not only as the enemies of the traditional civilisation of Europe, but also as the evil influences responsible for starvation and misery. In an address on the situation in the Netherlands, for instance, Dr Seyss-Inquart[6] stated that events had shown that the British, Americans and Bolsheviks were unable to maintain food supplies in liberated countries at the level attained during the German occupation.

5. William Joyce (1906–46) was an Irishman and a prewar member of the British Union of Fascists who moved to Germany shortly before the outbreak of war and worked as a broadcaster on English-language broadcasts beamed by Goebbels' Propaganda Ministry into Britian during the war. Popularly known as 'Lord Haw-Haw', he was arrested at the end of the war, convicted of treason and hanged.

6. Arthur Seyss-Inquart (1892–1946), an Austrian, was *Reichskomissar* for occupied Holland. He was convicted of war crimes and executed.

Hans Fritsche[7] twice attacked British policy. This, he declared, had betrayed the interests, not of Europe only but also of Britain herself; it could be explained only by the fact that Britain was in complete subjection to Bolshevism and international Jewry.

Britain's alleged complicity with Russia in the 'bolshevising' of Europe was generally considered fair game by German broadcasters, but attacks on the Anglo-American alliance were apparently considered less fruitful. The German people were even warned against attaching too much importance to Anglo-American disputes, which resembled 'the quarrels of a married couple who had no prospect of a divorce'.

Document 10/4[8]

Nazi Indoctrination Bulletin

Wartime Intelligence Officer's Comments

The following translation is part of 'Indoctrination Bulletin No. 9' dated 14 January 1945 issued by the NSFO (National Socialist Guidance Officer) of the 352nd Volksgrenadier Division.

SECRET

Soldiers are to be informed during the indoctrination period, that our offensive in the west was not launched for the purpose of gaining territory. The main purpose was to eliminate the direct threat by the great masses of American armoured units to the Ruhr District, the Saar District, and the Palatinate, and thus force the enemy to regroup his units along the entire front.

The Chancellery of the Nazi Party has published a letter of a Company Commander which he sent to the families of six German soldiers believed to have been captured by the Americans. The letter in part reads as follows:

7. Hans Fritzsche [*sic*] (1900–53) was a senior official in the Propaganda Ministry who supervised German news broadcasts.
8. ISUM 217, 2 February 1945, from Third U.S. Army.

> Your husband having taken part in the heavy defensive fighting in France has been missing since the 28th of August in the vicinity of Pogny. We were all in a difficult situation then and we had to try to save ourselves individually. In this confusion, several of our men were dispersed and to date have not rejoined this unit. There is a possibility that they have become part of another unit still in the front lines or they have been captured. In the latter case, your husband will be all right. The Americans who opposed us have been fighting fair, and they have treated and fed the German prisoners well. Several of our men who were in captivity and who later escaped have certified that fact. Should your husband be a Prisoner of War, you will probably receive news from him via the Red Cross.

The content of this letter will have a demoralizing effect upon large sections of the population, because the people at home may influence the soldiers at the front in this direction. Unit commanders are held responsible that biased information of this nature be suppressed.

Document 10/5[9]

This is Your Achievement . . . Or Is It?

Wartime Intelligence Officer's Comments

Two recently captured documents mark the high and low tide of the Wehrmacht's winter propaganda campaign. The first, captured by 2nd US Infantry Division, is an enemy leaflet entitled 'Western Warriors, This is Your Achievement'. The black, long list of Allied losses ends with the sentence 'The danger of a Western offensive coordinated with the huge Bolshevist drive, was averted'.

Hardly had the print dried on this fancy of the Goebbels mind when an Order of the Day by Rundstedt dated 13 February 1945 warns his dazed troops in the west 'the enemy is on the march for a general attack'. Small

9. ISUM 237, 22 February 1945.

wonder that the average Teutonic mind must now be reeling under a series of 'averted' offensives that just won't stay averted.

Now You See It . . .

When Germany opened its offensive on 16 December 1944, only a few of you knew what was occurring. Today you are informed. The Americans and the British were preparing to launch their final great drive. They intended to break through Aachen and Cologne into the Ruhr, and to smash through Strasbourg into southern Germany. Thus they expected to force a decision.

At the critical moment our offensive hit them. The surprise was perfect. The enemy armies were forced to fall back and go on the defensive. The danger to the Fatherland was averted. This, western warriors, was your achievement. You have transcended all difficulties of terrain and weather to prove that you are tougher than the enemy. Your leaders and your country know that they can place their faith in you.

The Success of your Offensive

By 27 December 1944, eleven days after the initial attack, the following American divisions had been destroyed:

128th Infantry Division
106th Infantry Division
9th Armoured Division

Badly mauled were:

1st Infantry Division
70th Infantry Division
5th Armoured Division
2nd Infantry Division
83rd Infantry Division
7th Armoured Division
4th Infantry Division
99th Infantry Division
82nd Airborne Division
8th Infantry Division
3rd Armoured Division
101st Airborne Division

Casualties suffered by American troops in Belgium and in Alsace-Lorraine between 16 December and 15 January were:

over 160,000 dead, 50,000 wounded, 35,000 PW
2,000 tanks, 450 heavy and medium artillery pieces
a countless number of anti-tank, AA guns, mortars and other infantry weapons

The enemy was forced to commit all his reserves. 65% of all enemy forces on the continent were rushed to the salient. After the airborne divisions had been smashed, the intended American assault towards Cologne and the Ruhr was impossible.

The danger of a western offensive coordinated with the huge Bolshevist drive, was averted.

Document 10/6[10]

Propaganda for Paratroops

Wartime Intelligence Officer's Comments

An interesting departure into the morale business is the following 8th Parachute Div document ordering its units to post slogans on all vehicles. The slogans are a curious mixture of faith, defiance, Aryanism and straight patriotism, but judging by the average prisoner, they take their place among the reasons for the unquestionably high paratroop morale.

'Combat Group Wadehn'

National Socialist Leader
Subject: Propaganda on Vehicles *28 January 1945*
To: See distribution

By order of the Divisional commander. In response to the enemy's planned agitation campaign, effective immediately, one of the slogans below will be painted on the sides or rear of all vehicles, trucks, armoured vehicles, H/T vehicles. Vehicles that are camouflaged white can be easily marked by using a wet rag. On vehicles not similarly camouflaged, preferably white paint should be used.

10. ISUM 255, 12 March 1945, adapted from XVI U.S. Corps.

The Divisional commander emphasized the fact that after the 1st of February NO vehicle of the Division should remain unmarked.

For the Div Staff
The NSFO
sig. Hammer, Leutnant

Inscriptions for vehicles:

1. We stand faithful to the Führer
2. Times are hard; we are harder
3. Rather death than slavery
4. We shall do it
5. Now is the time
6. To have faith aids victory
7. Strictly a question of nerves
8. We remain firm
9. The enemy lies
10. Just don't weaken
11. Nobody can beat us
12. Everything passes by
13. The *Panzerfaust* for the enemy
14. It's the Jews' fault
15. German and faithful

Distribution: Down to Battalion and independent units

Chapter 11

Morale and Discipline

Document 11/1[1]

Rewards for Apprehending Deserters

Wartime Intelligence Officer's Comments

Many references have already been made to the numerous and far reaching steps taken by the enemy to prevent defeatism and desertion in the Army. Although not as drastic as the stern measures taken by Himmler in eastern Germany, the system of 'rewards' referred to in the following translation is just one more attempt to discourage tendencies which by now must be causing great concern to all commanders.

246 VG Division
Commander Division HQ, 28 October 1944
SECRET
Subject: Unit Courts-Martial Procedure

1. Enclosed is a memorandum for Regimental Commanders and Commanders of independent units and battalions regarding the establishment of Courts-Martial.
2. Attention is called to the fact that measures indicated in the orders are applicable only at such times when temporary disbanding of

1. ISUM 224, 9 February 1945, from First U.S. Army.

troops becomes apparent. If such is the case, weapons must also be immediately resorted to, that is to say, without any judicial or Courts-Martial procedure.

3. Attention is called to the fact that pursuant to Army orders of 30 August 1944, up to M.100.00 can be granted during wartime by the convening authority and up to M.500.00 by the superior commander as rewards for alertness and courage in apprehending deserters.

A legal right to such reward does not exist. Only in exceptional cases will a reward be paid to members of the army, the SS and the police.

Claims are to be submitted to Division through channels, giving endorsement of the respective commander.

s/ Körte
Official
Judge Advocate

Document 11/2[2]

Morale of Ardennes-Weary Divisions

3rd Parachute Division

Two regiments of this division were virtually destroyed before its retirement into the West Wall. Only a few replacements have been received. The entire division numbers less than 1,500 men. Food, ammunition and all types of weapons and equipment are painfully short.

The majority of the personnel of this unit are becoming increasingly pessimistic and resentful. PW state they think it absurd to be expected to fight without ammunition, food, and adequate medical aid. Even one-time ardent Nazis speak of a 'betrayal' by the German war-lords. However, there is still a considerable minority which is clinging to the dim hope that this phase of the war will not be the final one. Such men easily fall prey to any promises of propagandistic statements made by their NCOs or officers. Thus, they were told by an NSFO (political commissar) that Marshal

2. ISUM 232, 17 February 1945, from First U.S. Army.

Timoshenko had revolted against Stalin and seized an important city in Russia. This announcement was taken at its face value and interpreted as the first attempt by Russian forces to unite with Germany against Stalin. Among these fanatics it is furthermore believed that Hitler has asked the Almighty to acquiesce in and pardon the 'last ten days of the war' which will see a crushing counterblow with devastating new weapons.

3rd Panzer Grenadier Division

In much the same condition as 3 Parachute Division. The bulk of its badly depleted personnel consist of GAF replacements.

Morale is definitely low. The food is inadequate, the men are under constant strain and have little time for sleeping. The platoon leaders don't know their section leaders, and the latter are not familiar with the capabilities of their men. MGs are available, but few men volunteer for the dangerous job of #1 gunner. The majority of the PW were captured in groups. Though the situation admittedly warranted surrender, escapes could in most cases still be attempted, according to PW. Normally, prior to group surrenders, discussions take place among the men evaluating the situation. During these discussions little opposition is offered to the decision to surrender. Another indication pointing to the present morale of the German soldier is the large number of stragglers circulating behind the German lines. As one PW put it: 'We have an army of stragglers in reserve, allegedly searching for their units.' These stragglers are now trying their best to remain this side of the Rhine, because according to PW, all stragglers caught east of the Rhine are sent to the Eastern Front.'

Document 11/3[3]

Masterly – But Not Masterly Enough

Wartime Intelligence Officer's Comments

The following letter indicates another in the long series of devices used to enable members of the Wehrmacht to desert. This incident's only claim to distinction is that even the fanatical paratroopers are not immune to the virus of desertion.

G Ops Franch	Regiment HQ
Grenadier Regiment 1062	21 January 1945

Reference Deserters

To: Ops Branch, 84th Infantry Division
Attached is the report on the desertion of three soldiers on 29 January 1945, submitted by III/Parachute Regiment 2.

The reason given, to get some chickens, is considered by the Regiment to have been merely an excuse for them to leave the trenches.

Moreover, the fact that they left the trenches without snowsuits is proof that the three soldiers intended to get neither chickens nor a PW. They were ingenious enough to camouflage their real intentions in a masterly fashion.

On the evidence of the facts the Regiment is convinced that the three soldiers left the trenches only for the purpose of deserting.

The evidence against Acting Lance Corporals Hiller and Beyer and Lance Corporal Bauer, together with their statements on cross examination, are being forwarded.

3. ISUM 236, 21 February 1945.

Document 11/4[4]

Stragglers, Please Note!

Wartime Intelligence Officer's Comments

In the following document, translated by 30 Corps, the Operations Branch of HQ, 7 Parachute Division reveals the understandable concern on the subject of 'rearward movement of individual soldiers.' It appears that too many 7 Parachute Division stalwarts were voluntarily taking on the status of stragglers from their units, and this latter is obviously a stern measure to curtail their activities.

G Ops 7 Parachute Division CP 14 February 1945

SECRET

The sharpest measures will be taken forthwith against the rearward movements of individual soldiers and small units which have been observed for the past two days.

Regiments and Battalions will arrange:

(1) The organisation of stragglers collecting points in B Echelon[5] areas.
(2) Handing over of soldiers convicted of cowardice for sentencing by Court Martial.
(3) If necessary, rapid setting-up of summary courts.
(4) Daily comb-out of Echelons and immediate dissolution and fusion of Echelons of units that have been destroyed.
(5) Stragglers returning from the front line may be fed only at stragglers collecting posts. It is forbidden to issue food from unit field kitchens.
(6) Daily check of unit ration states to ensure that these maintain their correct relation to strength states.

Signed: I. V. Paulsen, Major
for Chief of Staff

4. ISUM 236, 21 February 1945.
5. Rear areas.

Chapter 12

Humour (Such As It Was)

Document 12/1[1]

More About Model

Two PW of Army Signals Unit 605 captured on 29 March 1945 and interrogated at First US Army Cage have provided further shading to the character portrait of the Commander of Army Group 'B', Field Marshal Model.

According to them Model would like to be known as the saviour of the German nation. Ruthless with the officers of his staff (they change constantly) as well as with Divisional and Corps Commanders, he is an absolute power. He accepts no suggestions or explanations and demands obedience to the utmost. At one time he called Genlt Gerke (his communications officer) out of his bed in the middle of the night and asked him to report to him immediately. Still he bawled him out because he had the nerve to appear before the '*kommandierenden General*' unshaven. He is as rude in his telephone conversations as in person: one can always hear him say '*Sie müssen halten bis zum letzten*' ('You must hold to the last').

On 24 January, on his birthday, Model received a telephone call from his wife at Dresden, which, according to one PW who overheard it, went like this:

1. ISUM 286, 12 April 1945, from First U.S. Army.

Wife:	'Stop playing soldier and come home.'
Model:	'Don't say such things over the telephone.'
Wife:	'What am I going to do? The Russians are pretty close.'
Model:	'Wait and see.'
Wife:	'What shall I do with your uniforms and decorations?'
Model:	'Give them away. I don't want the Russians to get them.'

Document 12/2[2]

A Day at the Cage or Never a Dull Moment

It has become apparent to the interrogators at the First US Army PW Cage that German war-weariness has taken on an aspect of extremity. A decided increase in the number of mentally unbalanced PW has been found. Many interrogators eye each PW with suspicion and it takes a long conversation with the PW to ascertain his sanity.

This afternoon a strange character approached one of the interrogators and demanded immediate audience. The serious glint in his eye and the sincerity of his appeal arrested attention and the interrogator stopped to delve into the matter.

'I must speak to you about paragraph 362 immediately', said the PW.

The term 'paragraph 362' was totally unfamiliar to the interrogator and he felt faint pangs of guilt at his ignorance.

'Paragraph 362 as directed by the Soviet Union.' the PW further explained, obviously disgusted with our uninformed interrogators.

'What about it?' the latter queried.

'I'm an agent of Soviet Russia and I have important information for you', whispered the PW while casting furtive glances in all directions to make certain no one overheard what he was saying.

'How can you prove this?' questioned the doubting interrogator.

'Easily', came the prompt reply. 'Here! You can see my badge of identification'. With this he reached cautiously inside his coat and after a brief moment of groping withdrew his hand.

'There you are', he rasped triumphantly.

2. ISUM 286, 12 April 1945, from First U.S. Army.

His hand held absolutely nothing. The interrogator squirmed uncomfortably.

'What other proof have you?'

'Ah!' answered the Russian agent, 'I have a letter from Josef Stalin,' and he reached into his coat once more. Here ensued a slight struggle since the spy insisted on groping around inside his coat without unbuttoning it.

'Why don't you unbutton?' suggested the interrogator helpfully.

'Don't have to,' he snapped back, 'I won't be able to find it anyway.'

The interrogator fled in all haste.

Chapter 13

Miscellaneous

Document 13/1[1]

This is the Enemy

Interrogation on 22 December by 30th Infantry Division revealed the following atrocity committed in the Division zone. On 18 December the Engineer Platoon of the 1st Reconnaissance Battalion of the 1st SS Panzer Division was en route to attack the town of Stavelot K7100. Before passing through the town of Parfondruy K7000, the members of the platoon were ordered and instructed by their platoon leader to do away with all the civilians that came into their sight. It has been definitely ascertained that the military operations of the enemy were not hindered in any way by the civilians concerned. The Engineer Platoon then went to work and rounded up 20 civilians, two of whom were women, and took them into a barn. The soldiers then shot them all down in cold blood. The barn was thereafter set on fire in order to erase all incriminating evidence. The platoon then moved on to occupy their objectives.

Some members of the platoon taking part in the outrage were captured today. They showed no concern at all over their deeds, and confessions have been easily obtained which were signed and sworn to properly. One man of the group testified that he had shot two Belgians who were about 45 or 50 years of age. Another testified that he saw an NCO walking off with two Belgians 19–22 years of age to shoot them. The Belgians, when they realized

1. ISUM 181, 28 December 1944, from 30th U.S. Division.

what was up, tried to escape, and the PW states that he shot them both. The platoon leader of this platoon who was responsible for this outrage has been wounded seriously, and is now receiving medical aid. All POW are being fowarded to higher headquarters for a trial of their crime, and the punishment which their bestiality deserves.

Note: *This information is corroborated by a civilian who had escaped and was previously interrogated.*[2]

Document 13/2[3]

Please Use Your Influence

Wartime Intelligence Officer's Comments

The following curious letter was found on the body of Captain Günther Kessler of III/7th Parachute Regiment who was killed on patrol in the area south of Wageningen E5775.

Kessler, Günther
Captain *4 December 1944*

Dear Major

Remembering the happy hours at Corps HQ, especially at Niemes (France), I take the liberty by this letter to stress my request made by telephone.

Since the end of November, I command III Battalion Parachute *Jäger* Regiment 7 and have met there an old comrade. It is Captain Jupp Kahlen, born 27 March 1909, seniority 1 December 1941 No. 2, Battalion Commander since 27 March 1942 (Luftwaffe Feld Battalion z.b.V. 3, Russian Campaign). At the beginning of 1944 Captain Kahlen received the promise from General Schimpf that he would be given a regiment under the General's command. Kahlen has especially proved himself in all battles. I recognize his capabilities without envy and am convinced that he is equal to the stern task of a regimental commander.

2. See also Document 5/12, above.
3. ISUM 177, 24 December 1944.

Through our spies we have found out that our present Regimental Commander, Colonel Börsh is to be relieved and that we are to get Colonel Count Kersenbrock. Colonel K, too, led a Battalion z.b.V. in Russia and was relieved of his command there. We are here dealing with a Cavalier who never succeeded in appearing near the HKL during battle and who soothes his passions by liberal recourse to the bottle. Up to now Colonel K, who, by the way, is a 'Du'tz-Freund' (very intimate friend) of General von Waldau, has been employed in the Military Science Branch of the General Staff.

I would like to ask you to use your influence with the Corps Commander to see that Captain Kahlen will be given command of the regiment . . .

Hoping that my request will be acceded to, I remain

With German Greetings

Document 13/3[4]

From the File of Colonel Katzmann

Wartime Intelligence Officer's Comments

The following is a letter taken from the personal file of the elusive Colonel Katzmann, erstwhile CO of 1062nd Grenadier Regiment of the now badly shattered 84 Infantry Division. It gives an idea of the kind of intimate problems facing a German regimental commander.

Colonel Katzmann *Field, 2 October 1944*

Battle Group Commander
Unit 710
Training Centre Wahn
Cologne

To: *Kreisleiter* NSDAP, Paderborn
Subject: Confidential information about Frl Massmann

2/Lt Gerhard Rödiger is intending to marry in the near future *Fraulein* Wilhelmina Massmann, born in Paderborn on 7 July 1917 and now resident at

4. ISUM 230, 15 February 1945.

52 Abtsbrede, Paderborn, and has submitted an application for this to be approved.

I am therefore asking you to furnish the following confidential information: Whether the bride enjoys an unexceptionable reputation, whether she is in sympathy with the National-Socialist regime, whether this regime is approved by her parents, and whether she is altogether worthy to become the wife of an officer.

Thanking you in anticipation of this information.

Heil Hitler!
(Signed) Katzmann
Colonel and Battle Group Commander

Document 13/4[5]

Leave Instructions

Wartime Intelligence Officer's Comments

The following is a translation of instructions given by 176th Division to troops proceeding on leave:

Supervision of Foreigners

Keep a constant watch on foreigners!
It is forbidden to associate with foreign workers!
On Saturday afternoons and on Sundays foreigners are not allowed on the trams!
No foreigner is allowed to use a bicycle for private purposes!
Arrest offenders! Confiscate their bicycles!
Poles and workers from Eastern countries are forbidden to visit cinemas, churches and places of public resort!
Eastern badge on left arm denotes a decoration for distinguished conduct!
White stripe on left arm denotes PW levied for labour!

5. ISUM 208, 24 January 1945, from Second Army Intelligence Summary, 22 January 1945.

Association of German women with foreigners is forbidden! Intervene!
Curfew for Poles and Eastern workers 2000–2100 hours.
Foreigners are allowed to use the State Railways for local lines only for the purpose of proceeding to and from work, and on long distance lines only if in possession of a leave pass (home leave)!
Hand over drunken foreigners to the Police!
If you overstay your leave through intervening, obtain a certificate from the Police showing the time lost!
Report all incidents to troop commander!

Soldiers in the Home War Zone! Keep your eyes open! Intervene without regard to your surroundings! The peace and security of your homeland are at stake!

Document 13/5[6]

Lieutenant-General Richard Schimpf – 3rd Parachute Division

'Everybody in the American Army knows me,' boasted Lieutenant-General Richard Schimpf (48), Commander of 3rd Parachute Division, as he was welcomed at the First US Army Cage. In fact, we have been expecting him since 8 June when we first contacted 3rd Parachute Division in Normandy. As a compansation for his delay, the General brought along two General Staff officers instead of the usual one (they were in the process of relieving each other).

The General is a jovial kind of fellow: quite willing to talk politics but shrewd enough to evade questions of a military character. He seemed to be quite impressed by our appraisal of 3rd Parachute Division (First Army PWI Report, 12/13 December) which was personally handed to him by Generalfeldmarschall Model when he rejoined the Division at the end of December. General Schimpf stated that the report was very objective. (The PWI report was allegedly captured at Elsenborn: Feldmarschall Model is not on the official distribution list).

6. ISUM 256, 13 March 1945, from First U.S. Army.

General Schimpf is a professional soldier of the last war's vintage, one of the 100,000 Reichswehr members. His prominence began in 1933 when he helped Goering in the organization and formation of the Luftwaffe. In 1940, he was on Rundstedt's staff in charge of air operations, and he continued in this capacity throughout the German version of the French campaign. From 1942 to 1943 he was in command of Division Meindl in Russia. On 17 February 1944 he took charge of 3rd Parachute Division, the unit with which he gained quite a bit of recognition. He now rejoined his Division in captivity.

Many sources indicate that the General came into US captivity voluntarily. He states himself that he had ample time to cross the Rhine if he had wanted to; he remained behind because he had orders to that effect from his superior, General Püchler,[7] Commanding General of 74 Corps. General Schimpf told a 'friendly' PW Colonel, 'General Püchler ordered me to stay behind with my Division in order to save other units. If the German Command thinks that they have sufficient experienced generals and General Staff officers, it is all right with me. Püchler and Model messed this thing up anyway – they are amateurs'. It is known that General Schimpf contacted the Swiss Consul in Bad Godesberg, and it is rumoured that he arranged for the General's transfer into US captivity.

It is evident from the General's behaviour, his statements to other PW and from his lengthy conversation with the interrogator that he had given up all hope for German victory. He referred continuously to Germany's most difficult position of fighting a war on two major fronts, to our great superiority of men and materiel, and to the many mistakes of the German Command. He was also very anxious to show his western orientation and was most emphatic in stating that he never had any Party connections.

Asked to comment on Himmler, Model and the Party influences in the Wehrmacht, he responded ironically that these are long chapters about which many things could be said and written. He did not conceal the fact that the Luftwaffe is a thing of the past, and he said plainly that no secret weapons will turn the tide of the war. He expressed his doubts that Germany will ever resort to gas warfare and he said the reason for the German preparations along these lines was in fear that the Russians may resort to gas. Asked about the possibility that the Wehrmacht may refuse to continue the war, he said that only a direct order from Hitler can influence the Wehrmacht to stop the fight. 'You Americans don't and can't understand our mentality. The German soldier at present is an instrument

7. *General der Infantrie* Carl Püchler (1894–1949).

of politics, but I myself am non-political. I have been soldiering for 31 years: I served under the Kaiser, the Weimar Republic, and the Nazis, and I would be perfectly willing to serve under the Americans also. Make no mistake about it, I was not exactly an adherent of Reichspresident Ebert, just as I am not in accord with many people in the Nazi Party.'

The General opposes the association of the *Volkssturm* with the Party; he ridicules the military role of the Gauleiters and believes that most of them are cowards. While talking about the Wehrmacht, he insists that we differentiate between the old school ('*alte Generalstabschule*') and the new school. He is perfectly aware of the pitfalls of the new leadership, but he is ashamed to talk about this with the enemy. Towards the end of the discussion, the General could not refrain from making a few derogatory statements about Model. It was he who gave Schimpf a direct order to remain on this side of the Rhine. One of the General's last statements was: 'I am anxious to see how our prominent Party leaders will behave in the case of an American victory. I wonder whether their behaviour is going to be the same as that of some of the *Gauleiters* I know.'

Document 13/6[8]

A Nazi Sees The Light

An infantry officer PW who spent a week behind our lines before hailing a truck on the highway and reporting to our PW Cage has interesting comments to make on our occupation policy. Having spent nine years in the Wehrmacht, including many in Russia, he had swallowed quite a bit of Nazi propaganda until the last few days 'opened his eyes', as he put it.

He was recuperating at a military hospital near Haltern A55 when put in charge of some other patients and told to fight it out with our Shermans. He took up positions in the woods and did not have to wait long. Hardly had he realized what was happening, when our tanks had rumbled through, the infantry by-passed his position and he found himself in the middle of rear echelon troops. 'I would never have believed it possible', he says. The motorized equipment impressed him no end.

8. ISUM 286, 12 April 1945, from Ninth U.S. Army.

'There is no such disparity of force, no such overwhelming superiority on the Eastern Front.'

The behaviour of the population filled him with astonishment. Hardly had the tanks rolled by when he tried to look for a way out and saw the landscape dotted with white surrender flags hanging from every house. 'I confess, I wept bitter rears of disappointment. I am an officer and love soldiering but I realize that I had kept my interest too exclusively focused on military matters. I could not believe that things had come to such a pass on the home front. I thought that every woman and child would fight to the end.'

When he went to a farmhouse to procure some food, it was refused him. 'I was disappointed at first but the farmer told me that he would get into serious trouble with the authorities if he fed me. In fact he threatened to report me, if I did not leave'. Going from one house to the other in a vain attempt to get some food, he was told of Military Government's advice to all farmers to go on ploughing their fields. He saw cattle in the fields and chickens in the courtyards. A civilian told him that no food had been stolen and that it was being distributed to civilians on new ration cards. Life, in fact, was getting back to normal with very little interference. He saw no brutality, witnessed no looting, heard of no rape. His surprises grew daily. 'I must say, I am truly enthusiastic (*wirklich begeistert*)', he comments.

Having thus satisfied himself that all was well with the Fatherland and getting hungrier all the time, he hitch hiked a ride on a US truck on the highway and rode to the PW cage, the only place far and wide that would greet him with open arms and feed him hospitably.